Nuclear Statecraft

A Volume in the Series

Cornell Studies in Security Affairs

edited by Robert J. Art, Robert Jervis, and Stephen M. Walt

A list of titles in this series is available at www.cornellpress.cornell.edu.

Nuclear Statecraft

History and Strategy in America's Atomic Age

Francis J. Gavin

Cornell University Press

Ithaca and London

First published 2012 by Cornell University Press

Printed in the United States of America

Library of Congress Cataloging-in-Publication Data

Gavin, Francis J.
Nuclear statecraft : history and strategy in America's atomic age / Francis J. Gavin.
p. cm.
Includes bibliographical references and index.
ISBN 978-0-8014-5101-0 (cloth : alk. paper)
1. Nuclear weapons—Government policy—United States—History. 2. Nuclear nonproliferation—Government policy—United States—History. 3. Nuclear arms control—Government policy—United States—History. 4. United States—Foreign relations—1945–1989. 5. United States—Foreign relations—1989– I. Title.
JZ5665.G38 2013
355.02'170973—dc23 2012022113

Cornell University Press strives to use environmentally responsible suppliers and materials to the fullest extent possible in the publishing of its books. Such materials include vegetable-based, low-VOC inks and acid-free papers that are recycled, totally chlorine-free, or partly composed of nonwood fibers. For further information, visit our website at www.cornellpress.cornell.edu.

Cloth printing 10 9 8 7 6 5 4 3 2 1

For Olivia

Contents

Acknowledgments

This book could not have been completed without the generous support of several organizations: the Nobel Institute in Oslo; the Donald D. Harrington Faculty Fellowship; the Tom Slick Memorial Fellowship of the University of Texas; the Policy Research Institute of the LBJ School of Public Affairs; the Faculty Research Development program of the University of Texas; and, especially, the Smith Richardson Foundation, which awarded me a Junior Faculty Fellowship in International Security and Foreign Policy.

I am grateful for the wonderful research assistants who have done such great work for me over the years: Brent Chaney, Anya Cherkasova, Braden Civens, Ben Davis, Rex Douglas, Michael Gerson, Leslie Holmes, Katy Koch, Patrick McMillin, Colin Murphy, Justin Patrick, Megan Reiss, Yana Skorobogatov, Miha Vindis, and especially Jessica Mahoney.

My colleagues at the LBJ School and the Robert S. Strauss Center for International Security and Law at the University of Texas are the best one could find anywhere, and I have been lucky to benefit from their friendship and inspiration. I have been particularly fortunate to have two deans, Bobby Ray Inman and Jim Steinberg, who provided extraordinary support and mentorship throughout this project. Running a center while completing a book was possible only with the tremendous help of Jim Langdon, Greg Engle, and especially Celeste Gventer.

Many people read portions of the manuscript or heard me present portions of the book, and I am thankful for all the valuable feedback and advice I have received. While those who have helped improve this manuscript are too numerous to list, I am especially grateful to Melvyn Leffler and Mira Rapp-Hooper for their ideas and advice. Two scholars have had a profound influence on how I think about these issues, and their imprint is on every page of this manuscript. Robert Jervis has done more than anyone to shape how we think about nuclear weapons and international politics, and while we are all in his debt, I am particularly lucky to have received his encouragement and detailed comments on this book. Marc Trachtenberg taught me how to be a historian, and I continue to learn from him. Everyone should be so lucky as to have a teacher as wise, kind, and supportive as Marc. My biggest thanks go to my most important supporters—Natalie, Catherine, and Olivia.

Material appearing in chapter 2 appeared previously in "The Myth of Flexible Response: American Strategy in Europe during the 1960s," *International History Review* 23, no. 4 (December 2001): 847–75. By permission of *International History Review*. Material appearing in chapter 4 appeared previously in "Blasts from the Past: Nuclear Proliferation and Rogue States before the Bush Doctrine," *International Security* 29, no. 3 (Winter 2005): 100–135. By permission of *International Security*. Material appearing in chapter 5 appeared previously in "Nuclear Nixon: Ironies, Puzzles, and the Triumph of Realpolitik," in *Nixon in the World: American Foreign Relations, 1969–1977*, edited by Fred Logevall and Andrew Preston, 126–45 (Oxford University Press, 2008). By permission of Oxford University Press, Inc. Material appearing in chapter 6 appeared previously in "Wrestling with Parity: The Nuclear Revolution Revisited," in *The Shock of the Global: The 1970s in Perspective*, edited by Niall Ferguson, Charles S. Maier, Erez Manela, and Daniel J. Sargent, 189–205 (Cambridge, MA: Belknap Press of Harvard University Press, 2010). Reprinted by permission of the publisher; copyright © 2010 by Niall Ferguson, Charles S. Maier, Erez Manela, and Daniel J. Sargent. Material appearing in chapter 7 appeared previously in "Same as It Ever Was: Nuclear Alarmism, Proliferation, and the Cold War," *International Security* 34, no. 3 (Winter 2009–10): 7–37. By permission of *International Security*.

Nuclear Statecraft

Introduction

There is a widely held belief that we are at a profound and critical juncture in world politics. Nuclear proliferation, strategy, and policy have risen to the top of the global policy agenda, and nuclear issues receive more attention now than at any other time in recent memory. The Obama administration laid out a long-term vision of a world free of nuclear weapons. The United States and other countries continue to condemn Iran and North Korea for their nuclear efforts, and aggressive action to cripple their programs has not been ruled out. Fears of nuclear terrorism and concerns over nuclear tipping points are widespread. Arms control has taken on a new prominence, not seen since the Cold War, with the signing of the New START treaty with Russia in 2010 and efforts to strengthen the nuclear nonproliferation regime.[1] The Obama administration also conducted a vigorous internal review of US nuclear strategy and made significant changes. These policies are taking place in a dynamic international environment, where nuclear and nonnuclear powers from East Asia to the Middle East to Latin America are making crucial, and in some cases far-reaching, decisions about their own nuclear policies.

The United States is making make big bets in the nuclear arena, bets that could have lasting consequences. That nuclear weapons have had a profound influence on world politics is accepted by almost everyone. But there is a wide degree of difference as to the meaning and consequences of this revolution and what the appropriate policy responses should be. How should we evaluate various proposals and the ideas that animate them? The most important thing we can do to is to better appreciate the historical origins of our contemporary nuclear world. Understanding that past is my goal in this book. Surprisingly, this is rarely done. On the one hand, many policy analysts claim that the past has little to tell us about the new and frightening nuclear challenges of the twenty-first century. This view is wrong-headed. I do not argue that nothing has changed, but there is far more continuity than we acknowledge. Many questions that appear novel have in fact come up before, and those issues that are truly new often have their foundations in past experience. What is as alarming is that those who do base their arguments on the past often get the story wrong. Each of the chapters in this book uses history to break open long-held nuclear myths. Taken together, they challenge the widely accepted, stylized narrative about the "nuclear revolution" and its effect on international relations and US foreign policy since 1945. Bad history is almost worse than no history. We cannot begin to devise effective policies until we recognize the importance of our nuclear history and, just as important, get it right.

Many are skeptical that history can provide anything of use to policymakers. As I explain in chapter 1, "History, Theory, and Statecraft in the Nuclear Age," historians have for a variety of reasons not played a key role in understanding the nuclearized world we live in. As Jill Lepore has pointed out, "the American historical profession defines itself by its dedication to the proposition that looking to the past to explain the present falls outside the realm of serious historical study."[2] Even those historians who are interested in contemporary history may think they have little to offer decision makers. Historians emphasize complexity and uncertainty when looking at the past; they dismiss the possibility of predicting future events and even question whether it is possible to generalize. The military historian Michael Howard captured this view when he claimed he was "conscious above all of the unique quality of an experience that resulted from circumstances that would never, that could never, be precisely replicated."[3] Policymakers are understandably impatient with this way of seeing the world. Clear-cut policy guidance, parsimonious explanations, and reliable predictions would seem to better serve the needs of decision makers.

In this book I attempt to demonstrate how historical analysis can provide us with an understanding of the complex and at times contradictory ways nuclear weapons have influenced international politics in the past—and how it can also provide useful guidance to decision makers facing hard choices in the future. Like the integrated essays of John Lewis Gaddis, Robert Jervis, and Marc Trachtenberg, this book uses new historical evidence to wrestle with competing interpretations of the postwar nuclear order rather than simply telling a chronological story.[4] The historical lessons are both interesting and important in and of themselves, and they are crucial to making better policy in the nuclear arena today.

There are also observers who question whether there is much new to say about the fundamental question—"How do nuclear weapons affect international politics?" This issue had been deemed so important that it spawned its own field in the earliest days of the nuclear age, the field of security studies, which is marked by vigorous, sophisticated debate and analysis. Although scholars with a historical background contributed to these discussions, strategists, international relations theorists, economists, and scientists drove most of the work on nuclear issues. The sometimes ahistorical quality of this scholarship was not really that surprising: one of the key tenets of security studies was that nuclear weapons had revolutionized military affairs and world politics, and applying rigorous and at times cutting edge social science methods to the nuclear question was more important than having a deep understanding of the past.[5] And, really, after countless books and articles since 1945, what more was there to say about the nuclear age? As Steven Walt, a political scientist, pointed out when discussing the decline of scholarly interest in nuclear questions, "one reason is that there hasn't been that much new to say about the subject; the essential features of deterrence theory are well-established by now, and the infeasibility of any sort of 'nuclear war' seems to be pretty well-understood (at least let's hope so)."[6]

What were the essential features of the received wisdom? There were disagreements among scholars, of course, but a consensus of sorts emerged on what were the important questions and what were the best ways to assess various claims. The focus was on the nuclear weapons themselves—raw numbers, capabilities, deployment—and how their presence and the strategies to use them shaped incentives in the international system and drove state behavior. Of overriding concern was the interaction between the nuclear forces of the United States and the Soviet Union, the two powers that dominated what came to be called the bipolar order. In particular, analysts exploited innovative tools such as game theory to recommend what nuclear strategies the United States should develop to deter the Soviet Union from aggressive actions.

A narrative emerged, the rough outlines of which are well known. There was little in the way of "strategy" in the early days of the nuclear age. Policymakers struggled to come to terms with the enormous impact these weapons had on questions of war and peace. In the early to mid-1950s, the Eisenhower administration developed a strategy based on the massive preemptive use of strategic nuclear weapons to deter the Soviets and prevail in a possible war.[7] By the late 1950s, however, critics were arguing that the strategy of "massive retaliation" was not credible.[8] The emergence of what was called "secure second strike" meant that no matter how effective a massive preemptive strike against Soviet nuclear forces might be, the Soviet Union would still have enough atomic firepower to retaliate and cause unacceptable damage to the United States. Combining this belief with the fact of superior Soviet conventional forces in the European theater led many to doubt whether the US strategy could effectively deter the Soviets, particularly in Europe.

Enter the so-called whiz kids. The young and dynamic president, John F. Kennedy, along with his brilliant cadre of strategists and defense intellectuals, transformed US nuclear strategy in the early 1960s, as rigid "massive retaliation" gave way to the more nuanced and modern "flexible response." This new strategy included a wide array of nuclear packages, calibrated military responses, and more robust conventional force options up and down the escalatory ladder. Secretary of Defense Robert McNamara laid out the new strategy during speeches in Athens and Ann Arbor in the spring of 1962. Although intense debate and disagreements would continue in the decades to come, the new approach laid out the basic contours of US nuclear strategy for the rest of the Cold War.

There is a problem with this story, however: it is largely incorrect. Top US decision makers such as President Kennedy and Secretary McNamara, and later President Johnson, did not actually spend much time thinking about the issues that concerned those in the security studies field. When secret documents were declassified, it was revealed that they did not want more US conventional forces in Europe (quite the contrary), did not spend much time or effort on creating strategic nuclear options that were more flexible in any meaningful way, and had far more in common with the Eisenhower administration than anyone would have guessed. And, despite the obvious sophistication and brilliance of the security studies literature, there was little evidence that tools such as game theory captured the dynamics of how top decision makers made nuclear policies.

This was all quite surprising—virtually every major work in the field had highlighted the Kennedy and Johnson administrations' flexible response as a dramatic shift away from past strategies and had emphasized the influence of the strategic studies community in bringing about this change. If the documents told a different story, as chapter 2, "The Myth of Flexible Response," makes clear, could other aspects of conventional wisdom surrounding nuclear history also be called into question?

This question highlights the methodological power of historical work that looks at policy and strategy during the postwar period. I did not set out to study nuclear issues when I visited the archives. But while doing research on a book about US international monetary policy, I came across all sorts of evidence that called into question the received wisdom about how top policymakers thought about and made nuclear policy. Time and time again, for example, I found that each of the presidents I was looking at—Eisenhower, Kennedy, Johnson, and Nixon—pressed their aides to find ways to reduce the balance-of-payment costs of stationing US troops in Europe, even if it meant bringing troops home (a policy in direct contradiction to the received story about flexible response). This alerted me to surprising and previously unknown causal connections, referred to in the first chapter as "horizontal" history, which provided insights into how the policymaking process actually worked.

A fundamental issue underneath many of these causal linkages concerned the question of how nuclear weapons influence international politics. Are such weapons stabilizing or destabilizing, and under what circumstances? We have lots of international relations theories on this issue, but what did the historical record reveal? One way of testing these questions would be to reexamine what was arguably the greatest period of nuclear tension—the four years that began in late 1958 with Soviet premier Nikita Khrushchev demanding a change in Berlin's status and ending with the denouement of the Cuban missile crisis in 1962. What role did nuclear weapons play in both creating and resolving these terrifying tensions? Was the story of what actually happened, the policies actually pursued, at odds with the conventional interpretation? In other words, was there a gap between our theories and the history similar to the one that plagued nuclear strategy? Could a better understanding of the past close this gap, and perhaps even provide insight into how nuclear weapons influence international politics today?

In chapter 3, "Nuclear Weapons, Statecraft, and the Berlin Crisis, 1958–1962," I wrestle with these questions. I offer two tentative but provocative counterfactuals to help get at these important issues: First, how might a superpower crisis over Berlin have unfolded in a nonnuclear environment? Would it have happened at all? Second, and related, how would the nuclear dynamics between the United States and the Soviet Union have differed if there had been no disagreement about the status of Berlin? The goal of this exercise is not to provide a definitive answer to unanswerable questions: counterfactuals should be used, if at all, with great care. Instead, the idea is to explore whether the Berlin situation was simply unusual and perhaps sui generis, if only to give us pause before we try to extract generalizable lessons from the crisis. Much of our theoretical work on nuclear brinkmanship, crisis dynamics, and the role that the balance of power and resolve are taken from this unique period, and those theories play into our notions about how stabilizing or destabilizing nuclear weapons can be in the contemporary world. If, on the other hand, the lessons from Berlin are generalizable, the influence of nuclear weapons on the behavior of both the Americans and the Soviets between 1958 and 1962 can be understood as undermining arguments about the stabilizing effects of the nuclear revolution. Because these issues play such an important role in our thinking about the hazards of nuclear proliferation—far larger than we often recognize—understanding the real story from this volatile period is all the more important.

As I continued my historical work, a second serious problem with the conventional wisdom about nuclear weapons came into focus. When looking at the late 1950s and early 1960s, I saw that the security studies literature zeroed in on the strategic dynamic between the nuclear forces of the United States and the Soviet Union, almost as if this interaction took place in a political vacuum. The documents, however, made clear that decision makers were primarily concerned with the underlying geopolitical questions animating the standoff between the superpowers. Both the Eisenhower and the Kennedy administrations recognized that resolving contested issues could ease the sense of crisis between the superpowers. For example, if the superpowers could come to an understanding on the military and political status of Germany, many of the other issues, including arms control, would fall into place. This dynamic—far more than abstract notions of how nuclear weapons did or did not drive behavior—is crucial to understanding the crisis period of 1958–62.[9]

This emphasis on underlying political questions exposed a third problem with the conventional wisdom: policymakers focused far more on the spread of nuclear weapons, what came to be called nuclear proliferation, than on the strategic interaction between the Soviets and Americans. The subject of proliferation was not completely ignored by the security studies literature, but until the Cold War ended, it took an undeserved second seat to what has been called "vertical" competition between the superpowers. While the strategic community was slow to understand the importance of nuclear proliferation, by about 1960 profound changes in world politics were forcing policymakers to confront new nuclear challenges. US and Soviet officials began to recognize that their early, lackadaisical attitudes toward nonproliferation were no longer prudent. Who would and would not get access to nuclear weapons became an issue of fundamental importance, not only between the superpowers but also within each alliance and in the nonaligned world as well.

Although it is true that in the early days of the Cold War, US and Soviet nonproliferation efforts were less than vigorous, prospects for effective global nonproliferation policies improved in the early 1960s. There were four reasons for this change. First, as Lawrence Wittner has shown in his path-breaking work, *Resisting the Bomb*, grassroots antinuclear groups gained popularity throughout the world. The development of thermonuclear weapons, and the dangers associated with nuclear testing, brought emerging environmental groups together with peace advocates to demand that governments ban the bomb. Nongovernmental organizations in the West, as well as political leaders from the non-aligned movement, were especially important in advocating a nuclear test ban treaty.[10] This grassroots, global antinuclear movement expanded and increased its influence in the decades to come.

Second, the tense standoff between the Soviets and Americans between 1958 and 1962, initially over the status of Berlin and culminating in the Cuban missile crisis, brought the world close to the first use of nuclear weapons since 1945. Approaching the nuclear precipice—Secretary of State Dean Rusk called it "the most dangerous crisis the world has ever seen," the only time when the nuclear superpowers came "eyeball to eyeball"—both the Soviets and the Americans recognized the need to reduce tensions, halt arms racing, and limit the chances of an accidental nuclear war.[11] A world with fewer nuclear weapons and fewer atomic powers, it was thought, would be much safer. Both governments increasingly made both bilateral and global nuclear arms control a priority after the October 1962 missile crisis.

This led to the third concern—the idea that if proliferation were not stopped, there could be a domino, snowball, or tipping point phenomenon resulting in dozens of new atomic powers. President Kennedy told the world in 1963 that he "was haunted by the feeling that by 1970, unless we are successful, there may be ten nuclear powers instead of four, and by 1975, fifteen or twenty."[12] In 1961, the strategist Hermann Kahn claimed that with "the kind of technology that is likely to be available in 1969, it may literally turn out that a Hottentot, an educated and technical Hottentot it is true, would be able to make bombs."[13] In 1965, analyst Fred Iklé warned that if proliferation went beyond the "middle powers," it could lead to "owners of nuclear weapons who cannot be deterred because they feel they have nothing to lose."[14]

The fourth and most important reason for the shift toward stronger nonproliferation polices was geopolitical. Until the early 1960s, it could be argued that the countries that had developed nuclear weapons—the United States, the Soviet Union, Great Britain, and France—were status quo powers, unlikely to change postwar borders through force. Other potential proliferators—Sweden, India, Australia, even Israel—had understandable (if controversial) security motivations to acquire weapons for defensive and deterrent purposes. Two other potential nuclear powers, the Federal Republic of Germany (FRG) and the People's Republic of China (PRC), fell into a much different category. The possibility that either or both of these states might gain access to nuclear weapons threatened the stability of Europe and East Asia and challenged both US and Soviet interests.

The FRG, or West Germany, was part of a divided land, only a generation removed from the Nazi legacy of terror and war, feared by its Eastern bloc neighbors and mistrusted even by its closest European allies. The FRG demonstrated an interest throughout the 1950s in having access to the most modern weapons available.[15] At least West Germany was a liberal democracy; China was in many ways the original rogue state. Veering between the iron rule of Chairman Mao Zedong, the anarchy of the Great Leap Forward in the 1950s, and the Great Proletarian Cultural Revolution of the 1960s, China's successful program to develop its own atomic weapons worried both its neighbors and the Cold War superpowers. President Kennedy believed that a Chinese nuclear test was "likely to be historically the most significant and worst event of the 1960s."[16] Some argued that "the Chinese are the biggest problem of all," made "the rest of our problems seem academic,"[17] and that the United States should do whatever it could to "keep China permanently out of the business."[18]

But how could nuclear proliferation be slowed? Once again, the documents lead in an unexpected direction. While exploring the personal papers of former deputy secretary of defense Roswell Gilpatric (1961–1964) during a visit to the JFK Presidential Library (for the purpose of my work on the US balance-of-payments deficit), I found extensive notes to a commission he chaired that was tasked with recommending US policy in the wake of China's first nuclear test in October 1964. The deliberations of the so-called Gilpatric committee are detailed in chapter 4, "Blasts from the Past: Proliferation Lessons from the 1960s." They provide a window into how the US government wrestled with the challenges of nuclear proliferation.

The committee's recommendations laid the groundwork for a transformation of US policy, paving the way for the 1968 Nuclear Nonproliferation Treaty (NPT) that shapes global nuclear politics today.[19] It was not obvious or inevitable when the committee deliberated, however, that US policymakers would reverse their skeptical attitudes regarding nonproliferation and move in this direction. Three things were particularly surprising in the documents from this period. First, there was no shared faith among top decision makers that a robust US nonproliferation policy was possible or even wise. Second, they recognized that designing an effective nonproliferation policy would involve lots of difficult trade-offs and deep opportunity costs. Would a "no first-use" policy or missile defense system encourage or hinder proliferation? Should all potential proliferators be treated the same, or should the question of atomic spread be dealt with on a case-by-case basis? As a 1964 Hudson Institute report argued, "retarding the spread of nuclear weapons" is a situation where "the best may be the enemy of the good," and an "attempt to get 'everything' may risk achieving substantially less than . . . would be possible with more modest ambitions."[20] What was the role of different tools of statecraft, including appeasement, alliances, and preemption? The final insight was perhaps the most important one—once again, the question of nuclear proliferation could not be isolated as an "arms control" problem but needed to be viewed in the larger geopolitical context. The politics of the German question were central to the nuclear issue, without which the dramatic shift in policy that emerged during the 1960s cannot be understood.

The power of historical insight, however, is often found in exposing the exceptions rather than the rule. Eisenhower, Kennedy, and Johnson increasingly questioned the political benefit to the United States of nuclear weapons; but there was one president whose views on their utility were quite clear. On the surface, President Richard Nixon had what arms controllers would call an exemplary record. On his watch, the United States ratified the NPT, banned biological weapons, and negotiated the landmark Antiballistic Missile Treaty (ABM) and the Strategic Arms Reduction Treaty (SALT) with the Soviet Union. As is often the case with declassified records, however, the divide between public perception and actual policy turns out to be vast. Chapter 5, "Nuclear Nixon," highlights a leader dismissive of arms control and obsessed with finding ways to exploit nuclear weapons as a tool for his ambitious statecraft. Confronted and tormented by the realities of nuclear parity, Nixon nonetheless strove to find ways to manipulate the risk inherent in nuclear confrontations to his advantage. The Nixon period provides a fascinating laboratory for the question of how much the nuclear balance matters and whether strategies that seek to exploit the "balance of resolve" are effective.

Even if Nixon was unwilling to face up to the realities of nuclear parity between the superpowers, others were. In chapter 6, "That Seventies Show: The Consequences of Parity Revisited," I assess the three broad responses to the emerging strategic balance between the superpowers. The first—the mutual vulnerability/strategic stability school—believed that there was no point to seeking strategic superiority. The powerful structural pressures of a world dominated by the "security dilemma" required international arms control to save states from themselves. The mutual vulnerability school, which occupied the high ground among scholars and intellectuals, was a strange mix of realism and international law and not without its own deep internal contradictions. The second school—nuclear superiority/damage limitation—offered a wide range of arguments in favor of superiority, from the need to extend deterrence to the belief that a nuclear war might be fought and won. Adherents were often derided by the strategists, though they were sometimes embraced by certain policymakers. The third response—what I call beyond deterrence—was the least understood or well formulated in the 1970s, but it may have been the most important in the long run. Arising from diverse sources, it identified other factors, from nuclear abolitionism to globalization, that revealed that the whole question of deterrence might be less important than the strategists believed. In the end, all three responses were less important for their technical understanding of the nuclear order than for the starkly different view of world politics each represented.

Do these historical examinations have any relevance to the world we live in today? Can they help us construct better, more effective policies? Many analysts do not think so, arguing that we live in a second nuclear age, more dangerous than the first and dominated by the threat of rogue states, nuclear terrorism, and tipping points. The Cold War period was a much different world, with few lessons for today. In chapter 7, "Same as It Ever Was? Nuclear Weapons in the Twenty-First Century," I contend that this largely unchallenged view is wrong and based on four myths about our nuclear past. The first myth is that contemporary nuclear threats are new and more dangerous than those of the past, when in fact today's challenges often pale in comparison to what the world saw in the first decades after World War II. The second myth is that, unlike today, nuclear weapons stabilized international politics during the Cold War, when in fact the record—both today and in the past—pulls in different directions. The third myth conflates the history of the nuclear arms race with the geopolitical and ideological competition between the Soviet Union and the United States, creating an oversimplified and misguided portrayal of the Cold War. The final myth is that the bipolar military rivalry during the Cold War was the only force driving nuclear proliferation in the decades that followed the end of World War II. A better understanding of what actually happened in the past, of how and why the international community escaped calamity during a far more dangerous time and in a context of ruthless and powerful adversaries, might lead to more effective policies.

The final chapter, "Global Zero, History, and the 'Nuclear Revolution,'" analyzes the current divide over US nuclear and nonproliferation policy between what I call the nuclear sanguinists and the nuclear agonists. Agonists want a world with far fewer, and eventually no, nuclear weapons. For agonists, the nuclear question is far and away the most important global policy concern, and they are willing to pay a very high price to prevent proliferation, including the use of security commitments, sanctions, coercion, and even preventive force. Sanguinists are skeptical about both the prospects for and the desirability of a world free of nuclear weapons. In their view, nuclear deterrence has done a remarkable job of keeping the world safe, and they do not see any reason it will not do so in the future.

Which view is correct? It turns out that both views are based on particular readings of nuclear history, narratives that are often at odds with the documentary record. In fact, much of the agonist story is off base: the past was far scarier than the present, concerns about nuclear terrorism and rogues states are not new, tipping points are rare, and international treaties have been less important than security guarantees in limiting proliferation. Perhaps most important, a close reading of nuclear history reveals deterrence is robust and in many cases stabilizing, whereas certain kinds of nonproliferation policies can be dangerous and destabilizing.

There are also flaws in the sanguinist story. The record of the Cold War reveals less stability than is often acknowledged, and nuclear weapons not only made some crises worse but were the reason for the crisis in the first place. Nor can the sanguinist framework adequately explain US nuclear policy since 1945. Sanguinists overemphasize the strategic arms competition between the United States and the Soviet Union, focus too much on "mutual assured destruction," have unconvincing arguments for important US policies—including missile defense and the continued search for nuclear superiority, and in general underplay or ignore the fundamental political drivers of nuclear history. We cannot begin to assess the merits of critical policies, ranging from the goal of "global zero" to threatened use of preventive war to reverse proliferation, until we have a much better understanding of the historical forces that brought us where we are today.

In the end, readers do not have to embrace my version of the nuclear past to recognize what an important, though largely unrecognized, role historical thinking can play in analyzing contemporary and future global policy issues. It is important to remember that the value of historical work is not only in the answers and interpretations it offers. Good historical work provides a sensibility and an understanding of trade-offs, exposing unintended consequences and unexamined connections, recognizes uncertainty, and highlights the difficulties of accurately predicting and forecasting. If history teaches nothing else, it is that we should have humility and perhaps empathy: humility about our ability (or rather, inability) to provide clear-cut answers for those making policy, and empathy for those in positions of extraordinary responsibility who have little choice but to make decisions about an uncertain future. Although each chapter challenges conventional wisdom and widely held nuclear myths, this book as a whole raises as many questions as it answers, and often the conclusions pull in different directions. These issues are likely to dominate the contemporary global policy landscape, ranging from the nuclear programs of Iran and North Korea to the movement to abolish nuclear weapons from the planet. We face large and complicated choices. This may not seem like much, but I would argue the same humility that history teaches, would benefit all of us—scholar, citizen, and policymaker alike—and provide the wisdom that might make for wiser choices by all.

[1]

History, Theory, and Statecraft in the Nuclear Age

Questions of war and peace have driven modern world history.[1] It is often claimed that the creation and spread of nuclear weapons has fundamentally transformed the issue of international conflict.[2] Understanding why and how this is so should be a priority for any analyst of contemporary world politics. Yet we know far less than we think we do about this vital subject.

Many would dispute this claim. As mentioned in the introduction, there are scores if not hundreds of books; thousands of articles; and numerous foundations, think tanks, and research centers devoted entirely to questions surrounding nuclear statecraft and politics. Indeed, there is a whole field—nuclear strategy—that has, for decades, been devoted to this topic. What more could there be to learn?

To understand my assertion—that we know less than we think—we need to reflect on the three different types of analysis employed by people who have routinely thought about questions of nuclear statecraft since 1945 and compare the methods used and the kinds of assessments made. These analyses focus on theory and strategy, policymaking, and history.[3] While obviously they are related, generating theories, making policy, and undertaking historical inquiry have significant differences. In simple terms, theory and strategy attempt to explain how the world should work, policy and statecraft are about figuring out what to do in real time, and history seeks to understand what happened and why. Broadly speaking, theory is prescriptive, policymaking reactive, and history descriptive. Why do these distinctions matter? For one thing, what is claimed should have happened is often taken for what did happen, when in fact our understanding of what occurred in our nuclear past is, at best, incomplete. These different ways of thinking about nuclear issues are often conflated, leading to overconfidence in both our policies and theories about nuclear statecraft that are not warranted when one examines the historical record.

It is important, therefore, to separate these different modes of analysis, understand their similarities and differences, and recognize why nuclear history has been underappreciated. Whereas making policy and generating theories are obviously different, there are strong affinities in the way nuclear issues are approached by experts in both areas. Theory and policy are, broadly speaking, confident and certain.[4] Historical analysis, on the other hand, is often guarded, speculative, contextual, and unwilling to generalize. Who wants uncertainty when the subject is as important as the influence of nuclear weapons on world politics? Furthermore, personalities from the strategy community and the policy worlds have often interacted and even worked together. The same is not true for historians.

If, however, strategists and policymakers have often been wrong about issues for which we have a historical record—a key claim of this book—what does that say about their assessment of contemporary and future nuclear policy challenges? This should be reason enough to study nuclear history, though as we shall see, this task is easier said than done. The first section of this chapter explains why there has been so little sustained historical analysis of the atomic age, and it lays out why pursuing this worthy goal is fraught with challenges and difficulties. The second section highlights why it is important to try and suggests that some of the core ideas and frameworks used by theorists/strategists and policymakers to explain nuclear statecraft may not stand up to the light of history.

The Challenges of Nuclear History

I believe in the benefits of good historical work for understanding and even improving US foreign policy.[5] This is not an uncontroversial position, however, and there are powerful arguments—typically made by historians themselves—against this claim. One prominent skeptic argues that "history cannot in the first instance be concerned with navigating the ship of state."[6] Various arguments discount the role the study of history can play in improving our theories and policies of nuclear statecraft. To begin with, most historians are interested in the past for its own sake, do not like to generalize over space and time, and are no better than anyone else at making predictions—all positions at odds with those of strategists and decision makers.[7]

The comparative advantage of the study of history is in exposing complexity, nuance, and shades of grey. In addition, studying the past discourages efforts to simplify or forecast. Such insight may seem, at first glance, less accessible or useful compared to the parsimony and generalizability of theory and strategy. Furthermore, many historians hold a deep suspicion of power and those who wield it, arguing that the record of scholars who have been close to power in the United States has not always been exemplary.[8] Policymaking is only a small part of the past that diplomatic and military historians reconstruct and explain. Even scholars who focus on international history or US foreign relations are as likely to emphasize factors outside of the realm of policy such as geography, long-term trends including demographic and economic shifts, and cultural and intellectual variables including the changing role of race and gender. Finally, many historians believe it is artificial to study the history of a particular policy or to engage in what political scientists call "process tracing." Historians also lament the focus on "crises," as if singular events emerge out of nowhere and are to be understood in their own terms. These are all compelling barriers to bringing historians, theorists/strategists, and policymakers together to understand nuclear statecraft. The benefits, however, far outweigh the costs. Rigorous historical analysis allows us to see deeper connections between issues over both space and time, and to understand that events don't always unfold in a linear fashion. Such knowledge can lead to better theories, policies, and nuclear statecraft. What do I mean here?

When looking at a historical event or phenomenon, historians first look at its temporal, or "vertical," origins. Vertical history involves understanding the sequential notions of causality and agency. Why did a certain event or series of events occur, and what agents or combination of agents—forces, persons, institutions, and ideas—caused the event? While explaining how events unfold over time would seem to be straightforward, it is never a simple or uncontested process, as anyone who has studied controversial issues such as the causes of World War I, for example, understands. Identifying causes and agents depends on the perspective of the historian, including the spatial, cultural, and temporal angles. Causes can be either proximate or long term. Wrestling over these issues can provide a keen insight into what matters and how things work, and it can sensitize theorists/strategists and policymakers to complexity, uncertainty, and contingency.

An understanding of the past doesn't just reveal how things relate over time; history can also expose "horizontal" connections over space and in depth. In other words, good historical work can move laterally and reveal linkages between issues that are not readily apparent at first glance. This is the horizontal, or spatial-depth, axis on a historian's imaginary graph. Good horizontal historical work can reveal the complex interconnections and trade-offs that permeate most important foreign policies. This is rarely captured in studies that seek parsimony or to artificially remove "crises" from their historical context.

Furthermore, history reveals the unintended consequences of our policies, and it can provide a sense of when certain contemporary policy issues may not be as important as we think over the long run.[9] It may also reveal factors that are outside policymakers' control, such as culture and norms or long-term economic or demographic shifts, that are more important in shaping international relations than the discrete decisions of statesmen. These insights should be especially welcome in regard to a subject as important as nuclear weapons and their effect on international relations and US global policy. As Arthur Schlesinger Jr. wrote shortly before his death, "We are the world's dominant military power, and I believe a consciousness of history is a moral necessity for a nation possessed of overweening power."[10]

If historical work is so beneficial to understanding nuclear statecraft, why is there not more effort made to grapple with these extraordinarily important and complex nuclear issues, to get to the bottom of what actually happened and how things work? There are, of course, disciplinary and institutional reasons: for the most part, the field of academic history has moved away from focusing on questions of great power politics, war and peace, and national security. Diplomatic and military history are in the midst of a decades-long crisis. According to a *New York Times* article about the decline of diplomatic history, "job openings on the nation's college campuses are scarce, while bread-and-butter courses like the Origins of War and American Foreign Policy are dropping from history department postings."[11] Despite enormous student demand, the history of US foreign relations, grand strategy, and international relations is not taught by full-time faculty at many top-flight American universities. When it is, it is presented in a way that would be virtually unrecognizable to policy experts outside of academia. As the *New York Times* article laments, "In 1975, for example, three-quarters of college history departments employed at least one diplomatic historian; in 2005 fewer than half did."[12] Teaching and researching US foreign policy and international affairs, to say nothing of nuclear statecraft, is simply not a priority within many history departments where interaction with those connected with power is seen as corrupting.

Even within the subfields of foreign policy and international affairs nuclear questions have not received the attention they deserve. Campbell Craig points out, "The idea that thermonuclear war can put an end to everything plays a strikingly small part in the history of formal American thinking about international politics. . . . In the few histories that are available, nuclear war occupies a minor role."[13] Historians have often been as guilty as theorists/strategists in conflating the history of the nuclear age with that of the Cold War, assuming containment and deterrence were the same policies and focusing on blame rather than the causes of historical outcomes during the decades after World War II.[14]

Fortunately, and to their great credit, many political scientists have moved to fill this void left by professional historians. Young scholars trained in the same theoretical/strategic tradition I criticize at times in this book are actually writing some of the best historical work on the nuclear age. A younger generation of theorists and strategists are exploring the archives and acquiring skills in historical research.[15] There is far more to be done, however. Even if this kind of work were encouraged and supported in academia, there are substantial barriers that go beyond the ideological and political battles within the discipline of history. Undertaking the study of contemporary history is always a daunting challenge.[16] Assessing recent events often makes it hard to create the necessary distance for achieving a proper perspective. Current events, particularly when they are part of the policy process, can be emotional and polarizing. "Historical knowledge," according to historian Bruce Kuklick, "depends on a temporal perspective. Events take on their historical meaning with the passage of time."[17] The debates over nuclear strategy and weapons systems in the late 1970s and early 1980s, for example, were deeply politicized and part of partisan politics. Controversial policies, such as the Carter administration's decision to deploy medium-range missiles in Western Europe, or the Reagan administration's Strategic Defense Initiative (SDI), stirred deep emotions that often colored analysis. According to Robert Jervis, historians are more inclined than theorists and strategists to "make value and ethical judgments about the conduct of those they are studying."[18] If this is true, it is unfortunate: although difficult, rigorous scholarship demands that the historian distance himself or herself from the passions of the times in order to try to reconstruct the story as objectively as possible.[19]

We also face the challenge of periodization. We have a sense of when the nuclear era began—although one could argue that there are important substantive differences between the atomic and the thermonuclear ages or that the emergence of "mutual vulnerability" was the key marker or that there is a "second nuclear age" that began when the Cold War ended. But it is hard to place where we are in the story today. Unlike the history of feudalism or the Anglo-German naval race, for example, we lack an "ending," a full narrative arc or at times even a known direction, which forces our judgments to be tentative at best. It is like reviewing a movie before it is finished and without knowing how much longer it will go on: "One cannot write a history of a conflict until it is over."[20] And unless the global zero movement is successful—which is difficult to imagine—there is no end to this challenge, as the nuclear age will continue for some time to come.

There are four additional challenges to researching and writing nuclear history. First, the world of nuclear policy was and remains, for understandable reasons, veiled in secrecy, and getting access to the full documentary record is difficult. Furthermore, even in the case of the United States, the public rhetoric of nuclear strategy has often been quite different than, and often at odds with, the actual policy. Nuclear rhetoric was commonly used in the past to convey signals, reassure allies, and demonstrate resolve, making it even more difficult to interpret public speeches and pronouncements. Consider Secretary of Defense McNamara's 1962 speech to NATO in Athens, in which he condemned separate allied nuclear forces like France's.[21] Only weeks earlier, he suggested providing aid for France's nuclear program (see chapter 2). Or reflect on President Nixon's public embrace of arms control, which masked his private disdain for it, or his comment on US nuclear strategy: "Flexible response is baloney."[22] There is always a problematic, though some might say necessary, gap between what U.S. policy actually is and what the larger public is told, but figuring out the real story is particularly difficult with nuclear matters.[23]

Second, undertaking the writing of nuclear history involves assessing what did *not* happen, such as why there has never been a thermonuclear war or why nuclear weapons have not been used in battle since August 1945. It is close to impossible for historians to come to a consensus even on things that have happened. So how do we make sense of such a critical nonevent as (relative) peace and stability or, more pointedly, the nonuse of a weapon? In regard to the nonappearance of a phenomenon, it is extraordinarily difficult to assess competing claims and explanations.

Consider the absence of a great power war in post–World War II Europe, a nonevent of fundamental importance. Was it caused by nuclear deterrence, as many strategists claim? Or would great power peace have emerged, even without nuclear weapons, because Europeans had grown disgusted by war, a claim famously made by John Mueller?[24] Tony Judt has made the controversial suggestion that Europe's postwar peace may have been a product of the "success" of ethnic cleansing in the first half of the twentieth century.[25] There are other arguments as well—globalization, economic integration, technology, changing demographic patterns—that could explain the disappearance of great power war. But how can we explain something that did not happen, something we would presumably like to continue have not happening? We have a powerful intuitive sense that nuclear weapons must have been a driver, if the not the key one, but how can we prove it? The absence of measurable historical phenomena has made it natural for theorists/strategists to dominate the debate. As political scientist Richard Betts points out, "nuclear war spurred theorizing because it was inherently more theoretical than empirical: none had ever occurred. Except for Hiroshima and Nagasaki, where there was no question of retaliation, there was no messy store of historical evidence to complicate elegant abstractions."[26] Marc Trachtenberg makes this point as well: "The basic issues were analyzed on a very abstract level. One could work out in general terms the argument for 'strategic stability,' or for various nuclear war–fighting strategies. But at this level of abstraction there were no final answers—at this abstract level of conceptualization the most basic intellectual tensions could not be resolved."[27] Theorists/strategists may have made this more confusing by conflating theories about the causes of war and theories about the nuclear revolution, which, while obviously related, may not always be about the same thing.[28]

The third, and related, challenge is: How does one disentangle "nuclear history" from the history of the Cold War, decolonization, the rise of the global economic order, the spread of democracy, or sharp regional competitions in East Asia, South Asia, Europe, or the Middle East? The military and ideological competition between the Soviet Union and the United States was sometimes central, and at other times peripheral, to these histories. To what extent did nuclear weapons shape these histories? How did these histories drive nuclear questions? And what influence did the superpower arms competition have on decisions? This is obviously part of a far larger, more difficult problem—attempting to identify the causes and agents driving world politics since 1945, and explaining how these different causes and agents interacted with one another. These are not easy tasks, but we must attempt it if we are to comprehend the dynamics of nuclear statecraft. To make sense of this issue, imagine a history book written fifty or one hundred years from now: Will the nuclear revolution be at the core of this history or at the periphery? Or will it be so much a part of the assumed structure of world politics, that its transformative nature will hardly be remarked on?

To better understand how hard it is to "disentangle" history, think about a simple counterfactual: What would the Cold War have looked like, if it had happened at all, in a world where there were no nuclear weapons? This is not as implausible a scenario as it might seem—the US decision to pursue the Manhattan Project was not inevitable or uncontroversial. It was extraordinarily expensive, and it relied on assembling the most amazing collection of scientific talent the world had ever seen. Pursuing atomic weapons involved controversial strategic decisions and diverting critical resources from other important parts of the war effort.[29] Other national programs were nowhere near as advanced, and without a US program, the Soviets might not have had the motivation or the scientific information to develop their own atomic weapon.[30] In this imaginary nonnuclear war, would the odds of a large-scale land war in Europe after 1945 have increased measurably? Or were the keenest crises of the Cold War—in Berlin and Cuba—exacerbated and perhaps even caused by nuclear weapons? Were wars in Korea and Vietnam related to the need to establish credibility and commitment, qualities less important in a world where power was measured by the number of tanks and battleships a nation possessed, not by a willingness to demonstrate resolve? In short, was the history of the Cold War the same as the history of the nuclear arms competition between the United States and the Soviet Union? And, if they were different, how do we separate out the causal agents of each narrative?

The fourth challenge to nuclear history—arguably the most difficult and the one most highlighted throughout this book—is disentangling the interaction between the prescriptive/predictive, reactive, and descriptive and the dominating, even intimidating, position nuclear theory and strategy have had in scholarship on nuclear statecraft. As Campbell Craig suggests, "crossing into the world of political science is an adventure that is not going to appeal to most practicing historians."[31] This, according to Richard Betts, has left the ground wide open for the theorist/strategist: "With scant empirical grounds for testing propositions, nuclear strategy and deterrence seemed perfectly suited to deductive logic and game theory."[32]

Any historian of the nuclear age is immediately confronted by the legacy of these strategists, who have produced a powerful body of theories about why states seek nuclear weapons and how weapons shape states' behavior. These theorists and strategists were unusual because of their interest in policy and in believing that their ideas should be (and often were) incorporated into national strategy, at least in the United States. This is a further challenge to the historian. It was not that these strategists and theorists were particularly powerful or close to power, though they often were: many of them served in government or were employed by defense contractors, think tanks, and universities that were intimately connected to policy. The real challenge is that the theories they developed to understand the influence of nuclear weapons on world politics were believed to be so clear and so accessible that they were almost deterministic.[33] For example, theorists claimed that at a point at which two adversaries are both vulnerable to unacceptable levels of damage in a nuclear war even if they launched their weapons first, then governments would no longer feel a need to expand their nuclear forces. The whole approach to international politics would change. A national strategy that at one time sought to maximize power by adding military capabilities would change to one that seeks to avoid nuclear war and promote political stability through deterrence and arms control. These simple but powerful ideas were at the very heart of thinking about nuclear issues from the time that Bernard Brodie published *The Absolute Weapon* in 1946. People who suggested that these weapons be eliminated, on the one extreme, or used, on the other, were dismissed as failing to understand the powerful new logic of international politics in a nuclear world. They were not taken seriously by the inner circle of nuclear theorists and strategists.

Why understand what actually happened, how nuclear dynamics actually worked, when the theories made it clear there was only one way the story could unfold? "By the 1960s theorists had highly developed ideas about how to organize nuclear capabilities to stabilize US-Soviet deterrence. According to Betts, arguments among strategists from the ivory tower about logical effects of "invulnerable second strike capability," "reciprocal fear of surprise attack," "counterforce options," "mutual assured destruction," "graduated escalation," and "crisis stability" had a profound influence on civilian leaders."[34] And, as mentioned in the introduction, the very newness and profound impact of the nuclear revolution made the prenuclear world seem irrelevant. What could the Crimean War or the Boer War or the emergence of the Gatling gun possibly tell us about nuclear statecraft, especially compared to an elegant and parsimonious theory such as the stability-instability paradox or the spiral model?

And, in fact, the world of theory and the world of practice often seemed, from a distance, to walk hand in hand. Secretary McNamara's public embrace of "mutual assured destruction" (MAD) or the Nixon administration's negotiation of a treaty limiting both strategic offensive and defensive weapons seemed to be pulled right from the playbook of the leading theorists.[35] Of course, when policymakers wandered away from the core precepts of the theorists, as chapter 6 reveals, the criticism could be sharp. Policies premised on the idea that nuclear superiority could be translated into politically useful power or that strategic defenses could be an important part of national defense were ridiculed by many within the small but influential cadre of theorists and strategists as "illogical." These less-than-utility-maximizing positions were often dismissed as being produced by suboptimizing forces such as domestic or bureaucratic politics, ideology, or even autonomous structural forces outside the political process.[36]

This is not to dismiss the quality of either the theoretical work or the policies that have animated nuclear statecraft since 1945. On the policy side, we have not seen nuclear weapons used since 1945; the number of nuclear powers in the world is far smaller than anyone would have predicted fifty, forty, or thirty years ago; and we have a robust and impressive global arms control regime. No one would have predicted this remarkable result after the bloodletting of the first half of the twentieth century. Nuclear theorists have produced rigorous and insightful scholarship, much of which has been an aid to making nuclear statecraft more effective. The father of nuclear strategy, Thomas Schelling, was awarded the Nobel Prize in economics for his contributions to theory and policy: his efforts at understanding the nuclear arms race "have proven to be of great relevance for conflict resolution and efforts to avoid war."[37] The intellectual, policy, and institutional legacy of nuclear strategy theory is extraordinary.

Encountering such powerful ideas, ideas that appear to have been reflected in policy, is bound to intimidate a historian in search of documents to help understand exactly what happened and what it means. It is also necessary to historicize not just the policy process surrounding nuclear statecraft but the whole intellectual apparatus that created the theories, especially as this apparatus was born simultaneously with, or as the product of, the phenomena it was meant to study.[38] We should not, however, simply accept the claims made by theorists or policymakers at face value: Does the archival evidence reveal that what they say should happen actually did take place? And, if so, for the reasons they have posited? Did these theories accurately predict and explain the dynamics of a nuclear world and lay the foundation for the correct policies? Is the approach of the theorists and strategists, impressive as it is, the right approach to understanding the history of nuclear policy and politics? And if the documents reveal a story that varies from the explanations of the theorists, what is the historian to make of this?

What We Think We Know and Why We Need History

Armed with powerful theories and long-standing policies, we think we know much about the history of the nuclear age. Much of this narrative, however, has been based on the work of theorists and strategists and supplemented by public declarations of US policy. This story, which quickly became the received wisdom, was "apolitical" and "ahistorical." To the degree that history was considered at all, it "was more of a source of illustration than of insight."[39] But until we undertake more detailed historical research, these claims are, at best, unproven assertions. A better balance between description and prescription/prediction is needed; history can provide a powerful supplement, and even check, to the dominance of social science in matters of nuclear statecraft.

Look, for example, at the whole question of nuclear deterrence and its relationship to what historian John Lewis Gaddis termed "the Long

Peace" between the Soviet Union and the United States. A variety of assertions were made by theorists and strategists that often shaped policy in critical ways. First of these claims is that nuclear weapons in certain circumstances and under certain deployments can stabilize great power politics by making war unthinkable. In other words, in a nonnuclear world acrimony between the Soviet Union and the United States would have likely led to war. This simple and powerful claim is often repeated. Consider a more recent assertion of this view in a discussion of our policies toward terrorists and so-called rogue states: two prominent strategists claim "The threat of massive nuclear retaliation deterred the Soviet Union from directly attacking US interests and helped maintain a tense yet stable peace for nearly half a century."[40]

There are all sorts of reasons to question how we can know whether this was true or not, and without a careful historical reconstruction of how policy was actually made on both the US and Soviet sides, it is nearly impossible to determine what drove decision making. (And even with that reconstruction it is uncertain.) The important point here is that the powerful theory of nuclear deterrence was believed in, fed into the policy process, and created a sort of surface-level history of the period. Theorists said nuclear weapons deter war, and since there was no superpower war, nuclear deterrence must have been the key to preventing major armed conflict between the United States and Soviet Union. This theory shapes our view of the past and informs our policy debates today, from questions ranging to the global zero movement to the modernization of our weapons systems, and to responses to terrorism. But in actuality, we don't really know if these claims are true or not.

By "in certain circumstances and under certain deployments" I am referring to two separate but related claims made by well-respected nuclear strategists: First, that nuclear weapons make the so-called security dilemma worse and that this situation can best be abated by arms control. Second, that once each rival is no longer vulnerable to a devastating surprise attack with nuclear weapons, there is little purpose in adding additional nuclear capabilities.

The "security dilemma" is a situation in which one side takes measures it considers defensive but that are seen by an adversary as offensive and threatening; this can spiral out of control and lead to a destabilizing arms race and even a war neither side truly wants. Security dilemma dynamics are increased, according to theorists, by the particular characteristics and nature of nuclear weapons, which involve enormous incentives in a crisis to use them first and massively. This could produce enormous pressure on policymakers and pave the way for destabilizing misperceptions and misunderstandings. American theorists and policymakers alike feared a Soviet first strike, a bolt from the blue. At the very least, they worried that US nuclear weapons were vulnerable to attack—and, in later years, that command, control, communications, and intelligence systems were vulnerable.

The elegant and powerful theories that went into these ideas are well known and far better described elsewhere, but it is fair to say many strategists took them as the gospel truth. These theories, however, were based on a certain view of the world: that the international system was no longer solely driven by geopolitical competition between the great states. While these drives still mattered, international relations were now shaped by the existence of and interaction between rival nuclear forces. The weapons themselves—their lethality, their numbers, their deployments—drove the politics, not the other way around. The interaction could produce outcomes—arms races, dangerous crises, and even inadvertent war—separate from the political sources of the rivalry. These theories implied that the most effective policy might not be focusing on the underlying political dispute between rivals but to control their weapons and their interactions. One way was to pursue certain strategies and deployments that would signal relatively benign intents to one's adversary, such as eschewing defensive weapons and targeting population centers rather than the rival's weapons systems.[41] It also meant that mutual efforts had to be made to limit dangers and to negotiate, not about the core geopolitical issues driving the dispute, but control of the weapons themselves.[42]

This is an extraordinary way of viewing international relations, a view that has been the foundation for three generations of arms control officials. But does it accurately reflect the way the world works? It is interesting to reflect on how rarely the ups and downs of the superpower geopolitical competition mirrored the movements of the arms race. The Soviets pushed the United States aggressively on the issue of West Germany's military status by threatening West Berlin's viability at a time when the USSR was not only weak but potentially open to a US first strike in the late 1950s and early 1960s.[43] The Soviets left West Berlin alone after 1962, even as the US nuclear superiority that arguably helped protect the city disappeared. Why? Because the core geopolitical questions surrounding West Germany's military and political status were resolved, largely to the Soviet Union's satisfaction.[44] In fact, it is very hard to find any evidence that a security dilemma drove the rivalry between the United States and the Soviet Union in Berlin or that the Soviets ever considered launching a "bolt from the blue" against the United States.[45] As Trachtenberg suggests, "the strategists as a group . . . vastly overestimated the extent to which war could result from essentially military factors; the problem of 'strategic stability' had been greatly exaggerated."[46]

This framework—a focus on the weapons and strategies and not the underlying politics—still dominates the scholarly analysis of these issues. Compare three excellent articles from the prestigious journal *International Security* that assess the nuclear postures of China, Pakistan, and the United States. M. Taylor Fravel and Evan S. Medieros ponder the puzzle of why China's nuclear strategy has been rather unsophisticated for decades, not achieving the level of assured destruction that most US nuclear strategists and theorists would have expected. What could produce this "suboptimal" outcome? Since financial constraints cannot explain China's unexpected behavior, the authors focus on particular leaders, their ideologies, and persistent bureaucratic and organizational constraints as an explanation.[47] Vipin Narang tries to make sense of Pakistan's shift of posture from catalytic to asymmetric escalation, highlighting how Pakistan's eschewing assured destruction and embracing a strategy predicated on the early use of nuclear weapons in conventional conflict with India is extremely dangerous and destabilizing.[48] Looking at the United States, Daryl G. Press and Kier Lieber warn that the decline of Russia's nuclear forces, the quiescence of China's nuclear posture, and the continuing technological advance of US nuclear capabilities could lead to an American primacy that would be deeply destabilizing by offering powerful incentives for either or both sides to use nuclear weapons in a crisis.[49] Their analysis is premised on the idea that mutual vulnerability was the primary cause of stability and peace between the Soviet Union and the United States during much of the Cold War and that loss of the mutuality is to be avoided if possible.

Explicitly or implicitly, all three analyses generate their puzzles by identifying deviations from an idealized vision of the most "rational" and stabilizing nuclear posture, some variation on mutual assured destruction. Yet might this supposed puzzle—not embracing the optimal, or most stabilizing, nuclear strategy—be solved by understanding the political goals the state in question was seeking? For a China that is seeking economic growth, better relations with nearby trading partners, and inclusion in a world economic system dominated by the United States a minimal deterrent may suffice to guarantee its territorial security. Pakistan, seeking territorial adjustments against a bitter enemy with larger conventional capabilities, may desire a more aggressive nuclear posture, regardless of how destabilizing it is. The United States may seek primacy, less to threaten Russia than to assure and prevent proliferation by potential allies such as Germany and Japan. The absence of any fundamental existing political dispute between the United States and Russia, and the unlikelihood of one appearing soon, would seem to be a far more important indicator of future stability or conflict than the nuclear balance.

Whether these specific assessments are correct or not is not the point. Rather, my suggestion is that the puzzle emerges from the political goals each state is attempting to achieve rather than solely from the nature of the weapons themselves and that it is important to understand the ambitions of each state in question. Which framework one chooses—whether to focus on the weapons or the underlying politics—has enormous policy consequences. Consider potential approaches to a nuclearized Pakistan. What would be a more effective use of scarce diplomatic capital—to seek some kind of arms control and shift in Pakistan's military strategy, or to make an effort to resolve the underlying political issues driving the posture? Obviously, they are not mutually exclusive—the point here is that they are inextricably linked—but the nuclear posture does not emerge from a political vacuum.

To be clear, this is not to dismiss the profound impact of nuclear weapons on decision making or the shape of international relations—quite the contrary—or to deny that a deeper historical examination might uncover evidence for the theories favored by strategists. The point here is that until such evidence is found, a bit more humility about the claims for a particular kind of nuclear revolution may be in order. This humility is especially appropriate when applying these theories to non-US nuclear powers. There is a certain kind of myopia, a US-centric focus, in the strategy community on these questions. The mantra of US-based strategists and theorists has always been the need to develop secure second-strike forces.[50] A failure to do so—or an effort by the United States to exploit this vulnerability—is, it is argued, deeply destabilizing. Could it be, however, that a minimal deterrent is far more powerful than we have believed, at least in the eyes of non-US decision makers? Do larger, more sophisticated nuclear forces and forward-leaning strategies reflect a desire to do something more than simply deter an attack on the homeland, such as signal a desire to change the geopolitical status quo or to extend deterrence over another country? For that matter, might the whole US policy of extending deterrence through first-use nuclear superiority, strategic defense, and counterforce be seen by other states as an exercise in (irresponsible) brinksmanship? Historically reconstructing what went into these decisions and responses—not just in the United States, but in the Soviet Union, China, Israel, South Africa, Pakistan, India, and other states—could go a long way to telling us how universally applicable our body of nuclear theories really are across time and space.

Take another, related question of extraordinary policy importance—the role of the Nuclear Nonproliferation Treaty in world politics. Many see it as the ultimate bulwark against the spread of nuclear weapons, built on important norms and international law. Few commentators, however, understand the process that motivated the treaty. As I lay out in chapter 4, during the first part of the nuclear age, policymakers were not convinced the United States could do very much to prevent proliferation, even if it wanted to. Two complicated and potentially dangerous geopolitical questions emerged in the late 1950s and early 1960s to change this view—West Germany's and China's interest in obtaining nuclear weapons. Up until that point, aspiring nuclear powers were largely status quo oriented. West Germany, however, was a divided country that had caused two world wars and was committed to eventual reunification. China was seen as the ultimate revolutionary "rouge" state, and in recent memory it had fought US troops in Korea, attacked India, threatened Taiwan, and armed the Viet Cong. A nuclearized West Germany or China had the potential to destabilize the international system in ways an atomic France, Sweden, or Brazil would not. One cannot begin to understand the origins of the NPT without coming to grips with these issues.[51] How much of our contemporary policy or theory about nuclear statecraft takes this into consideration?

Or look at horizontal history, how things happen over space (as opposed to time). As detailed in chapter 2, the United States in the 1960s considered deep cuts in conventional forces abroad because the treasury was hemorrhaging dollars and gold. The balance-of-payments question was the foremost issue in US foreign economic policy, and overseas military deployment, particularly in West Germany, was the most obvious target for substantial savings. A withdrawal, however, could undermine West German confidence in the US commitment to protect it from the Soviets, increasing their temptation to acquire their own nuclear weapons. This was a deeply destabilizing possibility that no one—not the Soviets, the British, the French, or most Americans—wanted to see come to pass. The policies that emerged can only be understood by reconstructing the history of events and policies that were all occurring at the same time but which are rarely connected—US international monetary policy, nuclear and conventional military strategy, and political relations with West Germany.[52] It is from these horizontal connections that the strategy of flexible response emerged, something rarely recognized in theoretical studies of nuclear statecraft.

To complicate matters further, sometimes policies run against mainstream theories. Consider the much-debated question of nuclear proliferation. Most nuclear theories tell us that deterrence is a good thing and that, in many circumstances, it enhances global peace and stability. This might lead policymakers to be sanguine about the spread of nuclear weapons. Yet, as we know, the US government has vigorously pursued policies to prevent the spread of nuclear weapons, using treaties, security guarantees, sanctions, and even the threat of preventive military action to staunch and even reverse proliferation. If the theory is right, isn't the policy wrong?

Here is an area where developing a historical sensibility, what Trachtenberg calls a "historic sense or sensitivity," beyond simply going into the archives and finding primary documents can be helpful in understanding a complex issue and tying together divergent strands of a narrative. In reviewing US policy during the nuclear age, one notices a wide range of policies oriented at limiting proliferation. In some cases, these policies are coercive—there is consideration of preventive strikes, bold threats, and debilitating sanctions. In other cases, the tools are friendlier—conventional arms sales and extended deterrent guarantees to protect states willing to go without their own nuclear weapons. Negotiating international treaties, highlighted by the Nuclear Nonproliferation Treaty, and encouraging a norm of nonpossession might be seen as the "soft power" side of a rather one-sided, calculating strategy by the United States. Even decisions about nuclear strategy and deployments—from a never-ending interest in missile defense, an unwillingness to renounce the first use of nuclear weapons, and strategies that were, regardless of public rhetoric, oriented toward preemption and counterforce—look different when tied together with these other, seemingly unrelated decisions. A picture emerges from the documents of an overarching inclination (if not quite a fully formed strategy) to inhibit and even reverse the spread of nuclear weapons. Policies that made little sense before obtain a certain coherence in this new framework. Policies ascribed to suboptimal causes, such as ideology, bureaucratic politics, missile defense, or counterforce targeting, take on a new meaning when historical sensibility and archival research come into play.

Historians explore the archives expecting, indeed hoping, to be surprised or even proven wrong. I went into the archives to try to understand US international monetary policy and emerged with questions about US military strategy and nonproliferation policies. Over time, I changed my views on what motivated America's effort to stop and reverse the spread of nuclear weapons. I still see the potential nuclearization of West Germany and China, and the threats that posed to the international order, as motivating the United States to more vigorously pursue nuclear nonproliferation. But the more I look into the documents, the more I think the United States has often hoped to restrict the spread of nuclear weapons by foe and friend alike, not because of any enlightened notions of world peace, but because a state with nuclear weapons can cancel out every other form of US power. In the end, understanding whether different strands—from treaties to threats of preemptive strikes—of US policy were connected and what were the motivations is the kind of complex and important question historical research should grapple with.

A plea for a greater interest in and commitment to nuclear history is not a call to dismiss theory, ignore strategy, or criticize policies. It is important, however, to acknowledge how much uncertainty surrounds most of our theories and frameworks concerning nuclear statecraft. In the end, of course, policies have to be made, but these policy decisions, even if they are based on uncertainty, do create their own, often self-reinforcing, reality. Vigorous and critical historical analysis of our nuclear past can help us better assess the effectiveness and wisdom of these policies, and avoid an overreliance on elegant but untested theories.

Many questions surrounding nuclear statecraft would benefit from a historical, as opposed to a purely theoretical, perspective. Has the creation and spread of nuclear weapons decreased, if not eliminated, the prospect of great power wars of the type that killed tens of millions of people in the first half of the twentieth century? If so, how and under what conditions? Is it better for more states to possess these weapons, or for fewer to do so? Should these weapons only be held by great powers and not medium-size and even smaller states? Does the ideological orientation of the state in question, or its form of governance, matter? And, if so, in what ways? Why do some states eschew nuclear weapons while others take great risks to acquire them? Are nuclear weapons only useful for defensive or deterrent purposes, or can they be used for offensive ends, or in order to revise the international order? Can these weapons be used for purposes other than deterring an attack on a country's homeland? Can they be used solely to protect an ally? How effective has arms control been, what motivates it, and what are the prospects for, and wisdom of, complete nuclear disarmament? There are benefits in reconstructing how policymakers have thought about these issues, how decisions have been weighed and made—not just in the United States but in every country that has acquired or thought about acquiring nuclear weapons.

We have lots of impressive theories surrounding these questions but, in truth, very little certainty as to what the answers are. Historical work will not cure that problem. Even a concerted effort to uncover nuclear history may increase our certainty only at the margins, and only highlight for us what we don't know and what we can't really know. Even those meager results will not come easy. Good historical research will require scholars, not just to locate and work in the most appropriate archives, but to penetrate the secrecy and deceptive rhetoric found at times in declassified documents. Furthermore, researchers must contextualize thoughts and documents in their own times and avoid many of the same theologies that infect much of strategic theory. Finally, historical analysis will have to determine how much of this is an "American" story and what the parallels and difference are with nuclear statecraft in countries such as the former Soviet Union, China, and West Germany.

What is the payoff to this herculean effort? Perhaps the very humility such an exercise would provide, humility necessarily absent in both generating theory and making policy, might be the greatest reward of all. Michael Howard, who both studied and witnessed the destruction involved in total war, makes perhaps the most compelling argument for a historical perspective:

> People, often of masterful intelligence, trained usually in law or economics or perhaps political science . . . have led their governments into disastrous miscalculations because they have no awareness whatever of the historical background, the cultural universe of the foreign societies with which they have to deal. It is an awareness for which no amount of strategic or economic analysis, no techniques of crisis management or conflict resolution . . . can provide a substitute.[53]

Even a deep familiarity with history is no guarantee against disastrous decisions in matters of war and peace. Given the enormous stakes behind nuclear statecraft, however, it makes sense to bring all the methods and knowledge we possess to bear on these issues, even if absolute certainty continues to elude us.

[2]

The Myth of Flexible Response

American Strategy in Europe during the 1960s

How did US military policy change from the 1950s to the 1960s? Pick up almost any book on the subject and you find virtually the same answer: America's national security policy was dramatically transformed on January 20, 1961, when the incoming Kennedy administration began replacing Eisenhower's concept of "massive retaliation" with a new military strategy called "flexible response." Flexible response was seen as a radical departure from the policies of the past, especially in relation to the Soviet threat to Western Europe. The new strategy was supposed to enhance deterrence by providing the president with "flexible" nuclear options and increased conventional capabilities to deal with a variety of military crises in Europe.

This is the view of flexible response that is widely held by strategists and historians. Jane Stromseth, a leading expert on the question, for example, contends that flexible response replaced "the 'suicide or surrender' dilemma" of Eisenhower's massive retaliation strategy by providing "a genuine alternative to nuclear escalation in the event of a Soviet conventional attack."[1] The foremost historian of the period, John Lewis Gaddis, maintains that this new strategy required a buildup of US conventional forces in order to "increase the range of options prior to resort to nuclear war" and to avoid the dangers of nuclear "proliferation."[2] Robert McNamara's biographer claims that Eisenhower's readiness to "fire off American nuclear rockets at almost any Communist affront" was "highly dangerous." Kennedy believed "that the United States should build up its conventional forces to have the option of large-scale non-nuclear war, or what [General Maxwell] Taylor called flexible response."[3] Aaron Friedberg, the author of a landmark study of America's Cold War strategy agrees, claiming that a conventional buildup was "designed to increase the ability of the United States and its NATO allies to hold out against at least the initial stages of a Soviet-led thrust into Western Europe without resorting to the widespread use of nuclear weapons."[4] An important strategist concurs, suggesting that the "basic guidelines for the strategic doctrines of the Kennedy administration were derived from the critique of the strategy of 'massive retaliation' as it had evolved during the 1950's."[5] Kennedy "opposed massive retaliation," favored the buildup of "limited war" forces, and was "RAND's nearly ideal candidate."[6] These types of statements are found repeatedly throughout the scholarly literature dealing with the origins and impact of America's flexible response strategy in Europe.[7]

But the standard interpretation is wrong. A detailed examination of the evidence makes it clear that the operational changes in US strategy in Europe during the 1960s have been vastly overstated. Declassified documents and transcribed recordings reveal that top officials—including the president and the secretary of defense—did not buy into many of the core strategic arguments surrounding the flexible response doctrine. Like Eisenhower before them, they were not convinced that "controlled" nuclear war was possible; they entertained the possibility of assisting independent European nuclear programs; and they would have preferred to reduce rather than enlarge America's conventional forces in Western Europe.

The rhetoric of flexible response, however, was convenient to top US policymakers for reasons that had little to do with enhancing deterrence or winning a nuclear war. Although Kennedy, like Eisenhower, did want a wider range of military options to deal with the anomalous challenge of maintaining West Berlin's viability in the face of Soviet pressure, neither president believed the "flexible" options they desired for the Berlin crisis would be appropriate responses to a Soviet blitzkrieg or even a limited Soviet land grab, contingencies that would elicit from them an immediate nuclear response. The Kennedy administration's rhetorical adoption of the concept of flexible response, and the Johnson administration's efforts to get the NATO alliance to embrace the strategy, were motivated in large part by the need to ease difficult intra-alliance tensions over the two fundamental, intertwined questions of the Cold War in Europe: the German question and the nuclear question. By emphasizing conventional forces, controlled response, and centralized command and control of nuclear weapons, the new rhetorical strategy helped resolve a number of extraordinarily complex and potentially explosive political issues surrounding the military status of West Germany.

Understanding the real origins and meaning of the flexible response strategy is important for reasons that go well beyond simply correcting the conventional wisdom about the most significant strategic change of the nuclear age. This new evidence demonstrates that America's "strategy of containment" was not just meant for the Soviet Union. US policies on nuclear sharing and conventional forces in Europe were often shaped as much by the complexities of the "German question" as narrow military considerations vis-à-vis the Soviets, especially after the Berlin Crisis and Cuban missile crisis were resolved. This new understanding of flexible response also has important implications for international relations theory. Contrary to Waltzian neorealism, US strategy in Europe reveals that the Cold War was not simply a bipolar struggle and that balancing went on both within and between "alliances." Waltzian neorealism, which asserts that allies were irrelevant during this bipolar struggle between the superpowers, must come to terms with US strategy in Europe during the 1960s, since Waltz's arguments about the dynamics of bipolar systems and alliances are based entirely on the Cold War.

This aspect of flexible response has relevance today. The United States still maintains a significant conventional troop presence in places that were hot spots during the Cold War—including Germany—three decades after the collapse of the Soviet Union. Since America's "dual containment" policies in Japan, South Korea, and Taiwan may be challenged in the future, revisiting how America's restraint mission was handled in West Germany during the 1960s can provide guidance for this complicated situation in the years to come.[8]

Defining the Strategy of Flexible Response

What did "flexible response" mean more specifically in terms of US strategy in Europe? The term was quite vague, and it was rarely used in private meetings by top officials during the 1960s. National Security Advisor McGeorge Bundy, criticizing the process of rewriting the Eisenhower's Basic National Security Policy, told the US State Department's head of policy planning Walt Rostow that he had "grave reservations about the notions implied by the words 'doctrine' and 'strategy' in connection with basic policy."[9] During a White House staff meeting, Bundy also said "in the most serious way that he felt there was really no logic whatever to 'nuclear policy.'" In other words, "military planners who calculate that we will win if only we can kill 100 million Russians while they are killing 30 million Americans are living in total dreamland."[10]

The man responsible for implementing strategy in Europe, NATO's Supreme Allied Commander in Europe, Gen. Lyman Lemnitzer, actually "forbid the use of the term [flexible response] throughout SHAPE [Supreme Headquarters Allied Powers Europe] and Allied Command Europe." Lemnitzer complained that "so many of my people didn't really know what flexible response meant."[11] And the official history of America's nuclear command-and-control effort produced by the Institute for Defense Analysis contends that "to the extent it amounted to a doctrine, it was open to different interpretations, and it is not easy (if at all possible) to find a single coherent, clear statement of it, even among authoritative pronouncements of the President and the Secretary of Defense."[12]

In spite of this confusion, the term "flexible response" is normally associated with a certain cluster of ideas that had important implications for America's NATO strategy in Europe during the 1960s. In terms of general strategy, the idea was to move away from what was viewed as excessive reliance on nuclear weapons and to place greater emphasis on conventional capabilities.[13] Stronger conventional forces would allow NATO to respond credibly and effectively to Soviet provocations that did not merit full-scale nuclear attack, such as the seizure of a "hostage city" like Hamburg, or even a surprise Soviet conventional attack on Western Europe. In the narrower area of nuclear strategy, the idea was to shift away from a single all-out nuclear attack toward a policy of considering a controlled, discriminate nuclear war.[14]

This chapter will demonstrate that this view of flexible response is fundamentally misleading, at least for the 1960s. In the first section of this chapter I explore whether America's nuclear strategy really became more "flexible," by analyzing policy debates over controlled response, including damage limitation, nuclear sharing, and the military utility of tactical nuclear weapons during the 1960s. In the second section I investigate whether the United States, as is commonly argued, came to rely less on nuclear escalation and more on conventional options after 1961. This discussion analyzes the strong desire of Kennedy and McNamara to reduce conventional forces in Europe, and explains the specific connection between conventional forces and the crisis over Berlin's status. In the third section I examine the complicated relationship between flexible response, US conventional forces in Europe, and German nuclear politics during the Lyndon Johnson administration. I conclude with a summary of the myth of flexible response.

The Nuclear Dimension: Controlled Response

The strategy of flexible response demanded the ability to carry out limited nuclear options during a conflict. Flexible response was supposed to give the president the ability to deviate from preprogrammed attack packages in the "single integrated operational plan" (SIOP) with a less than all-out response. Could the United States "control and direct" nuclear forces in a crisis "as the military situation may dictate," as

McNamara claimed in a top secret statement made to NATO ministers in Athens?[15]

Despite widespread enthusiasm for the idea among defense analysts, it turned out that the ability to carry out "graduated" and "controlled" responses was simply not possible during the Kennedy and Johnson period. When McNamara first asked the Joint Chiefs of Staff (JCS) to prepare a doctrine that permitted controlled response and negotiation pauses, they replied that it could not be done.[16] In December 1961, the so-called Hickey group presented McNamara with a study that concluded that a controlled response could not be implemented before the late 1960s because of technical constraints.[17] Perhaps most surprising, very little was done to change the SIOP during this period. Historian David Rosenberg has shown that the actual changes made to the basic war plan during the Kennedy and Johnson administrations were relatively superficial.[18] Furthermore, the director of Joint Strategic Planning claims that McNamara allowed him and his staff to work out the war plan as they saw fit.[19]

Defense officials in the Nixon administration were shocked to find how little had actually been done in McNamara's Defense Department to provide for limited nuclear options. In early 1969, Nixon's Defense Department identified significant weaknesses in America's ability to respond flexibly to a less than all-out Soviet attack. The United States "had the number and types of weapons" but not the "planning and command and control capability" to respond with anything other than a large, preplanned nuclear assault.[20] The assistant secretary of defense for system analysis reluctantly concluded that the United States would not be able to respond "with strategic nuclear weapons at less than SIOP levels until 1975–76."[21] And when Secretary of Defense James Schlesinger laid out the Nixon administration's new nuclear strategy in 1974, he made it clear that it represented a dramatic change from the past:

> The thing that is different about the targeting doctrine that I have outlined to you is the emphasis on selectivity and flexibility. In the past we have had massive preplanned strikes in which one would be dumping literally thousands of weapons on the Soviet Union. Some of those strikes could to some extent be withheld from going directly against cities, but that was limited even then. With massive strikes of that sort, it would be impossible to ascertain whether the purpose of a strategic strike was limited or not.[22]

Despite the rhetorical emphasis on flexible nuclear response during the 1960s, it appears that Secretary McNamara quickly lost interest in the question of "controlled response" after his initial inquiries. Former government official Henry Rowen has pointed out that by 1963 McNamara no longer thought that efforts to produce flexible, limited nuclear options were worthwhile. The secretary of defense believed that the contingencies requiring nuclear weapons were so "unpredictable" that "nuclear planning could only be done when the contingency arose."[23] According to the 1975 report on nuclear command and control, the complex issues behind flexible nuclear options "that received major attention in the early 1960's" were "pushed into the background by the war" in Southeast Asia.[24] The period ended with "just as much, if not more" concern over the fundamental issue of survivability. In looking back on the 1960s, the report came to the conclusion that "the issue of flexible response seems to have been a less significant theme than it appeared at the time."[25] When Secretary Schlesinger was asked if the McNamara strategic plan involved a "a massive attack on cities and missile silos and other limited targets," which the Nixon administration was replacing with "a range of options which would range from attack on missile sites up to a massive attack on cities," he replied, "Yes, sir."[26]

The issues surrounding McNamara's calls for a second-strike counterforce capability—or damage-limiting force—are even murkier. In his first budget statement, McNamara suggested a strategic force that rejected both the extremes of a minimal deterrent and a first-strike capacity. The resulting compromise was a strategy known as "damage limitation," a posture that required strategic superiority in order to attack Soviet military targets after the United States had absorbed a Soviet first strike. This logic behind "damage limitation" was laid out to the NATO allies during the Athens meeting in May 1962.

It is clear that McNamara did not take the concept of second-strike counterforce seriously from the start. National Security Council staffer Carl Kaysen claimed in 1966 that McNamara presented a damage-limitation posture simply because he did not believe the public or the military would accept a minimal-deterrent policy. McNamara believed that "these figures were the lowest that he could consistently support and carry the military along with him."[27] An exchange between Department of Defense official Paul Nitze and McNamara soon after the Athens talk is also revealing. Nitze asked McNamara why he deleted the bracketed phrase, "relative to the US," from the following statement: "Attainment of a stable military environment requires strategic forces sufficiently effective so that Sino-Soviet leaders would expect—without question—the Bloc's present power position [relative to the US] to be worsened drastically as a result of a general nuclear war." Since the whole point of damage limitation was to demonstrate that the United States could survive a nuclear exchange with superior forces, Nitze wanted the deleted portion returned and the language strengthened. But McNamara refused, writing: "The concept of a 'worsened relative military position after a general nuclear war' is not a meaningful one to me when each side has the capacity to destroy each other's civilization."[28] It is important to remember that the Kennedy administration was confident of its overwhelming nuclear superiority at that time.

The question then becomes why the secretary of defense would argue for a nuclear strategy that he did not really believe in. An exchange with Britain's minister of defense, Peter Thorneycroft, is suggestive. When asked to explain his counterforce strategy, McNamara claimed that the whole point of the Athens talk was to convince the Soviets to harden their strategic forces. McNamara reasoned that the "Soviet forces were so soft that, if they believed the US were going to attack, the Soviets would have no option but to hit first. Therefore the Americans believed that the Russians would have to escape from this dilemma by hardening bases and sites and diversifying systems." McNamara believed that this "was because it would make for safety by reducing the pressure on the Soviets." McNamara concluded with the observation that "in the conditions of today neither side was likely in fact to resort to counter force strategy."[29] Thorneycroft found this a bizarre explanation and ascribed the real motives of the strategy laid out in Athens to US domestic politics.[30]

By the summer of 1963, the whole notion of a second-strike counterforce had been dropped. In a meeting on July 30, 1963, McNamara told Kennedy that such a strategy would no longer limit damage to the United States. When the president asked during a meeting with top officials what this did to the McNamara thesis—presumably the damage limitation strategy laid out at Athens—McGeorge Bundy jokingly replied: "That one was only good for about a year."[31] Over twenty years later, Bundy made the remarkable claim that that he and others in policymaking positions were "assiduous propagators of the fallacy of usable nuclear superiority. We owe some atonement for that."[32] And by the end of 1963, McNamara's budgets officially moved away providing for second-strike counterforce weapons to limit damage.[33]

The whole debate over second-strike strategies may have been irrelevant in any case. It appears that President Kennedy, unlike McNamara and Bundy, was far more interested in the mechanics and possibility of a US preemptive strike if a crisis with the Soviets got out of hand.[34] Kennedy told the JCS in 1961 that the critical point was to "use nuclear weapons at a crucial moment before they use them" and quizzed the JCS on the US capability of ordering a strike without letting the Soviets know.[35] The president stated that he had been told that if he ever released a nuclear weapon on the battlefield he "should start a pre-emptive attack on the Soviet Union," since "the use of nuclear weapons was bound to escalate and we might as well get the advantage by going first." During the

Cuban missile crisis, Kennedy pointed out that "everybody sort of figures that in extremis" nuclear weapons would be used. "The decision to use any kind of nuclear weapon, even the tactical ones, presents such a risk of it getting out of control so quickly, that there's . . ." Although the president's voice trailed off at this point, it seems clear that he was emphasizing the advantages of preemption.[36] This understanding of the logic of preemption is clear from Kennedy's comments a year later. When the president was told that a clean first strike was no longer possible, he asked, "Why [do] we need to have as much defense as we have?" since US strategy was now "based on the assumption that even if we strike first" the security of the US could not be protected in an ensuing nuclear war.[37]

While much of the evidence on this question has not been released, the question of replacing the SIOP with a limited first strike was investigated in 1961. New intelligence revealed that the Soviets had far fewer intercontinental ballistic missiles (ICBMs) than had been thought. Kaysen argued that a smaller, cleaner strike had a better chance of success and was more appropriate to contingencies arising out of the Berlin Crisis.[38] The president's military representative, Maxwell Taylor, forwarded Kaysen's analysis to the president with a covering report that was generally favorable. The day after receiving the report, the president quizzed his military advisers, including Gen. Thomas Power, chief of the Strategic Air Command, about the plan. Kennedy asked: "How much information did the Soviets need?" and "How long do they need to launch their missiles?"[39] Years later, Kaysen was asked if the point of this exercise was "an attempt to implement a relatively subtle strategy for controlled thermonuclear war," "the counterforce/no-cities" strategy that had been developed mainly at RAND in the late 1950s and that was later outlined by McNamara in his Athens and Ann Arbor talks in 1962:

> No, it was just, "Look, we may get in a war. We now know and have known for some months the Soviets really haven't got an operational missile force. Therefore, maybe we really can disarm them. Can we disarm them? It would be great if we could. By God, we can." That was all it was. I remember standing in the corridor outside the Cabinet Room in the White House with Harry [Rowen]. And, as I said, there had been some Berlin discussion and I don't know why I was there since I usually wasn't, but I was. And I said, "Look Harry, who the hell knows what's gonna happen? We ought to ask ourselves the question. We know the Soviets really have no missiles, that we can take care of them. Do we have a disarming strike and what will we need to do it?" And the point is, we didn't need all of SAC. That was the message. We just were saying, "Can we make sure that the Soviets can't launch a really serious heavy attack on the United States?" And the answer

was that in 1961 we could have made sure, with rather a high level of confidence.[40]

But it is important to point out that planning a clean first strike, with the goal of preempting the Soviets' ability to respond, is by no means the same thing as a flexible war-fighting doctrine. In the end, it appears that little was done with Kaysen's plan. And the next SIOP—SIOP-63—was changed in relatively superficial ways. While it did contain provisions to refrain from attacking certain Soviet satellite countries, SIOP-63 was not a radical break from the past, as has often been contended. At heart it was the same type of war plan as that approved by Eisenhower—a massive, preprogrammed strategic nuclear attack that contained almost no flexibility.

How did the flexible response strategy effect the explosive political question of possession and control of nuclear forces within the Western alliance? US policy on this question was often obscure during the late 1950s, but Eisenhower had been sympathetic to Europe's nuclear ambitions.[41] The Kennedy administration, however, was adamantly opposed to independent European nuclear forces, at least publicly. This stance was justified by the logic of strategy in the missile age. Small independent forces were unstable, invited preemption from the Soviets, and could only be effective against cities—not the types of military targets US strategists were emphasizing in their new counterforce plans. Most important, to successfully implement a strategy of graduated response and damage limitation, nuclear decision making had to be centralized. One needed very tight, centralized command and control to fight a flexible nuclear war. This view was forcefully laid out in McNamara's talk to NATO in Athens in May 1962: "In short, then, weak nuclear capabilities, operating independently, are expensive, prone to obsolescence, and lacking in credibility as a deterrent. It is for these reasons that I have laid such stress on unity of planning, concentration of executive authority, and central direction."[42] If flexible response was to be taken seriously, the United States could under no circumstances aid independent forces and should have made efforts to force the Europeans to abandon their nuclear programs. Quite surprisingly, however, the Athens talk did not reflect the real strategic views of either McNamara or President Kennedy about nuclear sharing. Only weeks before McNamara belittled small, independent nuclear forces in Athens, he was actively pushing a prosharing line within the administration. McNamara told the president that nuclear sharing with the French "would be justified on balance of payments reasons alone."[43] McNamara was not alone. Others in the administration, including Defense Department officials Roswell Gilpatric and Paul Nitze, US Ambassador to France James Gavin, and Kennedy's top military adviser, Maxwell Taylor, supported nuclear sharing.[44] Kennedy decided to maintain the no-sharing line, but for reasons that had little to do with military strategy—primarily, he "did not want to have the Germans clamoring for help in their turn."[45]

The administration's policy on nuclear sharing was an open question throughout 1962 and 1963. The president toyed with the idea of helping the French nuclear program in September 1962. During the Cuban missile crisis, Kennedy directed that the French be offered nuclear assistance.[46] Kennedy also authorized a shift in policy during the Nassau conference with the British in December of 1962. When McNamara's cancelled the Skybolt air-to-surface missile for budgetary and technical reasons, the president offered the British the Polaris missile. Since Polaris would extend the British deterrent well into the future, Kennedy, with McNamara's support, decided to reverse America's nuclear-sharing policy with France and directed US ambassador to France Charles Bohlen to open negotiations with French president de Gaulle. Kennedy made it clear to Bohlen that everything—including warheads and submarines—was negotiable.[47]

Despite the failure of the Nassau policy, the United States reopened the question of nuclear aid to France during the summer of 1963. Surprisingly, given the awful state of Franco-American relations, the Kennedy administration was ready to give the French "Polaris or Minutemen missiles . . . or Polaris submarine technology" if the French signed the partial test ban treaty.[48] Kaysen, who was intimately involved in the test ban negotiations, claimed that the administration was even willing to give the French "nuclear warheads for their bombs" if they supported the treaty.[49] While once again nothing came of this offer, it was clear that the Americans did not oppose France's nuclear efforts for the reasons McNamara laid out at the Athens meeting.

What explains this enormous gap between the rhetoric and reality of the administration's nuclear-sharing policy? It turns out that the whole question of America's attitude toward independent European nuclear forces was determined, not by military considerations per se, but by larger power political questions—particularly, the German question. If the United States helped the British with their nuclear program, the United States had to help the French. But if the French were helped, wouldn't the West Germans demand equal treatment? Kennedy, even as he made the decision to reverse US policy at Nassau and offer the French nuclear assistance, pointed out that the no-sharing policy had its roots in a fear of how US assistance might be interpreted by West Germany:

> The United States however had not supported the French in the nuclear field and the result of this policy had been to sour American relations

> with France. Rightly or wrongly they had taken this attitude because of Germany. . . . The United States were concerned at what would happen in Germany after Dr. Adenauer left the scene. . . . They regarded Germany as potentially the most powerful country in Europe and one whose future was in some doubt. . . . And if the United States did help France then pressure in Germany for similar help would rise.[50]

Similar dilemmas and contradictions emerged in administration debates over tactical nuclear weapons policy. Would a flexible response strategy be more or less likely to rely on theater nuclear weapons? On the one hand, tactical nuclear weapons provided another rung on the escalation ladder short of general war. As Taylor told McNamara, tactical weapons afforded a "'flexible nuclear response' short of the big ones."[51] This meant that utilizing tactical nuclear weapons should have been part of any "controlled response" or limited nuclear option. Yet, practically speaking, these weapons were inimical to the centralization vital to flexible response. In order for tactical weapons to be used effectively, authorization to use them had to be predelegated to commanders on the battlefield. McNamara skeptically wondered how "we preserve command and control in the tactical atomic environment?"[52]

Or consider another dilemma posed by tactical nuclear weapons for flexible response. Would tactical nuclear weapons be effective in a war limited to the European Continent? Military authorities argued that these weapons would cancel out the Soviet Union's conventional superiority. Furthermore, the Soviets might be deterred from mobilizing nonnuclear forces, since massed forces would be highly vulnerable to tactical atomic attacks.[53] On the other hand, given the pressures for escalation, there was a natural fear that the use of any nuclear weapons would increase the chance of a general war. Normally strong advocates of flexible response such as Carl Kaysen, Henry Rowen, and Alain Enthoven argued that tactical nuclear weapons were irrelevant since the *strategic* exchange would determine the outcome of a general war.[54]

Surprisingly, these puzzles and dilemmas were never fully worked out by the administration, and the policy regarding tactical nuclear weapons in Europe remained inconsistent. For example, in 1961, the Kennedy administration approved a policy for restricting the tactical nuclear buildup in Europe. In his May 1962 Athens talk, McNamara argued that tactical nuclear weapons would soon have little utility for Europe. But less than half a year later, in a speech to NATO ministers in Paris, McNamara stated: "I want to make it perfectly clear that it is our intention to maintain and increase tactical nuclear weapons in Europe." One military aide observed that this produced a situation "where our allies believe we have plans to increase nuclear weapons in Europe," while actual administration policy remained one of "reducing the number of deployed weapons if possible."[55]

Most of the civilian advocates of flexible response had deep reservations about the military uses of tactical nuclear weapons. But these weapons served a fundamental political purpose—reassuring the Europeans, and particularly the West Germans, that the Americans would not attempt to "de-nuclearize" Europe. As McGeorge Bundy pointed out when discussing tactical nuclear weapons for Europe, "the forces that one wants for war are not necessarily those which one may want 'diplomatically.'"[56] Ultimately, the number of tactical nuclear weapons was dramatically increased during the Kennedy/Johnson period.[57] In the end, America's tactical nuclear posture in Europe was determined, not by military needs, but by political and—in particular—alliance management demands.

Conventional Capabilities and Non-Nuclear Options

In terms of nuclear policy, therefore, the changes between the Eisenhower and Kennedy-Johnson periods were nowhere near as sharp as the conventional wisdom holds. But a key element behind the Kennedy and Johnson administrations' emphasis on flexible response was the need to enhance nonnuclear capabilities in Europe. By making a quick Soviet takeover of the continent more difficult and a forward defense of West Germany more realistic, increased conventional forces would both enhance deterrence and raise the nuclear threshold in the event of hostilities with the USSR. But did top US policymakers believe in the strategic, as opposed to political, logic behind this call for greater conventional capabilities? And did the United States increase its own conventional force presence in Europe? The answers to these questions are a test of how seriously leaders like Kennedy and McNamara took the strategy of flexible response.

It is often forgotten that the Kennedy administration inherited a sizable conventional force from Eisenhower—six large US divisions in Europe. Still, given the importance of defense issues in the 1960 election, one would have expected that McNamara's first defense budget would signal the strategic priorities of the new secretary of defense and his president with large appropriations to increase troop strength in Europe. To the surprise of the supporters of a conventional strategy, McNamara provided no additional money for new nonnuclear forces in Europe. Maxwell Taylor complained that he was "sorry to note the intention to cut back the level of conventional forces."[58] Dean Rusk complained that the secretary of defense's budget "actually projects a cutback in force levels, principally in the Army, below those currently approved."[59] Carl Kaysen pointed out that McNamara's five-year budget plan kept "limited war" forces static until FY 1969. Kaysen asked McGeorge Bundy, "Is this the New Look which corresponds to the President's program?"[60]

The battle to increase the permanent conventional force continued throughout the early months of 1962.[61] Due to the post-Vienna conference call-up of reservists and the mobilization of two National Guard divisions, the size of the US Army temporarily increased. But the secretary of defense refused to budget for the million-plus man permanent army desired by advocates of flexible response. Despite intense lobbying, McNamara "showed no great increase in his receptivity" to permanently increase America's conventional force strength.[62] McNamara' budgetary priorities prevailed, both in the 1961 budget and in those that followed.

More surprising, President Kennedy frequently threatened to remove large numbers of US troops from Europe. Almost from the start of his administration, he linked the continued presence of America's conventional forces in Europe to important US political and economic interests, particularly a resolution to the vexing problem of the US balance-of-payments deficit.[63] Bundes minister Heinrich Krone was warned that the United States would be forced to withdraw troops because of America's dollar and gold outflow.[64] In January 1963, the president told his National Security Council (NSC), "We cannot continue to pay for the military protection of Europe while the NATO states are not paying for their fair share and living off the 'fat of the land.'" It was time for the nation to "consider very hard the narrower interests of the United States."[65] And, in May 1963, General Franco told the German ambassador to Spain that the American president had warned that "the question of the American balance of payments constituted one of his greatest concerns." If he did not resolve the dollar and gold problem, Kennedy would be forced to "change his whole policy" and "dismantle the military support of Europe."[66]

The balance-of-payments problem was not the only issue that drove Kennedy to consider troop withdrawals from Europe. By 1962, both the French and West German governments were openly criticizing the administration's policies toward Europe, and the president was fed up. He told the British defense minister that if the Franco-German bloc were cooperating on a nuclear program, as he suspected, then perhaps the United States would simply "haul out" of Europe. If the Germans broke the 1954 Brussels treaty preventing their production of atomic weapons, the United States would "have to consider whether they should regard themselves still committed to their own obligations for keeping troops in Europe."[67] The president also warned French cultural affairs minister

André Malraux that if de Gaulle preferred a Europe dominated by Germany, then Kennedy would bring the troops home and save $1.3 billion, an amount that "would just about meet our balance of payments deficit." Kennedy informed West German chancellor Konrad Adenauer that "economic relations" were "possibly even more important to us now than nuclear matters," because the nuclear position of the West was strong enough to deter any attack.[68] And in a September, 1963 meeting with West German foreign minister Gerhard Schroeder, the president stated that "the U.S. does not want to take actions which would have an adverse impact on public opinion in Germany but does not wish to keep spending money to maintain forces which are not of real value."[69]

US troop withdrawals obviously contradicted the flexible response strategy, and many within the administration were puzzled by the president's desire to pull troops out of Europe. State Department official J. Robert Schaetzel asked how the United States could demand a "greater European contribution to a flexible strategy" while initiating steps "toward a détente with the Soviet Union," moving "unilaterally toward significant cutbacks in our present commitments and drift[ing] back toward the plate glass doctrine"?[70] Carl Kaysen pointed out that McNamara's troop withdrawal plan in the Far East would require US strategy to shift toward "an immediate nuclear response." Wouldn't troop cutbacks in Europe require the same shift in strategy?[71] White House NSC official David Klein pointed out the troop withdrawals made the Kennedy administration appear Gaullist:

> We are calling for the creation of the MLF [multilateral force], with the proviso that the contributions to the conventional forces will *not be reduced*. But then we go on to say, *either* you put more into the conventional pot, and support our strategy, *or* we'll pull back and support your strategy. And then before the Europeans can respond, we go on to the *or* of the *either-or* condition, and come out looking like good Gaullists.[72]

This seemingly contradictory policy was not so puzzling when it is understood that the president was far more concerned about America's political and economic interests than the effect of troop withdrawals on the flexible response strategy. In December 1962 the president told the JCS that Europe was getting a "free ride" on both the political and defense side, and that "this situation with our NATO allies had to be changed this year."[73] Two months later, he ordered them to examine "how much we can reduce our forces in Europe in the next twelve months."[74] Planning for these withdrawals continued throughout the spring and summer of 1963. The president ignored protests from the military and the State Department that these withdrawals would undermine America's military strategy in Europe. Kennedy did not want to endanger the US economy by defending countries that were undermining America's political and economic interests.[75]

It is not surprising that Kennedy considered troop withdrawals to protect America's international monetary position. But there is strong evidence that he did not even accept the military/strategic purposes of US conventional forces in Western Europe. By 1962 he appears to have concluded that the only military reason for the large numbers of US troops was the threat to Berlin. Since West Berlin was well within the Eastern bloc, NATO would have to initiate military action to restore access to the city by the West. America's nuclear forces, on the other hand, could do little to maintain the viability of West Berlin. But the situation in West Berlin was anomalous, almost bizarre. Kennedy thought that the strategic requirements for the defense of Western Europe were much simpler than the requirements for maintaining access to West Berlin. Kennedy believed that if the Berlin Crisis could be resolved, he could bring large numbers of US troops home.[76]

What if the Soviets invaded Western Europe? The president made it clear that any Soviet move against Western Europe would "lead promptly to nuclear warfare." For that reason, "the nuclear deterrent would be effective."[77] The Americans "would be forced to use nuclear weapons against the first Russian who came across the line."[78] Secret recordings reveal that Kennedy told Eisenhower in 1962, "If we did not have the problem, I say, of Berlin and maintaining access to that autobahn of ours, then you can say that any attempt to seize any part of West Germany, we would go to nuclear weapons." In order to maintain access to Berlin, one cannot suddenly "drop nuclear weapons the first time you have difficulty." Kennedy also told Eisenhower that de Gaulle would "be perfectly right in talking about our immediate use of nuclear weapons, it seems to me, if we didn't have [the] Berlin problem, because then obviously any Soviet intrusion across the line would be a deliberate one and would be a signal for war." Kennedy concluded that the unique and perplexing challenge the West faced in Berlin was the only "valid reason" for "our emphasizing the necessity of their building up conventional forces."[79] Kennedy told West Berlin mayor Willy Brandt that "the geography of Berlin was such that the disadvantage lay with us because it was we who would have to make the first military move. This detracted from the credibility of our threat of nuclear war and made necessary readiness to use our conventional forces."[80]

Kennedy fully understood that reducing the size of US conventional forces in a particular theater meant that nuclear weapons would be used sooner. During a September 25, 1962, meeting on US strategy in the Far

East, chairman of the JCS Maxwell Taylor argued that the United States should use nuclear weapons in Korea "at once" if the Chinese crossed the Yalu River. The president responded: "I don't think you could say if they came across the Yalu River, but you could say that we certainly use it [nuclear weapons] if they attack in force across the cease-fire line." General Taylor pointed out that where the US would use nuclear weapons was less important than that they would use them early. The point of the new posture in Korea was "that we would not be prepared to hold them back by conventional methods if they came en masse. How they got there wouldn't particularly matter." During the same conversation, McNamara strongly advocated lowering the nuclear threshold so that the United States could reduce its conventional presence and "free substantial Korean forces" that were being paid for through US aid: "In the long run it would greatly reduce our military assistance program because we're supplying air power to Korea and Taiwan, and we will have to supply it to Thailand if we continue the present policy, which wouldn't be required if we understood that we could use nuclear weapons, particularly nuclear weapons delivered by U.S. aircraft."[81]

When Bundy contended that this was the opposite of US strategy for Europe, Kennedy disagreed. The president argued that the only reason for slowness in using nuclear weapons in Europe was the fear of proliferation and the anomaly of Berlin. He concluded, "If you didn't have the Berlin problem, you just had a thin line, you would use nuclear weapons almost from the beginning if they came in force." Six months later, when McNamara claimed there might be a military need for conventional forces in Europe for contingencies other than Berlin, the "president did not seem persuaded."[82]

Proponents of flexible response wanted enhanced conventional forces for other "limited war" contingencies besides Berlin that would fall below the threshold of general war. It was often argued that nonnuclear options would be needed to deal with what strategists called the "hostage city" scenario. But Kennedy dismissed the idea that the Soviets would ever launch a limited attack to seize a West German town like Hamburg: "But, of course, they never will." To Kennedy's mind, there was a "great deal of doubt in the Soviet Union about whether or not we would use nuclear weapons and that it would be unlikely that the Soviet Union, with this doubt in their minds, would take up a venture such as the seizure of a city in Western Germany."[83] As the president told his National Security Council in 1962, it was the "credibility of our nuclear deterrent" that held the Soviets back—because "they think we might use the bomb if they pushed us hard enough."[84] It was only the "geography of Berlin" that would force the West to "make the first military move," which "detracted from the credibility of our threat of nuclear war" and made it necessary to "use our conventional forces."[85] Kennedy told the British chief of defense staff that the "Berlin situation distorted the whole Western military posture" and that all of NATO would only require "ten divisions in Central Europe" if not for the need to maintain access to West Berlin. British officials took Kennedy's statements so seriously that their military undertook a study of how many conventional forces NATO would need if President Kennedy's premises—a nuclear stalemate and a trusteeship arrangement for Berlin—came to pass.[86]

In fact, if West Berlin was attacked by the Soviets, as opposed to simply cut off, there would be no flexibility in the American response. When McNamara asked what would happen if US troops in West Berlin were overrun, Under Secretary of State George Ball stated, "It's perfectly clear" that the United States would "go to general war." When Kennedy asked if that meant a nuclear exchange, an unidentified speaker told him, "That's right."[87] Kennedy reaffirmed this strategy the next day. If the Soviets take "Berlin by force," then he would have "only one alternative": to "fire nuclear weapons" and "begin a nuclear exchange."[88] Kennedy reinforced this message in his meeting with the congressional leadership three days later. If Berlin were seized, he said, "our war plan at that point has been to fire our nuclear weapons at them."[89]

In the end, Kennedy undertook no major troop withdrawals from Western Europe. But this had little to do with military strategy in Europe. Instead, the president maintained six US divisions in NATO Europe because his two great concerns—the Franco-German revolt and the dollar and gold outflow—had been largely resolved by October 1963.[90] By agreeing to sign the partial test ban treaty the West Germans agreed to remain a nonnuclear state. This concession relaxed tensions between the West and the Soviets over the status of Berlin. For agreeing to this second-class status, the Federal Republic was given something in return, namely a large US troop presence. It was also agreed that the West Germans would take various financial and monetary measures to neutralize the balance-of-payments cost of this commitment. This complicated, interlocking arrangement protected both Europe and the dollar while helping to end the great East-West showdown over Berlin.[91]

The issue of America's conventional force commitment to NATO turned on geopolitical and international economic questions. Rarely were narrow military considerations—in this case, the strategy of flexible response—even discussed at the highest levels. Ironically, Kennedy's commitment to maintain large-scale conventional forces in Western Europe came after relations with the Soviets had improved dramatically and the danger of war had subsided.

LBJ, Conventional Forces, and German Nuclear Politics

The monetary-security framework that kept US troops in West Germany and made the rhetorical strategy of flexible response in Europe possible was delicate throughout the 1960s. The same questions that had consumed the Kennedy administration continued to plague the Johnson administration. Would the Germans continue to accept their nonnuclear status? Would they continue to make onerous payments to offset the foreign exchange costs of US troops? On the American side, would worsening balance-of-payment deficits and the war in Vietnam increase domestic pressures to redeploy troops? Could this three-layered game—deterring the Soviets, restraining the FRG, and winning domestic support for an expensive overseas commitment—be maintained in the face of an emerging US-Soviet détente, increased German resentment, and domestic pressures to return American troops from Europe? Ironically, this "détente" only magnified the dilemmas surrounding America's military strategy in Europe, particularly the question of America's conventional force commitment to NATO.

In fact, only three years later the alliance seemed to be coming apart. In 1966, France announced its intention to leave the integrated command, Great Britain declared that it would drastically cut the size of the British Army on the Rhine because of its own balance-of-payments problem, and the West Germans unilaterally abrogated the financial arrangement with the United States that had been the quid pro quo for America's expensive conventional force commitment. This came on top of a worsening situation in Vietnam, a deteriorating payments deficit, and calls within Congress for a reduction in the number of US forces in Western Europe.[92] Given these pressures, a US troop withdrawal from Europe could not be avoided. But how many troops would be brought back to the United States, and how would the redeployment be squared with the official strategy of flexible response?

The attitude of the man who in 1962 lectured the Europeans on the need for flexible response was quite surprising. The documents reveal that Secretary of Defense McNamara was far more concerned with the balance-of-payments component of the conventional force debate than with any narrow military or even deterrent considerations in the mid-1960s. To McNamara, the troop issue was simple—if the Germans did not meet their offset obligations, then the Americans would have to withdraw at least two divisions, regardless of the effects of such a move on NATO strategy.[93] Others within the administration—particularly in the State Department and the Joint Chiefs of Staff—worried that a troop cut would undermine America's political and military interests in Europe. But McNamara was more concerned about the dollar and gold drain than the effect of an American redeployment on the flexible response doctrine. As NSC aide Francis Bator told President Johnson, "McNamara believes a two division cut would be safe."[94]

At times, President Johnson appeared willing to go even further. In the midst of a disastrous summit with FRG chancellor Ludwig Erhard, Johnson asked McNamara to determine the savings a complete and total withdrawal of US troops from Western Europe would produce: "How much, when you pull all your troops out of there? Just suppose that you decided that we couldn't afford it." McNamara was taken aback by the request. He replied, "Of course, if we were going to pull them all out, it would be quite a difficult movement back because we just have . . . something like a million tons of equipment would be in Germany." Johnson was unfazed: "Looks to me, we ought to take advantage of this opportunity to make [Erhard] tell us that he cannot afford to have our troops there."[95]

The West Germans hardly knew what to make of the secretary of defense's "repeated explanations, threats, and disclaimers" about troop withdrawals. They found it "extremely difficult to induce McNamara, who has extremely a mind of his own, to take a cooperative position."[96] Would the secretary of defense really undermine his own flexible response doctrine that he had finally, despite great difficulties, convinced the Federal Republic to embrace?[97] "McNamara is totally aware of the fact that the enemy's fighting strength has not decreased, but rather increased. If he would concede to the domestic policy pressure on decreasing the troops in Europe too early, his concept of defense would be questioned."[98] Giving up on "the American concept of the 'flexible response' and thus to a decrease of the nuclear threshold" through troop withdrawals could "mean the deathblow for NATO."[99]

The Germans eventually came to recognize that McNamara and others in the Johnson administration were quite willing to pull troops out of Europe even if it contradicted the strategy of flexible response. The West German ambassador to the United States, Heinrich Knappstein, repeatedly warned officials back home that the Americans were quite serious about large withdrawals of US troops from Europe. The reasons included the balance-of-payments problem, the Vietnam War, "increasing discontent" with US-European attitudes, and even an alarming "neo-isolationist trend" that believed the United States "could defense itself only with the missile potential." Beyond these substantive issues, there was an "emotional position" that was not entirely new but that "gains weight and momentum" about the Europeans as "fat and lazy" and wanting to merely "enjoy their prosperity" under "the protection of the American nuclear shield." In the long term, these attitudes led the United States to seriously confront the question of a "substantial reduction of troops." "Twenty-one years after the end of World War II, the mood of the people is no longer simply to win in favor of further infinite stationing of troops. . . . The demand 'bring the boys back home' that Eisenhower successfully adopted . . . in 1952 . . . has still today an attractiveness that should not be underestimated."[100] America's efforts to undermine its own strategy led the German chancellor to tell US representative John McClay: "Flexible response is no longer believed in."[101]

In order to manage US troop withdrawals and avoid a complete unraveling of NATO, the Johnson administration began high-level talks with Great Britain and West Germany to discuss NATO's conventional force requirements and costs. Although one of the purposes of the negotiations was to examine NATO strategy, the real motivations for America's large conventional force deployment to Europe can be seen in documents detailing positions on US troop withdrawals. It is surprising how arguments about strategy against the Soviet Union—and in particular, the flexible response doctrine—were underplayed and at times ignored in these discussions. As Bator told President Johnson, "the military issue is only a small part of the picture." It was "Atlantic politics and US-German relations" along with "domestic politics" that were "the heart" of the debate over the size of US conventional forces in Europe.[102]

One of the key analyses from the State Department, which argued against McNamara's proposals for troop withdrawals, discounted the possibility of a Soviets decision to launch a massive invasion. The authors argued that the mobilization of large numbers of Soviet divisions would eliminate surprise and a quick victory. More important, the Soviets knew that a massive assault on Europe would risk, if not guarantee, a devastating response from the United States. The State Department also argued that "not even the dissolution of NATO" would prevent the US from intervening if the Soviets attacked Western Europe.[103] Detailed military examination of the European arena confirmed McNamara's analysis that US troops could be brought home without endangering the continent. A report prepared for the Trilateral negotiations concluded that even "a total reduction in NATO Central Region M-Day army manpower of 75,000–150,000 would not seriously weaken our conventional capabilities" to deal with the most likely contingencies. In the end, it was the "threat of nuclear response"—not conventional capabilities—that "provided and will continue to provide a highly effective deterrent against massive Soviet non-nuclear attack."[104]

Ironically, the State Department contended that the one particularly frightening scenario was a potential reduction of Soviet troops in the GDR. This would reverse the trend toward "greater stability" in the GDR and could prompt a West German intervention "with all the ramifications which that might have."[105] In other words, US and Soviet reductions could lead to instability in the region and even revolt in East Germany, which would tempt the Bundeswehr to intervene. Neither the Soviets nor the Americans wanted that. This is a dramatically different picture of the role that US troops played in Central Europe than the one that saw strategic nuances of flexible response.[106]

From a strictly military point of view, it appeared that America's combat troop presence in Europe could be reduced without tempting the Soviets to intervene. And McNamara believed that even a large Soviet nonnuclear thrust could be checked with three-plus US divisions. A report on NATO prepared for the Trilateral negotiations between the US, Great Britain, and West Germany to deal with these issues contended that "if the relationship between Western Europe and the U.S. had been based merely on common defense against the Soviet threat, it might be logical to conclude that the basic raison d'être of the alliance was rapidly being eroded." But the strong US presence in NATO served a political purpose that was perhaps becoming more important than its military function. One political function was to reduce the scope of "traditional power politics" as represented by de Gaulle's "hegemonic drive." But an even more important function was the contribution NATO and the US presence made to confront "the German problem." US power had allowed the Federal Republic of Germany to be "integrated into the West European political fabric" without upsetting the region's internal balance. As a background paper for the negotiations put it, "This factor contributing to NATO's strength seems to be growing more important as time passes."[107]

It was fears about the effect of a US troop withdrawal on the "German question"—and not its impact on the flexible response strategy—that terrified policymakers, who argued against US redeployments. In 1963, the West Germans had reluctantly agreed to arrangements that "precluded independent nuclear forces" so long as the United States guaranteed their security.[108] "The objective of German security policy is assurance that her borders will be defended by adequate and appropriate forces. As long as the German government and people are convinced that the United States will defend Germany, Germany does not need nuclear weapons." This fragile arrangement was based on the extension of the US "commitment to the defense of Europe"—a commitment that "should not and cannot be lightly made."[109]

But by the mid-1960s, discussions of US troop withdrawals made the Federal Republic increasingly doubtful about America's commitment to its security. A November 16, 1967, report prepared by Policy Planning entitled "Implications of a More Independent German Foreign Policy" claimed that "the mood underlying present FRG policies is, to a much greater extent than prior to 1966, one of uncertainty, resentment, or suspicion regarding the direction of U.S. policy." This was largely because the United States had threatened troop withdrawals from West Germany while simultaneously initiating a conciliatory policy toward the Soviet Union: "Many Germans fear deeply that the US will either progressively reduce its forces in Europe and thus make the Germans vulnerable to Soviet pressure, or strive increasingly for accords with the USSR at the expense of FRG interests, or both." The typical American rebuttal, that "the Germans have no place to go," only applied when the FRG had "confidence in US support for German security and reunification."[110] Many Germans feared this confidence was no longer warranted.[111]

Another policy planning paper, written three months later, was even more pessimistic. It indicated that "the Germans are convinced that the US will in the relatively near future make further substantial and unilateral reductions in its forces in Germany." The report predicted that the FRG would be increasingly willing to make dangerous concessions to the Soviets to win liberalization in East Germany, concessions that would purchase nothing but disappointment and eventually resentment within West Germany. It stated: "Disillusion in West Germany might well set in and produce radical movements of the right and left." The fear of US troop withdrawals would make the West Germans feel "intensely isolated." They would suspect that they were being forced to accept a neutralized status in which the division of Germany would be permanently institutionalized by East-West security-control arrangements. This could start West Germany down the very dangerous road of attempting to purchase confederation with the German Democratic Republic (GDR) from the Soviets at the price of neutralization and of far-reaching security concessions.[112] George Ball warned that US troop withdrawals would cause the Germans to "develop neuroses that can be catastrophic for all of us. They did it before and they can do it again. . . . A neurotic, disaffected Germany could be like a loose ship's cannon in a high sea."[113]

In the end, it is clear that these types of arguments—geopolitical as opposed to narrowly military—carried the day among US policymakers. The United States in the 1960s needed a strong military presence in Germany to guard US political interests in Europe, which included but went well beyond rebuffing a Soviet attack. This is the meaning behind such euphemisms as "maintaining the cohesion of the alliance" or "enhancing the stability of the alliance," which were given as the main purpose of the Trilateral negotiations. Given that the Soviets were not going to invade Western Europe any time soon, this meant essentially the management of the "German problem." American troops in Germany guaranteed that the FRG would remain allied to the West and could be prevented from making any destabilizing moves, such intervening in East Germany or acquiring a nuclear capability.

This also highlights the reasons that the Americans were desperate to maintain the British Army on the Rhine throughout the 1960s. Neither the Americans nor the West Germans thought very highly of the BAOR as a fighting force. Indeed, the British thought "a conventional defense in Europe is hopeless and therefore neither strong conventional forces nor war supply for more than 14 days are required in Central Europe."[114] Nor were the British concerned about the military consequences vis-à-vis the Soviets if NATO's conventional capability was downsized. The British thought that while "Soviet capabilities have not receded, the USSR has no intention to attack Europe today" and that Soviet doctrine "is based on the use of nuclear weapons from the outset." This left the British convinced that "a long conventional war in Europe is unlikely; any conflict there is likely to escalate to an all-out nuclear exchange very quickly. Even in the unlikely event of a Soviet attack with conventional forces, NATO forces would be compelled to use tactical nuclear weapons within days, if not hours." The British did recognize the power-political implications of a troop withdrawal, however: "London fully realizes that its contribution to NATO forces enables it to participate in Allied efforts to control West Germany's present and future place in Europe. . . . Some London editorialists have recently expressed concern that withdrawal of British (and US) troops would lead Bonn to argue that they should be replaced by Germans and 'properly' armed with nuclear weapons."[115] For the Americans, a strong UK presence put the management of the German problem in a multilateral—and less coercive—context. Furthermore, a British withdrawal would strengthen domestic political forces within the United States, such as US Senate majority leader Mike Mansfield, who wished to force the administration to withdraw US troops from NATO.

This is not to completely discount the military function of US and British troops in Europe during the mid-1960s. A Europe without a strong US combat troop presence might have been pressured or even blackmailed by the Soviet colossus without a shot being fired. A drift toward neutralism or, even worse, a revival of intra-European rivalry and conflict might well have resulted. But during a period of relative stability between the Eastern and Western blocs, it was thought unlikely that the Soviet Union would launch an attack or try to blackmail Europe, even if two or three US Army divisions were removed. Top officials in both the Kennedy and Johnson administrations seemed unconcerned about the effect large US troop withdrawals would have on the strategic logic of the flexible response doctrine.

The Myth of Flexible Response

The conventional wisdom surrounding the strategy of flexible response is thus deeply flawed. It is clear that on both the nuclear and nonnuclear side the shift in strategy between the Eisenhower and Kennedy/ Johnson eras was nowhere near as stark as the secondary literature contends. America's nuclear strategy did not really become more "flexible" in the 1960s. And the United States did not come to rely less on nuclear escalation and more on conventional options after 1961.

There is evidence that both Kennedy and McNamara recognized that they were pursuing far more strategic continuity with the Eisenhower administration than they wanted to admit in public. For example, it turns out that President Kennedy originally planned to retain Eisenhower's secretary of defense, Thomas Gates, for at least a year into his new administration. The plan also included putting the president's brother, Robert, in the Defense Department as undersecretary, where Gates would train him until Bobby was ready to take over. Despite Bobby Kennedy's keen interest, this plan was rejected on political grounds, because it was feared that Gates would use his position to build up his chances to win the governorship of Pennsylvania.[116] It would be hard to imagine a strategic revolution being ushered in by a holdover from the Eisenhower administration.

Robert McNamara also knew that the difference between the Eisenhower and Kennedy/Johnson strategies was oversold. McNamara and Kennedy were briefed by Gates during the 1960–61 transition and informed that America's capabilities for conducting limited war were considerable and that it was not necessary to "step them up."[117] During 1964 McNamara told the Democratic Party Platform Committee that in 1961 "we found military strategy to be the stepchild of a predetermined budget," with "no coordination" among the services and the nation's strategic nuclear force "vulnerable to surprise missile attack." Gates angrily responded with a letter to McNamara charging that the secretary of defense knew these charges were false:

> I cannot believe that you agree with these statements yourself. . . . If the conditions actually had been as you have described them, then I could not consciously have remained in office—nor would I have been allowed to; in fact, if our defense posture then had actually been in the state of disorder you have painted, I doubt that anyone could have corrected in to the time you have been in office. . . . If the allegations you made, at complete variance not only with the content of your dispatch to me but also with a number of statements you had earlier put on the public record, were inserted in your presentation to serve a political purpose, then

> August 17th was an unfortunate day for the process of government in this nation.[118]

There certainly were important changes in US strategy during the 1960s. The deployment of sophisticated weapons systems like the Polaris and Minuteman, which were authorized by Eisenhower but came on line in the 1960s, brought the Cold War into the missile age. New reconnaissance satellites dramatically improved targeting. And while conventional forces were not increased, they were supplied with more modern weaponry and supported by increased airlift capability. And, to be sure, there was an important shift in attitude toward the military utility of nuclear weapons between the Eisenhower and Kennedy/Johnson eras.

But it is important to emphasize what did not happen to US strategy in Europe during the 1960s. Nuclear sharing with the British and the French was not ruled out. A truly flexible nuclear strategy did not come into being, both because of technical constraints and, after 1962, a lack of interest. Despite all the rhetoric about moving away from massive preplanned attacks, the SIOP was not significantly altered to provide for limited flexible responses in the 1960s. The dilemmas behind complicated issues such as the utility of tactical nuclear weapons or the meaning of "damage limitation" second-strike counterforce targeting were never seriously worked out. And, not only was America's conventional force presence in Europe not permanently increased but threats of US troop withdrawals because of the gold and dollar outflow were a constant source of transatlantic tension. As we have seen, President Kennedy came to believe that the only military justification for large US conventional forces in Europe was the Berlin Crisis, a situation where the United States would have to go on the offensive to maintain the viability of a small enclave deep within enemy territory. After the Berlin Crisis subsided, many top US policymakers wanted to bring troops home. McNamara, a balance-of-payments hawk throughout his tenure as secretary of defense, finally succeeded in withdrawing significant US conventional forces in 1967—the same year that NATO formally embraced the flexible response doctrine!

Why did the Americans propagate a military strategy they didn't really believe in? One important reason was the tricky nuclear politics behind the German question. If the United States revealed that it did not believe in "controlled response," or in a viable first-strike policy, it would be obvious that the extended deterrent—America's nuclear guarantee to Europe—was fraudulent. The Europeans, including the West Germans, would demand nuclear forces of their own, which would undermine America's politically motivated struggle against German nuclearization. Furthermore, this meant that the Americans had to stress the importance of nonnuclear forces in order to support their arguments that the Europeans, and especially the Germans, would be making a contribution of real strategic value by augmenting their conventional forces. While many top policymakers questioned the military utility of six fully supplied US Army divisions in West Germany, US policymakers feared the political consequences within NATO, and especially the Federal Republic, if large troop withdrawals were ordered.

This story is more than a historical correction of how an important Cold War strategy originated and was implemented. The revised story of the flexible response strategy compels us to reconsider how we should understand the relationship between military strategy and power politics in the nuclear age. The field of security studies has too often viewed the Cold War as a bipolar conflict whose shape was dictated almost entirely by the military environment. We are often told that the Cold War's supposed stability was a result of this bipolarity and the robust quality of nuclear deterrence. This framework allowed strategy to be seen in a rather static and deterministic way, as if the Cold War was driven exclusively by military circumstances and devoid of any political content. But, of course, that was not the case at all. For example, a framework that focuses solely on the nuclear environment and bipolarity cannot explain why the Soviets perpetuated a dangerous crisis over Berlin and Cuba (1958–62) at a time of great strategic vulnerability, yet became a status quo power in Europe when they achieved strategic parity (after 1963). Nor can it explain why the United States made a permanent conventional force commitment to NATO only after the Soviet Union stopped putting pressure on West Berlin (again, after 1963). Soviet and American behavior was certainly conditioned by strategic circumstances, but their strategies were driven by core geopolitical interests, interests that were often quite complicated and even overlapping.

This does not mean that the Cold War in Europe cannot be explained through a realist lens. Intentions and capabilities mattered enormously, but they mattered in a multilateral context. Balancing went on simultaneously between alliances and within alliances. The primary concern of the Americans and West Europeans was, throughout the Cold War, the Soviet threat. But each of these players had other power political worries as well. Like the Soviets, France, Britain, and the United States could not help but have serious reservations about West German power. Likewise, the Western Europeans, including the Germans, were understandably troubled by US hegemony on the continent. To make matters even more interesting, it is clear that top US policymakers accepted many Soviet concerns—particularly their fear of a militarily resurgent Germany—as legitimate during the 1960s. For example, US Ambassador to West Germany George McGhee told Dean Rusk that the United States "would withdraw," the other NATO allies would "dissociate themselves from Germany," and the Soviets would "make such efforts the subject of a preemptive attack" if West Germany tried to acquire a national nuclear capability."[119] For their part, the Germans understood that there were a "number of mutual interests emerging between the US and the Soviet Union, which they feel could bring about a realignment in the post-war security pattern."[120]

At the same time, the Europeans, and especially the West Germans, were loath to see the superpowers come to any arrangements on these issues. A successful American strategy in Europe had to take all of these complex issues into consideration, as well as manage the domestic political and economic consequences of policy choices. And while issues such as strategic vulnerability, limited war, and controlled response played a certain role in shaping this strategy, it was the political considerations that dominated. Indeed, nuclear strategy was often the servant of political imperatives. How could the Soviets be deterred while at the same time the West Germans were restrained yet reassured? And could the United States maintain domestic support for a military strategy rhetorically based on containing the Soviets in the face of superpower détente and balance-of-payment pressures? It was these kinds of broad political questions that drove US policy on issues such as nuclear sharing, strategic targeting, tactical nuclear weapons, and US conventional force levels in Europe during the 1960s and beyond. Although concerns about all-out nuclear war have faded, these questions continue to shape policy regarding NATO's role in Europe, the military status of Germany, and America's relations with Russia. Policymakers would do well to recognize not just the continuities of the Cold War era but also between that time and our own.

[3]

Nuclear Weapons, Statecraft, and the Berlin Crisis, 1958–1962

> De Gaulle told Kennedy that he considered Berlin primarily a psychological question: "It is annoying to both sides that Berlin should be located where it is; however, it is there."
>
> —Frederick Kempe, *Berlin* 1961

President Dwight D. Eisenhower never hid his belief that the US position in Berlin was a poor one. The United States had "made an error in attempting to control Germany from Berlin, so far behind the Russian lines."[1] This position had emerged from "naïveté," and Eisenhower found it "ironic [that I am] now confronted with a crisis based on a decision against which [I] had recommended as a military commander."[2] He added, "We have a genius for getting in a hole to protect ourselves—we are always having to defend Matsu or some other out of the way place."[3] Later, President Kennedy appeared to agree, complaining that "of all the legacies of World War II which the West had inherited, Berlin was the most difficult."[4] He told British prime minister Harold MacMillan, "On Berlin we have no bargaining position."[5] Despite this, the crisis over Berlin created what Eisenhower's policy planning staff had warned would be "a period in which risk of world war will rise to a very high point, perhaps higher than any so far."[6] The United States found itself in a situation that Eisenhower said "can best be described as a 'can of worms.'"[7]

Both presidents recognized that the Berlin situation ranged from burdensome to absurd. West Berlin added nothing to the material strength of the United States or the Western alliance, and its loss would have no effect on the overall balance of military power. The city could not be defended if it was attacked by the Soviets or East Germans, nor was supplying the city viable without their cooperation. Both Eisenhower and Kennedy understood that the Soviet Union had a legitimate interest in stabilizing the situation in Berlin, and they engaged in negotiations to ease tensions. Yet both administrations were willing to risk a global nuclear war to defend its position. Rarely in history, Eisenhower thought, had the military policy needed to defend an asset been so out of whack with its inherent balance-of-power value. The president "expressed unhappiness that here is another instance in which our political posture requires us to assume military positions that are wholly illogical."[8] When confronting it, Kennedy agreed: "So we're stuck in a ridiculous situation. . . . It seems silly for us to be facing an atomic war over a treaty preserving Berlin as the future capital of a reunified Germany," when all of us "know that Germany will probably never be reunified."[9]

The primary point of this chapter is not to reinterpret the events between 1958 and 1962, as there is an excellent and growing literature on the crisis.[10] Nor is it only to explore the role nuclear weapons played in the origins and outcome of the clash, though that is a key component.[11] More broadly, in this chapter I attempt to put the interaction between the unique geopolitical issues driving the Berlin Crisis and the role of nuclear weapons in *historical context*, with a view toward shedding light on contemporary debates about nuclear weapons, statecraft, and international relations.

Analyzing the crisis over Berlin between 1958 and 1962 reveals many of the puzzles, dilemmas, and contradictions of how nuclear weapons influenced international politics in the post–World War II period. The struggle was at once both an enigma and the signature crisis of the Cold War, underlining the profound and unique influence of atomic weapons, while highlighting the traditional geopolitical questions about the nature of German power. It also occurred at precisely the time when the full effects of the so-called nuclear revolution came into play, which, according to many, reshaped the fundamental nature of statecraft and international relations. As chapter 2 demonstrated, this was also when—at least rhetorically—the United States initiated a dramatic shift in its nuclear strategy from massive retaliation to flexible response. Several of the most contested issues surrounding the nuclear age came into play during the Berlin Crisis: What role, if any, did the balance of military power play in the origins, course, and outcome of the crisis? Or was the "balance of resolve" more important, and, if so, how was it measured? Did nuclear weapons stabilize great power relations and prevent the crisis from escalating into a thermonuclear exchange, or were they a cause of the crisis or at least a dangerous irritant between the superpowers?

I explore these issues by comparing the claims made by the advocates of the "nuclear revolution" against what the historical evidence reveals about US policy during the Berlin Crisis of 1958 to 1962. In particular, I try to determine what mattered more in both the origins and outcome of the crisis—the balance of power or the balance of resolve—while assessing whether nuclear weapons were ultimately stabilizing or destabilizing. Finally, if the historical evidence does provide clues about these important issues, I will ask whether we can generalize the lessons of Berlin in order to better understand the influence of nuclear weapons on international politics today and in the future. In other words, was Berlin sui generis or the ultimate laboratory to understand how we should think about statecraft in the atomic age?

The Nuclear Revolution and International Politics

Advocates of the concept of nuclear revolution focus on questions of fundamental importance: Under what conditions, if any, do the existence of nuclear weapons stabilize international politics, ameliorate crises, and prevent great power war? When, and in what circumstances, does the "deterrent" value of these powerful weapons outweigh their many dangers? The answers to these questions should determine how we assess a wide range of important contemporary issues, including how worried we should be about nuclear proliferation, what nuclear postures make the most sense, and whether the world should work to rid the planet of these weapons.

One way to explore these questions is to look to the past, to examine how nuclear weapons influenced world politics during a time of great tension—the Cold War. Many have argued, however, that we are living in a "second nuclear age" with different types of actors (such as rogue states and nonstate organizations) operating in different regions (the Middle East and East Asia as opposed to Europe) with a different distribution of international power (unipolar, nonpolar, or multipolar, instead of bipolar). These differences from the past have been vastly overstated. To a greater extent than is often recognized, our current theories and policies are based on this history. Rogue states are not new; neither is the fear of nuclear use by nonstate actors. Policymakers during the Cold War wrestled with many of the same questions surrounding nuclear weapons. Even when the issues were different, there is much we can learn from this history.[12]

What are the commonly held views and lessons? Scholars routinely characterize the Cold War in Europe as the Long Peace.[13] The relationship between the Soviet Union and the United States was marked by deep tension, ideological competition, and geopolitical disagreements. Yet this rivalry never led to a full-scale war between these superpowers. Given how bloody international politics had been during the first half of the twentieth century, with two world wars that killed tens of millions in

Europe and elsewhere, the absence of conflict demanded an explanation. Two ideas buttress the idea of the Cold War in Europe as a Long Peace. First is the notion of bipolarity. The Soviet Union and the United States were the only global superpowers, and a system dominated by only two powers that are roughly balanced is, according to some analysts, more likely to be stable. The second is what Robert Jervis calls "the nuclear revolution." Nuclear weapons, and particularly thermonuclear weapons, are so devastating that their use for anything other than deterrence is almost inconceivable.[14]

According to the nuclear revolution advocates, the nonusability of nuclear weapons has had a profound impact on statecraft. States are less likely to engage in behavior that could provoke crises that might lead to war. If they do find themselves in crises, they are apt to behave with more prudence than they might have had in the nonnuclear age. The nuclear revolution, many strategists believe, explains the extraordinary caution demonstrated by the United States and Soviet Union during the Cuban missile crisis, where actions that could lead to a war were avoided. That such a crisis was resolved without weapons being fired is evidence of the influence of the nuclear revolution, as is the absence of any nuclear crisis between the superpowers in the three decades that followed.

The nuclear revolution/Long Peace advocates make a series of other claims as well. Nuclear superiority is of limited value, particularly once a condition of "mutual vulnerability" exists. The outcome of a crisis should not hinge on who has more nuclear weapons, since even if only a handful of weapons survive a nuclear first strike, they would be able to cause enough catastrophic damage to deter most rational actors. A crisis is much more likely to be determined by the balance of resolve, according to this argument. In other words, the state with more at stake and more willing to take risks will succeed in a test of wills, which nuclear revolution advocates contend is apt to make the crisis less dangerous. In terms of the Cuban missile crisis, for example, a combination of greater interests and resolve, combined with local conventional superiority, allowed the United States to prevail and compel the Soviet Union to remove their nuclear weapons from Cuba. America's nuclear superiority, we are often told, was not decisive. In sum, according to Robert Jervis: "If nuclear weapons have had the influence that the nuclear-revolution theory indicates they should have, then there will be peace between the superpowers, crises will be rare, neither side will be eager to press bargaining advantages to the limit, the status quo will be relatively easy to maintain, and political outcomes will not be closely related to either the nuclear or the conventional balance."[15]

In short, according to this theory, nuclear weapons create what Stephen Van Evera has termed a "defense-dominant world." Since conquest in a nuclear world is almost impossible, the chance of great power war is dramatically lower.[16] Advocates of the nuclear revolution theory also believe that these weapons are so fearsome, and nuclear deterrence is so robust, that deterrence can be extended to cover allies quite easily and without needing to seek overwhelming nuclear superiority.

Not everyone accepts these views. Some analysts argue that nuclear superiority does matter, especially in circumstances where a state is trying to extend deterrence. Others argue that one cannot judge the stabilizing qualities of nuclear weapons simply by asking whether or not they lead to great power war; there are behaviors and crises *short* of war (or that risk war) that are extraordinarily dangerous and that one would hope to avoid. There may be times when nuclear weapons create destabilizing conditions that dramatically increase the chance of general war.

The Berlin crises that took place between 1958 and 1962 offer an excellent opportunity to test many of these claims about the Long Peace/nuclear revolution. Did the leaders of the superpowers exhibit more caution than they otherwise might, respecting each other's core interests and avoiding actions that could lead to war? And as the crises played out, what factors determined the outcome? Did nuclear superiority matter, or was the balance of resolve more important? And did these factors—alone or mixed—make war less likely? If the nuclear revolution/Long Peace view is correct, we would expect leaders on both sides to be very cautious, both in initiating a crisis and in behavior throughout. We would not expect the nuclear balance between the Soviet Union and the United States to shape the crisis; in other words, nuclear superiority should not matter. The balance of resolve should be the most important factor in determining the outcome. Crises shaped by the balance of resolve should be more stable and predictable than those determined by the balance of power.

The Background of the 1958–1962 Berlin Crisis

The status of Berlin was contentious from the early days of the Cold War. The future of Germany had been discussed during the conferences in Yalta and Potsdam, and it was decided that the defeated country would be divided into three (and later, four) occupation zones, to be held by the Soviet Union, the United States, Great Britain, and France, based largely on the location of allied troops. In addition, Berlin was to be divided into four occupation zones.

The problem was that Berlin was located in the heart of the eastern occupation zone, which was controlled by the Soviet Union and miles away from any western zone. It was completely surrounded by overwhelming conventional Soviet military power, was dependent on the eastern zone for supplies, and was virtually indefensible. While there was a treaty providing air and traffic corridors from the western zones to Berlin, no formal agreement guaranteeing rail and road access through the Soviet zone was ever reached. This vulnerability provided the Soviets with a convenient tool to harass the West. They impeded travel and shipments into the city on several occasions until they installed a comprehensive land blockade against the city in 1948 in reaction to the Marshall Plan, the creation of a new West German currency, and moves to integrate and eventually merge the three western sectors into a single unit. The Western allies responded to the land blockade with a massive airlift to supply the vulnerable citizens of Berlin; it was so successful that the Soviets ended their blockade less than a year later.

Despite this success, Berlin's vulnerability and indefensibility meant it would remain susceptible to Soviet pressure. In November 1958, Soviet premier Nikita Khrushchev demanded that Western soldiers leave Berlin and that access to the city be controlled by East Germany. Scholars have identified several important motives for Khrushchev's ultimatum. Two stand out: First, Berlin's status allowed dissatisfied citizens of the Eastern bloc and particularly East Germany to leave for the West. Both the sheer numbers and the high quality of those leaving threatened to undermine the German Democratic Republic.[17] Another, perhaps even more compelling, motive was to signal the Soviet Union's great concern and displeasure over what appeared to be the nuclearization of the Bundeswehr, West Germany's army.[18] This crisis lasted for four years with several key phases.[19] The first took place at the end of the Eisenhower administration and saw both threats as well as attempts at negotiation. The second took place between the spring and fall of the first year of the Kennedy administration. The final phase took place the next year and culminated with the October 1962 Cuban missile crisis. Many of the issues animating the crisis over Berlin were de facto resolved in negotiations between the Soviet Union and the United States in the summer of 1963, although the de jure resolution of the situation did not come until the quadripartite agreements of 1971.[20]

Were the issues separating the Soviets and Americans vis-à-vis Berlin between 1958 and 1962 intractable? And, in particular, did the Americans have no "give" in their position? Did they find the status quo ideal and have no regard at all for the views of the Soviet Union? Given the length and severity of the crisis, one might have expected US policymakers to dig in their heels, ready to maintain their position at all costs. In the prenuclear age, such circumstances made for the most dangerous crises. But that was not the case with US policy toward Berlin. President Eisenhower made it clear he thought the original decision to maintain a western zone in Berlin unwise. The president argued that "we should not have committed ourselves as deeply as we had to Berlin, where he said the situation was basically untenable, as in the case of Quemoy and Matsu."[21] President Kennedy took a similar view.[22] He said, "God knows I am not an isolationist, but it seems particularly stupid to risk killing a million Americans over an argument about access rights on an Autobahn in the Soviet zone of Germany, or because the Germans want Germany reunified."[23] Even those who held relatively hawkish views, such as US ambassador David Bruce, conceded that the US position in Berlin was not ideal. According to Bruce, the "existence of [an] island of West Berlin, surrounded by hostile territory, results from political determination many years ago more remarkable for naïveté than long range judgment."

Nor did the Americans necessarily assume that the Soviets were unremittingly hostile or that their demands were outrageous. As the US ambassador to the Soviet Union Llewellyn E. "Tommy" Thompson argued at the start of the crisis, "I believe Khrushchev seeks a détente of long duration and a real measure of disarmament if this can be had without jeopardizing [the] Communist empire in Eastern Europe."[24] Great emphasis was put on convincing the Soviets that the United States was open to reasonable negotiations to change a status quo no one liked. As one analysis put it, it was important to get "Khrushchev to understand the Western position and the reasons for it more accurately, and showing him that we understand his problems better than he evidently thinks we do, and are prepared to deal with him on a frank and realistic basis with regard to problems on both sides."[25] There were even those, such as former head of policy planning George Kennan, who thought that the Soviets had far greater interests than the West in Berlin and that, as upsetting as it would be to the population of West Berlin, those interests should be accommodated. He wrote, "In general, I have never been able to go along with the tendency of some people to look to the populace of Berlin as an unfailing source of sound instructive wisdom about the realities of the Cold War."[26]

In fact, both Eisenhower and Kennedy engaged in negotiations with Khrushchev to end the stalemate, a stance neither would have taken if there had been no give in the American position. As Eisenhower put it, there was "no choice but to resume negotiations so long as we in fact say we do not seek a perpetuation of the situation in Berlin; clearly, we did not contemplate 50 years in occupation there."[27] The key for both presidents was that they be treated with respect. Even if the "present situation was admittedly abnormal, until the United States could discharge its responsibilities to the German people it could not accept unilateral action on the part of another party."[28] Secretary of State Dean Rusk even acknowledged the larger absurdity underneath the US-Soviet clash over Germany: "The U.S. had not been the Soviet Union's ally in World War II against the Nazis in order to fight a third world war over the German question. That would be foolish."[29]

Part of the issue was trying to figure out how expansive Soviet goals were. On the one hand, Khrushchev's effort to revise the legal status of Berlin, while serious, was clearly not in the same category as a Warsaw Pact blitzkrieg through the Fulda gap. The Soviets had legitimate concerns in Central Europe, including the mass outflow of refugees from the Eastern bloc through Berlin that was undermining the German Democratic Republic; fear of what the Soviets called German "military revanchism," which was actually a not unfounded concern that the West German military sought access to nuclear weapons; and the understandable desire to tie up the loose ends from the World War II. As Khrushchev himself said, he "could not understand the President's reference to Western Europe. The USSR does not wish any change; it merely wants to formalize the situation which has resulted from World War II."[30] Dale Copeland has argued that declassified documents reveal that Soviet motives during the crisis were not expansionist: "The Soviets were acting defensively to protect their position in Eastern Europe from the rise of West Germany and the steady decline of the GDR."[31] Yet others saw the USSR's motives differently: the "fact that Khrushchev kept threatening to alter the status quo in Central Europe was strong proof for both Taylor and Kennedy that the Soviet leader believed the United States was too afraid of the consequences of massive retaliation to fight for anything but its homeland."[32] This view lent support to those who argued for rigidity in dealing with the Soviets. French president de Gaulle told Kennedy, "*Any* retreat from Berlin, *any* change of status, *any* withdrawal of troops, *any* new obstacles to transportation and communication, would mean defeat. It would result in almost a complete loss of Germany, and in very serious losses within France, Italy and elsewhere."[33]

In such a difficult position, Kennedy, like Eisenhower before him, had to "avoid the risks inherent both in hardline nuclear missile-rattling on the one hand and a weak-seeming negotiations-at-all-costs stance on the other."[34] While no president would allow the United States to be forced to liquidate its position under pressure, there certainly was plenty of room for compromise. As Ambassador Thompson pointed out, given the "real risk of nuclear war," flexibility was a better alternative than the "Russian roulette in which Khrushchev threatens to engage us."[35] Kennedy understood the high stakes for the Soviet leader: "Khrushchev is losing East Germany. He cannot let that happen. If East Germany goes, so will Poland and all of Eastern Europe."[36]

Why then would an issue that was, arguably, a core interest of the Soviet Union's that the Americans were not wedded to be tinder for a nuclear war? How could a top US government analyst posit that America's position in the Berlin Crisis meant that the United States "must be prepared and ready, if all else fails, to wage nuclear war," while *simultaneously* suggesting that it would be wise to seek common ground "to avoid such a catastrophe"? "This may sound impracticable, but governments might do unexpected things, if [the] alternative appeared to be [the] destruction of most of [the] human race."[37] Why was it so hard to do the unexpected, and did nuclear weapons play a role in making it difficult?

The Role of Nuclear Weapons in the Crisis: Superiority vs. Balance of Resolve

US leaders left little doubt that nuclear weapons might be used if a crisis over Berlin got out of hand. When West Germany's chancellor Konrad Adenauer insisted that using nuclear weapons was inconceivable, US secretary of state John Foster Dulles chastised him: "It was essential that we employ the necessary counterforce. . . . This required that we must face up to the possibility of a general nuclear war in which he [Dulles] noted the United States would prove to be the main target . . . it would be disastrous for us to be committed to a conventional war in Europe. Surely this would please the Soviets with their great superiority in manpower and conventional weapons."[38]

Once significant military forces were engaged, the pressures to escalate to the use of nuclear weapons would be difficult to resist. Eisenhower warned that when political actions were replaced by military responses, "there are really no limits that can be set to the use of force."[39] The president, an avid poker player, made it clear that there would be no controlled escalation: "In order to avoid beginning with the white chips and working up to the blue, we should place them on notice that our whole stack is in play."[40] A purely conventional strategy was out of the question. "[The] President convinced them of the fact that we cannot fight a ground battle around Berlin with the Germans and the Russians—that is out."[41] Even de Gaulle understood that "there is no possibility of a military victory for us in the area of Berlin. What we must make clear is that if there is any fighting around Berlin, this means general war."[42] Despite some modifications in contingency planning, the Kennedy administration also understood a major conflict over Berlin would escalate quickly. As the Supreme Allied Commander in Europe, Lauris Norstad said, "War over Berlin was going to be a nuclear war—or an immediate and ignominious defeat."[43]

How could the use of US military force still be on the table if a ground war would lead to a devastating defeat? Simply put, the United States possessed what policymakers believed was a meaningful superiority in strategic nuclear weapons. In the end, this would force the Russians to back down. According to the Joint Chiefs of Staff at the time, "the Soviet Union is unlikely to risk general war to evict the Allies from Berlin, particularly at this time when the Soviet leaders probably recognize that the United Sates has a greater capability to inflict damage in general war upon them than they upon us."[44]

It was also understood, however, that this meaningful nuclear superiority was not a permanent feature of the Cold War and would eventually wane. In other words, the United States had a "window of opportunity" in which its strength would allow it to prevail. "[The] JCS had concluded that our negotiating position, from a military point of view, would be stronger now than two and half years from now, and that this was also the conclusion of an ad hoc committee consisting of State, Defense, JCS and CIA."[45] If anything, this sense of nuclear superiority increased from the Eisenhower to the Kennedy period. According to Secretary of Defense McNamara, the "USSR's hesitancy in pushing its Berlin objectives by precipitate action is that the Soviet leaders appear now to realize that the shift if the political-military relation of forces in the world has been less significant than they anticipated two or three years ago."[46] This meant that the issue of Berlin had to be pushed to a resolution sooner rather than later. President Eisenhower "was of the opinion that the US and NATO were stronger from the nuclear standpoint now than they would be in another two or three years."[47] As David Bruce wrote, "If they undertake to dislodge us from it at the risk of general war, I should rather accept the risk now than later."[48] In the summer and fall of 1961, the United States crafted a plan that would allow it to launch a "disarming strike" against Soviet strategic nuclear forces if the situation in Berlin escalated.[49]

Did this mean that the balance of resolve was not important during the crisis? Not at all; in fact, one is struck in the documents by the constant references to the need to demonstrate "will" in the crisis. Given how much the Soviets had at stake over Berlin—arguably more that the United States—the United States had to make it clear to Khrushchev that nuclear weapons could and would be used if it was pushed too far: "We must, however, have the will (which he could assure the Chancellor the United States possessed) to use those elements of force in which we are superior."[50] As Richard Betts has argued, the United States had to "convince Khrushchev that he was dealing with a leader ultimately willing to undertake what the Soviet note had said 'only madman' could contemplate."[51]

Former secretary of state Dean Acheson believed demonstrating resolve was the key issue: "The central problem was that Khrushchev did not believe the risk of acting today was as great as it formerly was." This was because the Soviet premier believed "we would not oppose him with nuclear weapons." Simply saying we would use them would not work: "The threat to use nuclear weapons did not increase the belief that we would use them." "Nuclear weapons should not be looked upon as the last and largest weapon to be used, but as the first step in a new policy in protecting the United States from the failure of a policy of deterrence."[52] Acheson argued that "Berlin was a general test of will and if the West failed it, Germany would be prized away from the Western alliance."[53] Interestingly, Acheson believed it was the US failure to demonstrate resolve, or will, and not the strategic nuclear balance, that emboldened the Soviet Union: "The capability of U.S. nuclear power to devastate the Soviet Union has not declined over the past two years. The decline in the effectiveness of the deterrent, therefore, must lie in a change in Soviet appraisal of U.S. willingness to go to nuclear war over the issue which Khrushchev reiterates his determination to present."[54] More or better nuclear weapons would not improve the situation; instead, deterrence would only be enhanced if the US government demonstrated it was "really prepared to use nuclear weapons for the protection of Berlin on which we had staked our entire prestige."[55]

How could the United States demonstrate its resolve, its will? Once again, the answer was not clear. Eisenhower had eschewed any mobilization of conventional forces for fear it would be both an overreaction and signal a lessened willingness to use nuclear weapons. When Sen. Lyndon B. Johnson pointed out "the seeming inconsistency of the current force reductions," Eisenhower responded "that when we reach the acute crisis period, it will be necessary to engage in general war to protect our rights."[56] Acheson recommended exactly the opposite course to Kennedy—mobilization and sending increased conventional forces to demonstrate American resolve and willingness to use nuclear weapons. McGeorge Bundy, surprisingly, responded to Acheson's recommendation by agreeing with the *Eisenhower* position: the crisis was "one of political unity and firmness of will." Increased military preparations might "divide the alliance, stiffen the Russians, frighten our own people" and, most worryingly, undermine the "shield of nuclear deterrence."[57] Herein lay one of the crucial problems with any crisis determined by will and resolve—how, short of launching a war, do you demonstrate this quality? Would mobilization and increased conventional capabilities show Khrushchev the United States was willing to use nuclear weapons if necessary, or would it reveal an unwillingness to use nuclear weapons?

At heart, then, the handling of the crisis turned on each side convincing the other it was willing to use nuclear weapons to defend its position. Was a crisis that turned on the balance of resolve more stable or predictable than one determined solely by the balance of military forces? One problem with balance of resolve is that it is hard to measure; it is largely subjective and in the eye of the beholder. In the spring of 1961, the leaders of both France and Great Britain believed the Soviets had the upper hand in terms of resolve. De Gaulle argued that "Mr. Khrushchev may think that we would not dare to go equally far" as we did in 1948–49; and MacMillan pointed out that "the West seemed to the Russians to be weaker and Mr. Khrushchev might no longer believe in the West's firmness of purpose."[58] Others saw the same situation in a completely different light. As military aide Lawrence Legere told General Taylor, "above all, General Clay is so eternally right when he says that if we stand up to them like men they will back down, not bomb New York and Washington."[59] But Kennan disagreed with those who assumed "the Russians are bluffing over Berlin" and that "if confronted with a flat no" can "be depended upon to back down."[60]

What if the Soviets were motivated by the same desire to demonstrate willingness to see the crisis through to the end? In fact, Khrushchev's strategy was based explicitly on exploiting the balance of resolve, even in the face of America's nuclear superiority. Through this period, the Soviet Premier believed that "so long as the Soviet Union was the weaker superpower, it had to practice brinkmanship to keep its adversary off-balance."[61] After putting the Soviet Union's first armed intercontinental ballistic missile into service in July 1958, Khrushchev thought he could initiate a crisis over Berlin: "Although the force was tiny in comparison with the US arsenal, it had symbolic meaning. The Soviet Union finally had the ability to launch a nuclear missile attack on the United States. Khrushchev hoped that only a few nuclear weapons of this kind would be necessary to reach rough parity with the United States."[62] At the same time, Khrushchev rejected plans to undertake a massive military buildup, relying instead on "minimal deterrence." Why waste money on a program that the Soviet Union could hardly afford when no sane leader, he believed, would ever risk war with the USSR so long as it had a few nuclear missiles? " 'Missiles are not cucumbers,' he liked to say, 'one cannot eat them and one does not require more than a certain number in order to ward off an attack.' "[63] This logic had a certain similarity to the arguments made by Eisenhower and Bundy to avoid mobilizing and increasing conventional forces during a crisis.

How could one tell if Soviet and also US threats were bluffs? When Khrushchev's son, Sergei, asked his father if his ultimatum would lead to war, the Soviet premier replied, " 'Of course not! No one would want a war over Berlin.' . . . Before that time came, his threat would scare the West into negotiations." When his son asked what would happen if the negotiations failed, Khrushchev was irritated: "Then we'll try something else."[64] As Frederick Taylor points out, thermonuclear weapons made Khrushchev "more, not less, bold in his foreign policy calculations." This was based on his belief that "Secretary of State Dulles's threats of massive retaliation were also bluff—brinkmanship based on the fact that both sides knew where the brink was and would act accordingly."[65] But as Daryl Press points out, the United States went to great lengths to convince its own allies that they meant what they said. Great Britain's ambassador to the United States reported that the American position had "no element of bluff" and that they were "inclined to play to the end of the game of chicken."[66]

As ambassador Thompson pointed out in a telegram, this created the real possibility of misperception: "Both sides consider [the] other would not risk war over Berlin. Danger arises from [the] fact that if K[hrushchev] carries out his declared intentions and we carry out ours, [the] situation [will] likely get out of control and military as well as political prestige would become involved making retreat for either side even more difficult."[67] Khrushchev expected the Americans to back down before things got serious, but leaders in the United States expected the same kind of restraint from the Soviets. However, it was recognized that while the Soviet leader may want to avoid a nuclear war "the real danger is that he might risk just such a war without realizing he is doing so."[68] Nonetheless, the US commander in Berlin, Lucius Clay, told Washington that he "felt he could count on Khrushchev and the Soviets to act carefully and to pull back in a real crunch."[69]

However, it was not even clear who would be the aggressor in a conflict over Berlin, making it even more difficult to calibrate who had the upper hand in terms of resolve and will. When Khrushchev told Thompson he could not believe "we would bring on such a catastrophe," the ambassador retorted, "it was he who would be taking action to change the present situation." Khrushchev disagreed, arguing that "we would be [the] ones [who] would have to cross [the] frontier."[70] To whom did the status quo in Berlin matter more? When Thompson told Khrushchev that "U.S. prestige everywhere in the world was at stake it its commitments to Berliners," Khrushchev understandably scoffed: "Berlin was really of little importance to either America or the Soviet Union, so why should they get so worked up about changing the city's status?"[71]

The competition between the Soviet Union and the United States was marked by great uncertainty and contradictions, made worse by nuclear weapons. From the American side, the Soviet concerns were not unreasonable, but their methods were unacceptable; it was unclear who would be the aggressor and who the aggrieved, and whose core interests were more at stake. Nuclear superiority mattered, but resolve and will seemed to matter more. Yet it was unclear how to demonstrate this resolve, and policies such as negotiations or conventional force buildups created mixed messages. Neither side thought Berlin worth a nuclear war, but both sought to manipulate the risk inherent in a nuclear crisis to get what they wanted. As Secretary of State Rusk said, "one of the quickest ways to have a nuclear war is to have the two sides persuaded that neither will fight."[72]

Nuclear Revolution or Traditional Power Politics? Or Both?

In the end, what was the role of nuclear weapons in the origins, evolution, and outcome of the 1958–62 Berlin Crisis, as opposed to, or in combination with, purely political drivers? The evidence pulls in several different directions. On the one hand, it is hard to see how nuclear weapons stabilized relations between the Soviet Union and the United States in the late 1950s and early 1960s, especially if we define stability as the absence of crisis, uncertainty, and risk-taking behavior that could lead to war. As Dale Copeland argues, "to make a theory of major war relevant to the nuclear era, as well as to the pre-nuclear era, we must explain why states would move from peaceful engagement to a destabilizing cold war rivalry, or from such a rivalry into crises with the types of risks witnessed in the Cuban missile crisis."[73] One of the primary motivations for Khrushchev's posture was his fear that West Germany was going nuclear; in a nonnuclear world, the FRG's military status would have certainly been important to the Russians, but a nuclearized Bundeswehr was an especially grave threat.[74] In traditional balance-of-power terms, Berlin should not have been an issue of great note. The loss of West Berlin—or more likely, its conversion to a "free city"—would have had little impact on the overall economic and military power of NATO. Instead of undermining NATO, a loss of Berlin would just as likely have brought the Western allies closer together, more willing to build the military forces necessary to fend off a Soviet attack.

Furthermore, both Presidents Eisenhower and Kennedy recognized that key Russian interests were engaged in the struggle over Berlin. While they did not like Khrushchev's ultimatums and bluster, they conceded that the jurisdictional situation in the city was an unfortunate relic of World War II. Over time, they came to understand, and even share, Russia's concern over German nuclearization, and they were not keen to see East Germany simply collapse. Finally, they understood that Berlin was military indefensible with conventional forces. From a political perspective, all of these factors might have pointed to the US taking a more conciliatory posture, working to avoid a most unappealing military confrontation.

Yet the crisis was extraordinarily dangerous, and US policymakers appeared willing to consider the use of nuclear weapons. Despite what nuclear revolution advocates argue, nuclear superiority was a key factor in US decision making; without it, the Americans feared their commitment to defend Berlin lacked credibility. They recognized this superiority would not last forever and that it was better to act while they still had such a significant nuclear advantage. Even with this impressive superiority, US policymakers thought they had to go to great lengths to demonstrate their resolve, will, or capability in ways that strengthened their position. Nuclear weapons were key drivers both of the origins and the outcome of the crisis.

In terms of the origins of the crisis, for example, it is hard to imagine how the United States could have prevented an East German/Soviet takeover of Berlin with only conventional weapons. The Warsaw Pact nations had superior conventional forces, and Berlin was deep in Eastern bloc territory. The United States was unlikely to risk a major conflict to hold onto a city whose loss, while a political and ideological blow, would do little if anything to worsen the military balance of power.

The same logic held for Cuba—in the absence of nuclear weapons, the United States would likely have moved quickly and relatively easily to eliminate a Soviet presence in Cuba, though it is hard to imagine what the Soviets would hope to gain from such an action in a nonnuclear, non–Berlin Crisis world. As the crisis in Berlin did unfold, it is clear that the focus on the balance of resolve was destabilizing, as both sides often appeared to underestimate or misperceive how far each was willing to go or how much "will" the other had.

This may provide an important lesson that is applicable to contemporary nuclear statecraft. When nuclear weapons are deployed on behalf of clear and obvious vital interests, such as deterring an attack on a state's homeland, then the stabilizing qualities of nuclear weapons should be clear. Waltz's logic that nuclear weapons prevent large land invasions is probably true. But what if a state tries to do more with its nuclear arsenal than simply deter an attack, such as trying to extend its deterrent over far-flung territories, or manipulate risk in order to change the status quo? Could elements of the Berlin dynamic come into play in a crisis between the United States and China over Taiwan, or in South Asia between India and Pakistan? It is hard to see how any crisis that encourages adversaries to manipulate the risk inherent in a nuclear standoff, where the focus is on such subjective and immeasurable factors as "will," credibility, and resolve, can be stabilizing. Khrushchev believed he could get what he wanted in the crisis, despite possessing far smaller nuclear forces, because he could demonstrate greater resolve. The United States, despite have arguably a smaller interest in what happened to Berlin, also thought it could prevail if it possessed superior will. The possibilities for misperception and disaster were clear. It is not hard to imagine a contemporary nuclear crisis unfolding in a similarly dangerous manner.

The story does not end there, however, and there is a further puzzle that demonstrates how the historical evidence rarely provides simple and clear-cut answers to questions about the nuclear age. Only a few years after the 1958–62 crisis, the Soviet Union reached strategic parity with the United States, ending the ability of the United States to wield nuclear primacy in a conflict over Berlin. West Berlin was as vulnerable as ever, and the dynamics surrounding the German question appeared, on the surface, to be just as volatile. Shouldn't we have expected to see the Soviet Union reignite tensions over Berlin, given its vastly improved strategic position? If nuclear primacy and nuclear brinkmanship determined the outcome in the 1958–62 period, shouldn't the change in circumstances have produced an outcome far more favorable to the Soviet Union?

US decision makers certainly feared such a move. As the Johnson administration's ambassador to West Germany, Henry Cabot Lodge, told Richard Nixon before the 1968 Presidential election, the "Soviet Union has some very strong cards to play." Lodge argued that it would be very hard for the United States to prevent the Germans from accepting a Soviet offer "to unify East and West Germany and to locate the capital of the newly unified state in Berlin." In fact, the Soviets might not even have to pay that high a price. Referring to the 1922 Rapallo Treaty and the 1930 Hitler-Stalin Pact, the ambassador warned: "Twice in our lifetime Germans and Russians have reached agreement."[75] West Berlin was an obvious pressure point. As Henry Kissinger told President Nixon, "given the city's vulnerabilities" the Soviets could "manufacture pretexts for harassment whenever they choose." Kissinger warned that the Soviets could "strangle the city."[76] The United States would have had far less leverage if such a situation arose. As Nixon told the West German chancellor, due to "disturbing developments," US strategic superiority had been eliminated while Soviet conventional capabilities had increased. "In 1962, at the time of the Cuban missile crisis, the US lead in strategic missiles had been so massive that no rational decision makers on the Soviet side would have risked war." By 1969, the new president recognized this was no longer the case.[77]

A strange thing happened, however. Despite small-scale tensions surrounding West Berlin, the Soviet Union pursued a mild, even conciliatory policy and sought an agreement to stabilize the status quo. The

Soviet ambassador to West Germany stated that "the Soviets respected the fact that West Berlin was occupied by US, UK, and French military forces."[78] Their ambassador to the United States, Anatoly Dobrynin, made it clear that the Soviets had no "intention of undermining the status quo in Western Europe" and did not "care about formal recognition of Eastern Germany."[79] Soviet Foreign Minister Gromyko assured Nixon that the Soviet Union had "no intention to weaken the status of the allied powers in West Berlin."[80] Soviet leader Leonid Brezhnev even offered that any agreement on Berlin would have to meet the "wishes of the Berlin population."[81] The Soviets offered a settlement that West German chancellor Willy Brandt pointed out was more favorable than what "was discussed in Geneva in 1959" or what Dean Acheson's Berlin report to President Kennedy posited as a goal in 1961, when the United States possessed nuclear superiority. Kissinger agreed: "I feel that we're doing better than I thought possible." This success was possible, in spite of the fact, as Brandt pointed out, "that we all know the military position rather is more favorable for the Soviet Union than it was then."[82]

What are we to make of all this? Why was it that only a few years after a dangerous crisis shaped by the nuclear balance and brinkmanship the same issue was being resolved in a relatively amicable manner in which nuclear weapons appeared to play no role at all? Both US and West German policymakers speculated that this later Soviet reasonableness was shaped by other political concerns, such as a desire to see the FRG ratify the Nuclear Nonproliferation Treaty or its concern over the growing threat it faced from the People's Republic of China. While we would need far better access to the Soviet archives to give a definitive answer, it is clear that by the late 1960s and early 1970s, the Soviet Union was satisfied with things as they were—a divided, nonnuclear Germany within a divided Europe—and wanted to see that status quo solidified. As Trachtenberg has convincingly explained, the power-political issues that led the Soviets to threaten Berlin in the Eisenhower period had been resolved. As a result, the "world at the end of 1962 was very different from the world of November 1958."[83] The Soviet leadership no longer saw a need to threaten West Berlin, and, as such, nuclear weapons played little role in the negotiations that led to the quadripartite agreement on Berlin in September 1971.

In the end, it is hard to know what to make of the 1958–62 Berlin Crisis. Based on the documents, one can argue that the Berlin Crisis might have played out much differently, and might never have happened at all, in a nonnuclear world in which Soviet conventional superiority and greater interest in the issues at stake surely would have led them to prevail. Preserving West Berlin in the nuclear age, on the other hand, required the

United States and NATO to think about nuclear weapons and military strategy in much different ways than they did for other contingencies, including defending the Federal Republic of Germany and Western Europe. Likewise, it is interesting to reflect on how the Cold War conflict between the Soviet Union and the United States would have unfolded if Berlin had not been an issue, if the victors of World War II had managed to resolve the city's political and legal status before tensions between the Soviet Union and the United States intensified. While there were many points of disagreement between the superpowers in the postwar period, Berlin was the most dangerous and exposed flash point of the bipolar struggle. A Cold War absent the struggle over Berlin might have led to different military strategies than those that developed; the Berlin contingency put pressure on the United States to possess the nuclear primacy necessary to credibly extend its deterrent capability over an asset that was otherwise indefensible. It is impossible to know.

While it may be unsatisfactory for those looking for parsimony and clear-cut answers, the historical evidence about the crisis over Berlin leaves us with an intertwined mix of traditional power politics and the extraordinary and often contradictory effects of nuclear weapons on international politics. It is almost impossible to disentangle. Consider Kissinger's 1970 assessment of Berlin (italics in the original): "*In the final analysis, our position in Berlin will depend on our own will to defend it and on the price the Soviets put on a continuing period of détente in West Europe.*"[84] In other words, any outcome in Berlin depended on two very different things—the challenge, temptations, and dangers of demonstrating resolve in a nuclearized environment, and the play of old-fashioned great power politics. In some sense, nuclear weapons both mattered greatly and very little. Only by understanding and assessing the role of each of these factors—traditional geopolitics and the profound influence of the nuclear revolution, both alone and in a highly interactive combination—can we begin to make sense of the 1958–62 Berlin Crisis, and of any international crisis between nuclear states since then.

[4]

Blasts from the Past

Proliferation Lessons from the 1960s

The National Security Strategy document issued by the George W. Bush administration in 2002 portrays a world far different from that of the past. The Cold War was dangerous, but according to this document, its lessons are largely irrelevant to the making of contemporary US strategy. After the 1962 Cuban missile crisis, the United States faced a "status quo, risk-adverse" adversary—the Soviet Union—that believed that weapons of mass destruction should be used only as a last resort. In contrast, in 2002 the United States is confronted by "rogue states" that "brutalize their own people," "threaten their neighbors," "sponsor terrorism," and "hate the United States and everything for which it stands." Most important, rogue states "are determined to acquire weapons of mass destruction" to "achieve the aggressive designs of these regimes." In so doing, they have created a world that is far "more complex and dangerous" than the international system of the 1960s. As a result, Cold War concepts such as deterrence are ineffective in a "security environment that has undergone profound transformation."[1]

US policymakers responsible for assessing international politics following the testing of an atomic device by the People's Republic of China on October 16, 1964, would have been puzzled by the Bush administration's characterization of their world. Four decades earlier, the threat posed by a nuclear-armed China under Mao Zedong was far more terrifying than anything Iraq's Saddam Hussein or Bush's "rogue" rulers can muster. China, with a population of more than 700 million in 1964, had already fought the United States in Korea; attacked India; and threatened Indochina, Indonesia, and Taiwan. It supported violent revolutionary groups around the world whose goals clashed with US interests. Mao's internal policies had led to the deaths of millions of Chinese citizens, and he had already declared that nuclear war with the United States was not to be feared. In Mao's words: "If the worse came to the worst and half of mankind died, the other half would remain while imperialism would be razed to the ground and the whole world would become socialist."[2] To the United States, such actions and statements made the PRC appear not only irrational but perhaps undeterrable.

It is well known that the United States considered a wide array of responses to China's 1964 atomic test, including a preemptive attack. What is less well known is that the ascension of this "rogue" state into the world's nuclear ranks inspired a searching debate within the US government over how to respond to emerging and potential nuclear powers. The issue went beyond the question of how China would behave with atomic weapons to the core questions that policymakers continue to grapple with today. For example: Could the United States slow the pace of nuclear proliferation, and, if it could, would the price be too high to pay? Is the prevention of nuclear proliferation so important that it trumps other policy considerations with no effort or expense spared to achieve it?

Under President Johnson, the United States transformed its nuclear nonproliferation strategy to meet these challenges. Starting with the creation of a little-known but highly influential group of experts known as the Gilpatric committee, the administration laid the foundations for a far more robust nonproliferation policy, which eventually led to the negotiation with the Soviet Union of the Nuclear Nonproliferation Treaty.[3] This shift, which has been missed almost entirely in the historical and strategic studies literature, was not inevitable. Indeed, contrary to the conventional wisdom, the Johnson administration's nonproliferation policy represented a clear departure from that of the Kennedy administration, which did little to halt proliferation. Nor was it a policy that would be embraced by Nixon administration, which downgraded nonproliferation as a priority. During its evolution, the Johnson administration's nonproliferation strategy encountered opposition both within and without the US government because it marked a shift away from traditional Cold War policy. Success demanded cooperation with the United States' sworn enemy, the Soviet Union, to constrain American allies. In particular, this new strategy required the United States to put heavy pressure on West Germany to accept permanent nonnuclear status without receiving anything in return.

The risks for the United States of doing nothing after China's 1964 atomic test, however, were considered too great to ignore. As one member of the Gilpatric committee stated, nuclear proliferation demanded that the United States "reexamine thoughtfully and objectively all of our NATO and East-West-China and nuclear postures with a clear and untrammeled mind. If, in the course of our thinking, we have to give up past thinking or past theories, then let us weigh the consequences of change" to determine whether a new strategy would leave the nation "better or worse off."[4] Despite intense opposition and significant risks, the Johnson administration crafted a strong nonproliferation policy that, for the most part, was a success, laying the groundwork for détente with the Soviets while constraining worldwide nuclear proliferation.

In this chapter the history of a crucial period in US foreign policymaking is rewritten in several fundamental ways. First, it reveals the consideration by a US administration to condone, and in some cases aid, nuclear proliferation in the 1960s; it also assesses the strength of arguments in favor of such a strategy. Second, it explores the reasons why the Johnson administration ultimately adopted a robust nonproliferation policy despite the many obstacles to success. Third, it shows how the Johnson administration's nonproliferation policy often challenged assumptions about US relations with allies and enemies alike, revealing a much more complex international order in the 1960s than simplistic accounts of the Cold War portray. Finally, it highlights some of the important lessons that policymakers today may find useful as they continue to address the pressing issue of nuclear proliferation in states such as Iran and North Korea.

The first section of this chapter examines the varied reactions of Johnson administration officials to China's 1964 atomic test, in particular their great concern about the potential regional and global consequences of the nuclear arming of this "rogue" adversary. The second section details the wide range of policies—from actively aiding proliferation to encouraging nuclear rollback—considered by the Gilpatric committee. The third section chronicles the broad disagreement within the Johnson administration over how to handle nuclear proliferation and the committee's efforts to address these differences. The fourth section reveals the obstacles the US government faced in trying to prevent other states from acquiring nuclear weapons, many of which still pose challenges today. The fifth section charts the most explosive issue for the Johnson administration: the possible effects of a revised nonproliferation policy on US relations with the FRG. It also chronicles the furious struggle that influential policymakers in Washington and Bonn waged to undermine the eventual adoption of this policy. The sixth section examines the Gilpatric committee's recommendations and discusses why, despite the barriers to success, the administration decided to adopt many of its proposals.

China's Atomic Test and Worldwide Proliferation

US intelligence had been aware of China's desire to test an atomic device for some time. During the Limited Test Ban Treaty talks between the

Americans and the Soviets in the summer of 1963, US negotiator Averell Harriman attempted to gauge Soviet reaction both to the increasing likelihood of China becoming a nuclear power and to the possibility of a preventive strike by the United States, either alone or with the Soviet Union, against China's nuclear infrastructure. US government officials revisited the idea of a preventive strike in the months before China's October 1964 detonation.[5]

Several factors help to explain the Johnson administration's growing concern over the possibility of China acquiring nuclear capability. First, the PRC was already pursuing an expansionist foreign policy: it had attacked India in 1962; it was continuing to threaten Taiwan; and it was seeking to influence events in Indonesia. Of even greater concern, its support for North Vietnam and the Viet Cong insurgency against the US-sponsored government in South Vietnam made a future military clash with a nuclear-armed PRC a distinct possibility. According to National Security Advisor McGeorge Bundy, a nuclear-armed China would be "the greatest single threat to the status quo over the next few years."[6] President Kennedy agreed: China's nuclear program, he said, was "the whole reason for having a test ban."[7] China's leadership had denounced the easing of tensions between the United States and the Soviet Union following the peaceful resolution of the October 1962 Cuban missile crisis, while US policymakers increasingly viewed Mao's regime as both irrational and extremist. One US analyst asserted that a nuclear-armed PRC would become even more aggressive and harder to deter. In his view, the Chinese appeared "determined to eject the United States from Asia" and were sure to "exploit their nuclear weapons for this end." The same analyst predicted that China would have "thermonuclear weapons" by 1970, and that by 1980, "it [would] be necessary to think in terms of a possible 100 million U.S. deaths whenever a serious conflict with China threatens."[8] Given Mao's "doctrine of the inevitability of nuclear war," John McCloy, an occasional adviser to the Johnson administration, argued that unless the Western alliance was strengthened to meet this threat, nuclear war was "almost inevitable."[9] In the early 1960s, therefore, China possessed all the features of what is commonly referred to as a "rogue" regime. To many, the US strategy of containment and nuclear deterrence, which had kept the Soviet Union at bay for so many years, appeared inapplicable to the Chinese.

In the wake of China's 1964 atomic test, fears within the Johnson administration that other states would want to follow the PRC's lead only grew. According to a 1964 National Security Council report, four countries—India, Israel, Japan, and Sweden—had "the technical capability to produce nuclear weapons" and were "considering whether or not to do so."[10] Around the same time, Gilpatric committee staffer Russell

Murray painted an even bleaker picture: "At least eleven nations (India, Japan, Israel, Sweden, West Germany, Italy, Canada, Czechoslovakia, East Germany, Rumania and Yugoslavia) have or will soon have the capability of making nuclear weapons, given the requisite national decision. Within the foreseeable future . . . the number will grow substantially. The Union of South Africa, the United Arab Republic, Spain, Brazil and Mexico may be included."[11]

For Japan, which already felt threatened by the Soviet Union, the entry of its ancient rival, China, into the nuclear club was a cause for great concern. Recognizing this predicament, US under secretary of state George Ball reported that as a result of the Chinese detonation, Japan would be "under some pressure" to develop its own nuclear capability. Japan's new prime minister, who declared that "Japan should provide herself some nuclear deterrents," only reinforced this view.[12] India, despite its public support for a nonproliferation treaty, had even more incentive than Japan to develop atomic weapons, having lost a conventional war to China in 1962 and lacking an alliance with either the Soviet Union or the United States. According to Ball, the Chinese atomic test meant there "was a fifty-fifty" chance that the Indians would seek to develop nuclear weapons.[13] Pakistan would then have little choice but to follow suit. China's nuclearization could also push Indonesia into pursuing a similar course, which in turn could force Australia into having to decide whether to develop an indigenous nuclear capability.[14] South Korea and Taiwan might also want to acquire atomic weapons, especially if a nuclear-armed China diminished US power and undermined the credibility of US defense commitments in the region. Nor could the United States rely on domestic and cultural taboos against nuclear weapons to prevent proliferation in Asia. As Murray noted at the time, "though public opposition may be strong, the governmental-military elite in some countries (e.g., India, Japan) is far ahead of the public. A nuclear decision may be made and advanced under the guise of a peaceful program while public opinion is shifting."[15]

The Chinese test also convinced many US officials that nuclear proliferation would not be confined to Asia. Israel already had a weapons program, and Egypt was expected to launch one as well. Argentina, Brazil, and even Mexico were considered candidates to develop atomic bombs. Intelligence officials believed that Sweden, Switzerland, and even Italy were contemplating nuclear weapons programs. Without a change in US policy, the dangerous but predictable nuclear standoff between the United States and the Soviet Union would be replaced by an atomic weapons race including medium-size and even small powers.

Whether the United States could adapt its Cold War policies to meet this new threat would largely hinge on perhaps the most pressing issue of the bipolar standoff: the possibility of West Germany coming into possession of atomic weapons. Facing the Soviet behemoth, the FRG had a tremendous incentive to acquire nuclear weapons. In addition, the possibility of widespread proliferation, particularly by less-developed states, could challenge German national pride and prestige, adding to the pro-nuclear pressure building in the country.[16] As one US official noted, "should India, Israel, Japan or Sweden acquire an independent nuclear capability, the Federal Republic of Germany would doubtless come to feel that it had accepted second-class status by not acquiring its own independent nuclear force."[17]

At the same time, both the nascent US-Soviet détente that emerged following the successful conclusion of the Cuban missile crisis, as well global stability more generally, depended critically on West Germany remaining nonnuclear. In the words of an unidentified US official, "German national nuclear capability is virtually a Soviet obsession, based upon a deep-seated emotional fear of resurgent German militarism."[18] The Soviets went so far as to argue that they were convinced the "Germans desired to have a nuclear capability because of their territorial claims against Czechoslovakia and Poland."[19]

Despite not wanting to embarrass a close ally, the United States also did not wish to see the FRG become a nuclear power. Secretary of State Rusk told Khrushchev, "The Germans should not have a national nuclear capability."[20] Under Secretary of State Ball conceded, however, that preventing German nuclearization would be very hard if China's test provoked widespread proliferation. But he also noted that it was not "safe to isolate Germany or leave it with a permanent sense of grievance," which would be an all-too-likely outcome from "her forced exclusion from the nuclear club." Such policies, Ball remarked, "would provide a fertile ground for demagogues."[21]

In sum, China's ascension to the nuclear ranks threatened to weaken the United States' position in Asia, unleash worldwide proliferation, and undermine geopolitical stability in the heart of Europe. US grand strategy, oriented toward containing the Soviet Union largely through nuclear deterrence, appeared inapplicable to the dangers and dilemmas that these threats posed to the existing international order. For the Johnson administration, new policies based on fresh thinking were needed.

The Gilpatric Committee and Its Four Policy Options

Within a week of China's atomic blast, President Johnson convened a meeting of his foreign policy advisers to discuss its consequences. The administration was surprised to learn that the PRC had exploded a U-235 device, not a plutonium weapon as the Central Intelligence Agency had predicted. In a meeting with the president, CIA director John McCone stated that the agency was "intensely reexamining all the evidence" as to how they had missed this key piece of information and to determine how the PRC had "obtained sufficient U-235." In addition, he cautioned that the Chinese were "farther along" in "developing a nuclear capability" than the CIA had believed. The discussion turned quickly to the consequences of the atomic test for China's military power, the worldwide proliferation of nuclear weapons, and the proposal to develop a multilateral force (MLF) in Europe.[22] McCone asserted that, although they had yet to do so, the "Germans probably possess sufficient nuclear technology to develop weapons" and could do so quickly if "the political situation so dictates."[23]

One week later, President Johnson commissioned a high-level group of "wise men," led by Wall Street lawyer and former deputy secretary of defense, Roswell Gilpatric, to reexamine every aspect of US nonproliferation policy and to predict the likely influence of China's test on international politics.[24] Johnson asked the Gilpatric committee "to explore the widest range of measures that the United States might undertake in conjunction with other governments or by itself" to limit the spread of nuclear weapons.[25]

The committee's members included John McCloy; Arthur Dean, chairman of the US delegation to the Conference of the Committee on Disarmament; former White House science adviser George Kistiakowsky; scientist and former director of defense research and engineering Herbert York; former CIA director Allen Dulles; IBM chairman Arthur Watson; and Gen. Alfred Gruenther, former military commander of NATO. The committee was supported by a strong senior staff that included Spurgeon Keeney of the NSC, who, according to Glen Seaborg, chairman of the Atomic Energy Commission (AEC), was a main drafter of the committee's final report. Other staff members included Raymond Garthoff, Russell Murray, George Rathjens, and Henry Rowen. Harvard Law School professor Roger Fisher, along with others, acted as an outside consultant. In addition, the committee consulted widely with officials from the Department of State, the Department of Defense, the NSC, the AEC, and the Arms Control and Disarmament Agency (ACDA).

The committee began by grouping the most vital proliferation policy issues into six categories. The first category dealt with proliferation in Europe, in particular the contested issues of the MLF and German nuclearization. The second concerned proliferation beyond Europe, especially in India and Japan but also in the Middle East. The third involved US policy toward existing nuclear powers and included the question of whether Great Britain could be convinced to abandon its nuclear program and whether China's and France's nuclear programs could be rolled back. The final three categories—US nuclear weapons policies; the peaceful uses of atomic energy; and safeguards, inspections, and technology transfer—were more technical.

The committee then identified four broad policy options. Option one, "permissive or selective proliferation," assumed that proliferation was inevitable and that in some cases the United States might benefit by facilitating the process. As one analyst asked at the time, "[Is] it [in] the U.S. interest in all cases" to prevent other countries from obtaining nuclear weapons, "or might it be in the U.S. interest for particular nations to acquire such capability?"[26] If India and Japan were determined to develop nuclear capabilities in response to the Chinese test, then the United States might win their favor by offering them assistance with their programs. At the other extreme, option four called for an "all-out" effort to prevent proliferation and to make it the most important foreign policy goal of the United States. The logic underpinning this option was that the short-term costs of an all-out strategy, which would include angering close US allies, was justified to avoid the long-term costs of a world with dozens of nuclear powers. Option two, also referred to as the "prudent course," advised the United States to take steps to slow proliferation, but only if they did not involve major risks or sacrifice other US interests. Ultimately, the United States would have to "learn to live" with the consequences of nuclear proliferation. The third option envisaged US acceptance of "substantial costs and risks" to halt the spread of nuclear weapons. It did not, however, go as far as option four.[27]

All four options had consequences for existing US Cold War policy. Option one would end US attempts to police the world. Countries such as India, Indonesia, Japan, and Pakistan could pursue a nuclear capability, as could Australia (with British help), Brazil, and even Mexico. Israel and Egypt could push forward with their atomic efforts unimpeded. Proliferation on this scale could eventually lead to the withdrawal of US (and Soviet) forces from regions populated with new nuclear powers. Under option one, the nuclear arming of the PRC would lead to "the U.S. departure from Southeast Asia," which would then "fall under Chicom [Communist Chinese] hegemony." Western Europe would integrate politically and militarily, possibly forcing US withdrawal from the continent. Although the danger of nuclear war might increase, the Gilpatric committee speculated that it was "conceivable new regional groupings and balances, coupled with the responsibility which may come with nuclear accession, may create a new stability."[28] Option one was realpolitik in its purest form.

Option four would also carry profound geopolitical consequences. To prevent non-European countries such as India and Japan from developing nuclear weapons, the United States would need to offer "really serious guarantees and deployments to back them up," including US nuclear weapons. If that did not work, Washington would have to resort to "bribes" and "threats of economic and military abandonment." Egypt and Israel, for example, would be treated in a "brutal" manner if they sought a nuclear capability.[29] Option four also considered the possibility of nuclear rollback. The United States might use military force to eliminate China's nuclear capability; failing that, an all-out effort could be made to win Chinese cooperation through appeasement, including United Nations membership and promises of trade and territory. France, on the other hand, would be expelled from NATO and the Common Market and treated "like Cuba" if it did not acquiesce to US nonproliferation policies.[30] Roger Fisher, special consultant to the Gilpatric committee, suggested the adoption of more "vigorous measures against French testing," including "covert operations" against France's nuclear facilities. According to Fisher, the United States could always call on Indonesia's president Sukarno, with help from Australia, to "undertake some dirty work" to undermine the French nuclear program, thus allowing the United States to avoid "a major war with France."[31]

US pursuit of option four had the potential to transform power politics in Europe. The MLF proposal would be dropped, and West Germany, faced "with [the] threat of U.S. security withdrawal," would be forced to remain nonnuclear. If Bonn resisted this pressure, Washington would push "hard for a European settlement" that included the removal of a "neutral" and reunified Germany from NATO and the establishment of a nuclear-free zone for Central Europe. This fundamental shift might "make Europe look safer and perhaps loosen Soviet ties to satellites." But if a reunified Germany ever remilitarized, "[it] would pose a serious threat to [the] Soviets (and West)." The Soviets "might try to step in, precipitating large-scale conflict."[32]

Aspects of option one and option four found support from members of the Gilpatric committee. Both options, however, contained elements that were fraught with uncertainty and danger. The policy the United States was pursuing, however—option two (i.e., continuation of the "prudent course")—was seen as deeply flawed. Under this option, the United States would continue to pursue nonproliferation efforts that could be made "without substantial cost."[33] Discussions toward creating an MLF in Europe would proceed, but "with hints of U.S. continued veto." The United States would remain "ambivalent" about a European deterrent, leaving "open" the idea of trading the MLF for German reunification, but in the end avoid a confrontation with the FRG. Because the United States would not make any specific military commitments, it would be hard to "stop India, Israel, Japan, and other Nth nations" from developing nuclear weapons. The United States would still be "forced to withdraw from Southeast Asia," but at a higher cost than assumed in option one.[34]

This left option three, which went well beyond option two in its recommendation that the United States should accept substantial costs and risks, short of nuclear rollback, to stem proliferation. According to this option, the effort to establish an MLF in Europe would have to be dropped, a move that would be sure to anger West Germany. France, meanwhile, would be irritated by increased US efforts to stop worldwide nuclear testing. In addition, the administration would have to strengthen US guarantees to Japan, as well as consider making promises to protect India. Despite the significant shift these changes would entail, US expectations were, in some cases, modest. According to one assessment, "U.S. pressure and slowed proliferation elsewhere would keep [the] FRG in line for an extra 5–10 years (and perhaps longer)." If India remained nonnuclear, "other nations might be kept in line," and nuclear weapons acquisition might be delayed "at least 5–10 years." On the other hand, adoption of option three might "delay Israel/UAR [United Arab Republic] acquisition indefinitely," with similar results for Japan. Africa, save for South Africa, would become a nuclear-free zone.[35]

The most important aspect of option three was its potential to facilitate the emerging détente between the United States and the Soviet Union. Neither the Americans nor the Soviets alone could halt proliferation, but "both ha[d] much to lose" if "lesser powers" acquired nuclear capabilities. The Soviet Union could face "simultaneous encirclement by [a] nuclear-armed China and Germany" and thus had a "vital interest" in reaching a "limited détente that could neutralize one or both threats." At the same time, the United States needed to find "ways to strengthen its deterrence of China and to maintain stable behavior in Western Europe." Both superpowers could benefit "from a lessening of ideological competition and national involvement in Asia, Africa, the Middle East, and perhaps Latin America." These "multiple, overlapping interests" suggested the "timeliness of early steps to achieve an essentially bipolar entente, resembling the Concert of Europe, the informal coalition based on limited mutuality of interests that kept the peace in Europe for more than half of the nineteenth century."[36] This opened up the possibility that a "European settlement and German reunification" could be achieved.[37] Only two years had elapsed since the Cuban missile crisis, yet some policymakers believed that US and Soviet interests were converging around the question of nuclear proliferation, which in turn could lead to greater bilateral cooperation on a variety of other geopolitical issues.

Bureaucratic Battles over Proliferation Policy

The Gilpatric committee quickly discovered that the government's bureaucracies were deeply divided over the direction of US nonproliferation policy. The ACDA, for example, argued that preventing the spread of nuclear weapons was more important than almost any other US foreign policy goal. The State Department, on the other hand, did not want to threaten important US interests, such as relations with West Germany and Japan, to achieve nonproliferation. And while the ACDA thought that a comprehensive nonproliferation policy would be most effective, the State Department wanted to tackle the issue on a country-by-country basis.

To better understand the different positions within the government, the Gilpatric committee organized a series of staff briefings and interviews with high-level political and military officials to solicit their views. At his briefing, the head of the ACDA, William Foster, was the most supportive of the committee's mandate. Foster emphasized the urgency of the nuclear proliferation problem created by China's atomic test and disagreed that proliferation could be slowed after India and Japan developed the bomb, as articulated in option two. He also suggested that the Soviet Union would join the United States in signing and promoting a worldwide "non-dissemination non-acquisition" agreement if it were not for the MLF proposal. Finally, he argued that the United States and the Soviet Union would need to limit their own nuclear programs because "it was unrealistic to expect to control proliferation as long as the great powers continued a nuclear arms race."[38]

Under Secretary of State Ball took a far different approach in his committee briefing. Although "non-committal" on the "prospects of deterring India and Japan from 'going nuclear,'" Ball did not think that a US-Soviet nonproliferation pact would influence their decisions. Instead, he proposed making available a "pool of nuclear weapons which could be drawn upon by India or Japan for use by their dual purpose delivery vehicles." Ball vehemently disagreed with the idea that the MLF proposal should be dropped, and he did not want the Johnson administration to give in to French and Soviet pressure on this issue. The MLF, according to Ball, would not make the US goals of nonproliferation or German reunification more difficult. As he stated at the time, "we cannot make the Germans into second-class citizens. We cannot subject them to a discriminatory state of original sin."[39]

In his appearance before the committee, Secretary of State Rusk also cautioned against changing US nonproliferation policy. Rusk argued that it "was easy for the U.S. to speak out against proliferation, but the Prime Minister of India or Japan must look on the question quite differently." The West German ambassador to the United States had told him that his country would withhold support for US nonproliferation efforts "as a bargaining counter for reunification." When CIA Director Dulles asked Rusk if the United States should make a "big effort, with many kinds of measures" to achieve nonproliferation, Rusk replied, "No." The United States had not been able to prevent France from developing nuclear weapons and had "not struck China to deal with its nuclear program." In addition, India was probably already working "on the first stages of preparations for nuclear weapons," and there was little the United States could do about it. For Rusk, "nonproliferation [was] not the overriding element in U.S. relations with the rest of the world."[40]

Secretary of Defense McNamara was sympathetic to the goals of both the ACDA and the Department of State. Although he offered only lukewarm support for the MLF, McNamara believed that President Johnson could overcome congressional opposition to its creation in the same way President Kennedy won over Congress on the Limited Test Ban Treaty in 1963. McNamara opposed "national" proliferation, but he believed that "starting with Australia and the Philippines" a collective nuclear organization should be created for East Asia. Perhaps most surprising, McNamara also suggested that the development of an "ABM might make sense" if the system were "thinly and broadly deployed" against the rising Chinese threat. His overriding objective, however, was bilateral arms control negotiations with the Soviet Union, a concern beyond the scope of the Gilpatric committee's mandate.[41]

In sum, the briefings exposed deep differences within the US government on the issue of nonproliferation. According to the head of policy planning, Walt Rostow, the State Department still believed that a country's decision to develop nuclear weapons emerged from "a complex politico-military calculus at the highest and most sensitive levels" and that nonproliferation would succeed only if the United States examined "the specific factors which affect that calculus in different capitals and operate directly upon them."[42] The arms control professionals disagreed: "It should be a prime objective of U.S. policy in all cases to prevent the acquisition by other countries of an independent nuclear capability. To make exceptions in special cases would frustrate the entire objective of such a policy." Therefore, if "Japan is to be treated as a special case, it is hard to believe that Germany and Italy would" remain nonnuclear.[43]

Obstacles to a New US Nonproliferation Strategy

The nuclearization of international politics gave rise to a number of puzzles and dilemmas that the Gilpatric committee had to address in its proceedings. The question before the committee went well beyond whether the United States had a right to dictate to other states how they should deal with their security. At the very time that US policymakers had concluded that nuclear weapons were unusable, and therefore had little military or political value, the US government was devoting tremendous energy to preventing other nations from acquiring them. The more effort the United States made to halt proliferation and the more political capital it spent, the more attractive these weapons must have seemed to smaller powers. If a single atomic detonation by China, a country with no conceivable means of delivery and decades away from a secure second-strike force, could provoke grave concern and prompt a shift in policy from the world's most powerful country, it would be very difficult for the United States to be convincing that these weapons had no political utility.

The Gilpatric committee wrestled with the following dilemmas when deliberating its policy recommendations: Should the United States appease or punish potential nuclear states? Should it employ the same nonproliferation standards to all states, or should proliferation be allowed in some cases? Was the United States wise in undertaking new security commitments to dampen proliferation? Should US strategy be transformed to de-emphasize the use of nuclear weapons? Would missile defenses deter or encourage proliferation? And how should the escalating conflict in Vietnam be viewed?

Appeasement vs. Punishment

In deciding on its response to China's atomic test, the Johnson administration considered two options: (1) appeasement, which could include offering the PRC an assortment of economic and political incentives such as UN membership if it stopped its testing; and (2) threats of force. While some in the administration urged a preemptive strike, others wanted to "explore what we need to [do to] bring the Chinese Communists into a nuclear détente" similar to that achieved with the Soviets.[44] In some cases, both options were recommended. One briefing paper insisted that the United States had to either "keep China permanently out of business or induce her to behave responsibly."[45] Another document noted that worldwide nonproliferation would be difficult to achieve unless the United States either could eliminate China's "nuclear-strategic capabilities and keep them eliminated" or succeed "in persuading China to cooperate responsibly in arms control measures." As the document's author noted, however, the choice was hardly satisfactory: "The latter program looks improbable; the former program is burdened with major risks; and the two are mutually inconsistent."[46]

US threats to use force against a state that developed a nuclear weapons program furnished that state with a great incentive to acquire the bomb, if only to protect itself from US pressure. Appeasement, however, was unlikely to work with a state that was determined to develop nuclear weapons. The United States continues to confront this same dilemma as it pursues policies ranging from preventive war to accommodation with countries such as Iran and North Korea.

Blanket vs. Case-by-Case Application

Another challenge the United States had to address was distinguishing among the ambitions and abilities of various potential nuclear powers. Should the United States apply its nonproliferation policy across the board, or should it examine states' nuclear programs on a case-by-case basis? Sweden was a stable, democratic status quo power that wanted atomic weapons purely as a deterrent. Should it be prevented from acquiring such a capability? As for countries in East Asia, Secretary of State Rusk doubted that a blanket nonproliferation policy made sense, given the region's high security needs. Rusk wondered, "Should it always be the U.S. which would have to use nuclear weapons against Red China? He could conceive of situations where the Japanese or Indians might desirably have their own nuclear weapons."[47]

Japan was a particularly complex case. In fall 1964, US intelligence warned the Johnson administration that Japan's incoming prime minister, Sato Eisaku, and foreign minister, Etsusaburo Shiina, were "hot for proliferation."[48] In 1965 the prime minister told President Johnson that "nuclear weapons in Japan just make sense."[49] He "personally felt that if the Chicoms had nuclear weapons, the Japanese should have them" as well.[50] A US assessment of Japan's nuclear capabilities suggested that Japan could "test its first nuclear device as early as 1971" and produce "as many as 100 nuclear-equipped MRBM/IRBMs [medium-range ballistic missiles/intermediate-range ballistic missiles] by 1975." Indeed, Japan's capacity to build nuclear weapons was "a near certainty." Even more worrying, recent indications were "discouraging with respect to [the] Japanese leadership or even support of a nonproliferation agreement."[51]

Similar pressures also existed in India, with some US policymakers having already expressed sympathy with the Indians' efforts to address their security concerns. As early as 1961, State Department official George McGhee suggested "that it would be desirable if a friendly Asian power beat Communist China to the punch" by testing a nuclear device first, and there was "no likelier candidate than India."[52] McGhee noted, however, that if India developed nuclear weapons, it could unleash "a chain reaction of similar decisions by other countries, such as Pakistan, Israel, and the United Arab Republic. In these circumstances, it is unrealistic to hope that Germany and other European nations would not decide their own nuclear weapons [*sic*]."[53]

The Johnson administration therefore understood that granting exceptions to Sweden and India, although understandable, would weaken the effort to prevent West Germany from acquiring atomic weapons. This puzzle applied to whole regions: while many saw the MLF as aiding proliferation in Europe, similar collective multilateral nuclear solutions were seen as a way to prevent proliferation in East Asia.

New US Security Commitments

Another dilemma involved whether to extend new US security commitments to certain states and concern over the effect such offers could have on US nuclear strategy. To convince countries to abandon their nuclear programs, the United States would have to guarantee their protection under its extended nuclear umbrella. But an extended deterrent strategy worked best if the United States maintained both nuclear superiority and a willingness to use atomic weapons, factors that would both accelerate the arms race between the United States and the Soviet Union and undermine global nonproliferation efforts. This dilemma clouded the debate in Washington over the role of nuclear weapons in the defense of Europe. Gilpatric committee consultant Roger Fisher argued that, so "long as the NATO powers behave as though the operation of a nuclear deterrent was the most important problem in the world, other countries will be influenced in a nuclear direction."[54]

The case of India highlighted the extraordinary challenges in linking US security commitments with the pledge not to proliferate. If India were truly threatened, only an explicit US commitment to come to its defense, backed by deployed forces, would convince New Delhi to forswear the acquisition of nuclear weapons. The Johnson administration, however, did not want to assume the risks associated with such a commitment. Llewellyn "Tommy" Thompson, the former US ambassador to the Soviet Union, advised: "It is doubtful that a country which feels really threatened and is capable of building nuclear weapons will indefinitely refrain from doing so merely in exchange for general or conditional guarantees.

I would not like to see 100 million American lives placed in escrow for renewed hostilities in Ladakh, at some distant time when the Chinese might have reestablished an effective military alliance with the Soviet Union."[55]

New security commitments could also threaten existing relationships. Here again, India epitomized the administration's dilemma. William "Bill" Bundy, a senior adviser to President Johnson, cautioned that "any parallel or joint assurances to India involving the US and the USSR would strongly tempt Japan to move towards a nonaligned position" (i.e., away from the United States). Bundy went on to warn that if such a strong security commitment were extended to a country—India—that had not made the painful choice of choosing sides in the Cold War struggle, it might "undercut our relationships with our allies."[56] Similarly, if the United States made commitments to every nonnuclear power, its credibility might be challenged. As McCloy pointed out, "the character of our determination will be diluted if we have 20 such commitments and our fundamental image of capability to defend the free world might be impaired."[57]

Arms Control and No First Use

A growing international demand that the United States reduce its own nuclear arsenal posed yet another dilemma for the Johnson administration. Although the shrinking of US strategic force levels would be a "great power quid pro" in efforts to convince smaller powers to embrace "nuclear denial," administration officials worried that a smaller strategic force would weaken the United States' extended deterrent and "make it easier" for a small country to become a "first-rank nuclear power."[58] To prevent Japan from acquiring nuclear weapons, for example, the administration had to "maintain a clearly superior U.S. nuclear capability in Asia."[59] In Europe, "repeated statements by responsible Americans from the President on down about the catastrophic consequences . . . of a U.S.-Soviet nuclear exchange," combined with a new emphasis on "conventional response[s]," only strengthened "European doubts about the credibility of our willingness to risk our destruction by using nuclear weapons." Some within the administration feared that a US denuclearization of Europe could "create the need for European independent capabilities."[60]

Another dilemma confronting the administration was whether to adopt a no-first-use nuclear strategy. Nonproliferation advocates hoped that the declaration of such a policy would demonstrate to the world the US position that nuclear weapons were unusable and therefore worthless. Moreover, as long as the US government continued to emphasize "nuclear weapons and nuclear superiority" and promised a nuclear response to a Soviet conventional attack, the United States was "teaching the world" that "nuclear weapons are 'superior' to the [nonnuclear] weapons they have," thereby strengthening "national incentives for acquiring nuclear weapons."[61] A no-first-use strategy, however, would weaken US security guarantees in the face of the Soviet Union's conventional force superiority. A background paper on the possibility of Japanese acquisition of nuclear weapons argued that "a manifestly effective U.S. nuclear 'umbrella' will obviate the need for Japan to create a nuclear force on its own. The doubts which may arise over the U.S. deterrent will not involve its strength, but rather our willingness to use it in defense of Japan."[62]

Proliferation and Missile Defense

The Johnson administration considered construction of an ABM system for each of the four options outlined by the Gilpatric committee.[63] Papers prepared by supporters of option one—that is, permissive or selective proliferation—recommended building up a "damage-limiting capability, including ABMs."[64] A similar recommendation was made regarding option two, the so-called prudent option.[65] The option three paper recommended that the administration "continue development of ABM for possible use against limited threats."[66] Defense Secretary McNamara, who would later become a fierce opponent of missile defense, argued that the "ABM might make sense for [the] U.S. if thinly and broadly deployed."[67] At one point, an outside expert even suggested that the United States should work "in concert with the USSR" to "deploy ABM systems which might be effective against minor powers."[68]

Missile defenses, however, could have complex and contradictory effects on nuclear proliferation—a fact rarely noted today. On the one hand, a light ABM system might be useful against weaker states, raising the bar to becoming an effective nuclear state too high for all but the greatest powers to clear. According to this argument, the deployment of an ABM system by the United States would "decrease U.S. vulnerabilities to possible Chinese threats of attack and thereby enhance the credibility of our [U.S.] commitments to Japan and other friendly nations."[69] An ABM system would be an "alternative to expensive" security "guarantees to discourage Nth country" proliferation.[70] It could also enhance a strategy of nuclear superiority and the credibility of US extended deterrence guarantees to nonnuclear powers.

Those who argued against US deployment of an ABM system cautioned that it could encourage proliferation by protecting the United States while leaving vulnerable unprotected nonnuclear powers. A West German government official, for example, told a US delegation that "the establishing of ABM systems in the Soviet Union and the United States, [would leave] Europe 'naked in the cold', [and] constitutes a reason for [membership] withdrawal" from a nonproliferation treaty.[71] Soviet ambassador to the United States Anatoly Dobrynin argued that it would be impossible to convince states "to sign a nonproliferation agreement if they saw the U.S. and USSR entering another major round of [the] arms race [implying the development of ABM systems on both sides]."[72] Furthermore, the message that nuclear weapons were "useless" would be undermined if the United States responded to proliferation by "minor powers" by deploying a technologically sophisticated multibillion dollar defense system. In the view of some Johnson administration officials, if the United States built an ABM system because of the nuclear threat posed by China, other nations would wonder why "we [would] consider undertaking a massive expansion of our strategic defensive forces in the face of a relatively weak Chinese threat when we have not chosen to do so against our much stronger Soviet opponent."[73] Deploying an ABM system against the Chinese would greatly magnify the image of China's military power, possibly inducing India and Japan to seek heavily subsidized ABM systems of their own.[74]

Finally, the ABM issue could expose contradictions between two initiatives with the same ostensible goal: achieving both a nonproliferation treaty and a comprehensive test ban treaty. One of the arguments against a complete test ban treaty was that it could "inhibit the development of ABMs and other devices which could afford a successful defense against second-class nuclear capabilities."[75]

The Credibility Conundrum in Practice—Proliferation and Vietnam

The dilemmas associated with nuclear proliferation influenced US military strategy throughout the world, most obviously in Europe. But a linkage also existed between a more active nonproliferation policy and the US military presence in Southeast Asia. The Gilpatric committee discussions took place when the Johnson administration was debating whether to escalate US military involvement in Vietnam. China's atomic test was bound to influence these discussions. President Kennedy had considered a nuclear-armed China a grave threat that would "so upset the world political scene [that] it would be intolerable."[76] Convinced that China was "bound to get nuclear weapons, in time, and from that moment on they will dominate South East Asia," Kennedy feared that even a minimal Chinese nuclear force could prevent US military intervention. As Kennedy had once noted, just a few missiles in Cuba had "had a deterrent effect on us."[77]

President Kennedy's analysis implied that once China acquired a nuclear capability, the United States would likely withdraw from Vietnam. In fact, the Gilpatric committee's option one policy envisioned a US withdrawal once India and Japan developed nuclear weapons (with US help). But government officials, as well as members of the committee, wanted to make clear that the United States would not break its commitments in the face of a nuclear threat. If the United States acquiesced to a nuclear-armed adversary, the incentives for small powers to develop nuclear weapons would increase exponentially. Vietnam would be the test case of this new commitment. In a paper for the Gilpatric committee, the deputy assistant secretary of defense for international security affairs Henry Rowen wrote, "A U.S. defeat in Southeast Asia may come to be attributed in part to the unwillingness of the U.S. to take on North Vietnam supported by a China that now has the bomb. Such a defeat is now much more significant to countries near China than it was before October 16."[78]

In a memorandum dated November 4, 1964, policy planning chief Walt Rostow laid out the argument in greater detail. As he saw it, dealing successfully with nuclear proliferation "hinge[d] greatly on the outcome of the crises in Southeast Asia and in the Atlantic Community." If the administration could make "U.S. military power sufficiently relevant to the situation in South-east Asia," the "impulse in India and Japan to go forward will be substantially diminished or postponed." If there was a stalemate or a setback in Southeast Asia, the impulse in India and Japan to move toward some national form of deterrence would be enhanced.[79] Two weeks later, Rostow again made the connection to the Gilpatric committee: "Can we enhance [India's and Japan's] sense of confidence in the relevance of U.S. military power as an effective check on Chinese Communist expansion?"[80]

The commitment to maintain US security agreements with countries facing a nuclear threat was also included in the first official presidential statement issued after the Chinese detonation. In the statement, President Johnson declared: "The United States reaffirms its defense commitments in Asia. Even if Communist China should eventually develop an effective nuclear capability, that capability would have no effect on the readiness of the United States to respond to requests from Asian nations for help in dealing with Communist Chinese aggression. The United States will also not be diverted from its efforts to help the nations of Asia to defend themselves and to advance the welfare of their people."[81]

This logic demonstrated perhaps the biggest dilemma of making security policy in the nuclear age: the United States needed to fight a conventional war in an area of little strategic interest (Vietnam), during a period of détente and cooperation with its main adversary (the Soviet Union), to convince an ally (Japan) and a neutral state (India) not to develop nuclear weapons, because if they did, the pressures on West Germany would mount, tensions with the Soviets would escalate, and détente would be undermined.

Some analysts even hoped that a new US nonproliferation policy might deter China from intervening in Vietnam. Discussing a proposal to ban the use of atomic weapons against nonnuclear states, analysts argued that a nonproliferation agreement could "underscore the exposed position" of China. According to this view, "by becoming a nuclear power it [China] has destroyed—or at least substantially reduced—the political inhibitions which have existed against using nuclear weapons against it."[82] In an obvious case of wishful thinking, the proposal's authors asserted that a ban on the use of nuclear weapons against nonnuclear states could "increase the reluctance of 'national liberation forces' in various countries of Asia to see Communist Chinese forces involved with them since [this] would mean exposure to the American nuclear arsenal."[83] More astute analysts such as Thomas Hughes, the director of intelligence and research at the Department of State, recognized, however, that the United States would be deterred from using nuclear weapons against China regardless of the latter's atomic capabilities. In the end, Mao's view that "the U.S. is actually deterred from the use of nuclear weapons by world opinion and possible Soviet retaliation" proved correct.[84]

"Concessions from the Wrong Side and to the Wrong Address"

The greatest challenge to a proposed shift in US nonproliferation strategy was that it would require the help of an enemy, the Soviet Union, to hinder allies such as France, Japan, and particularly West Germany in their efforts to build nuclear capabilities. A worldwide nonproliferation effort signaled an easing of Cold War tensions and emerging cooperation between the superpowers. Japan, and especially West Germany, had to be concerned that their basic national interests, to say nothing of any nuclear ambitions, would be sacrificed on the altar of bipolar détente. Because of their unresolved geopolitical conflicts with the Soviet Union, a US effort to achieve a nonproliferation agreement with the Soviets might unleash powerful incentives for both countries to acquire nuclear weapons.

One of the most outspoken critics of this proposed shift was John McCloy. It was "fantastic," McCloy argued, to think that the problem "of European security is solvable by the 'other side.'" Sacrificing West German interests to win Soviet approval, McCloy asserted, risked "losing both the Alliance and nonproliferation." It was this type of thinking, he averred, that "opened the door to German insecurity in the 1920s."[85] In a stinging letter of rebuke addressed to Chairman Gilpatric, McCloy disputed the notion that "a world in which there was a proliferation of nuclear weapons" was a disaster, particularly considering the "price we [i.e., the United States] might be willing to pay" to achieve it. McCloy argued that sacrificing the MLF to appease the Soviet Union would incur risks that were "at least equal, if they do not exceed" the risks of proliferation. Taking the attitude that "we owe nothing to the Germans and 'to hell with them anyway," he warned, threatened a return to the dangerous instability of the interwar period. McCloy reminded Gilpatric, "Germany has been allied with Russia before and if Germany cannot find a solid berth as a member of a Western partnership, she might try again."[86]

This struggle emerged from an even larger issue: whether the most fundamental question of the Cold War—the political and military status of Germany—had become less worrisome than the potential consequences of widespread nuclear proliferation. McCloy's position was clear: "We can talk and speculate about the effects of India having the bomb, or Israel, the U.A.R., or Pakistan, but these effects are less ominous compared with those which would flow from further acquisition of nuclear power in Europe." National nuclear deterrents in Europe were "more dangerous than proliferation in Asia, considering the past history of Europe."[87] Supporters of the MLF within the Johnson administration agreed. Under Secretary of State Ball told the British defense minister and foreign secretary, "We should avoid making concessions in European policy in an effort to accomplish solutions to Asian problems, only to find these solutions ineffective."[88]

As the Gilpatric committee's recommendations moved closer to becoming US policy, McCloy warned of the consequences. Writing to Rhode Island senator John Pastore, an ardent supporter of a nonproliferation treaty, McCloy asked, "Why should we make any concessions in respect of our security or that of our allies for a nonproliferation agreement (of doubtful efficacy at best) when we know the Soviets are no more disposed to proliferate their nuclear weapons or 'know how,' particularly after their Chinese experience, than we are or indeed anyone else is who has the weapon?"[89] After watching a television debate between Robert Kennedy, senator from New York, and West European officials, McCloy wrote, "Proliferation will certainly increase the chances of a nuclear disaster, but I think it is an oversimplification to associate all evil with proliferation and all good with nonproliferation."[90] Kennedy, who had seized on the nonproliferation issue in the Senate, responded that although there were risks in placating the Soviet Union's "morbid fear of nuclear weapons being shared with Germany in any way," a nonproliferation treaty was necessary to encourage "nations like India, Israel, Sweden and others to abstain from developing nuclear weapons themselves."[91]

McCloy's stature led nonproliferation skeptics both inside and outside the administration to seek him out. State Department official and MLF advocate Henry Owen wrote to McCloy that he was "struck by the amount of absolute nonsense which is being written" about nonproliferation.

Owen suggested that McCloy write an article for the journal *Foreign Affairs* laying out the dangers of a dramatic shift in US nuclear policy. Owen cautioned, "If we lose the public opinion battle on this issue, much of what we have been trying to accomplish in Europe over the past twenty years will be in grave jeopardy."[92] Robert Bowie, father of the original MLF concept and a government consultant and director of Harvard University's Center for International Affairs, offered to help McCloy in this effort. Bowie recommended a "case by case" approach to nonproliferation and argued that a treaty could unintentionally "accelerate" the efforts of have-not states such as Germany, India, Israel, Japan, and Sweden to acquire atomic weapons capability. Moreover, West Germany could expect a "British-French-U.S.-USSR" effort "designed to keep her in second place," which was "not a formula for a stable peace."[93] As Bowie's alarm continued to grow, he wrote to McCloy to say that because of the Johnson administration's nonproliferation efforts, Atlantic relations were the worst they had been since 1950. Sacrificing the long-term health of the alliance, Bowie asserted, would lead to "disaster—not in some dramatic defeat, but in the gradual, inevitable erosion of the Western position."[94]

McCloy's fears were not groundless. A number of German officials, for example, had already expressed long-standing concern about US attitudes toward nonproliferation. An FRG embassy official had told an ACDA representative in early 1964 that it was "completely unrealistic" to expect that "countries will forego the power that accompanies nuclear weapons." The Americans "had touched a very sensitive nerve in the German body politic" and should expect no progress on the "non-acquisition question" until "the MLF is achieved."[95] Twenty months later the West German ambassador to the United States told a high-ranking official from the State Department that the "FRG would not consider participating in [the] NPT unless [the] nuclear problems of [the] alliance have found satisfactory solution." The "defense of Europe" had to take "priority over accommodation of [the] USSR." He went on to say that the Soviets must make concessions in the "political or security field" first.[96] During a heated conversation with White House consultant Henry Kissinger, West German chancellor Ludwig Erhard stated that although he did not want his country to have nuclear weapons, he did not want to "stand before history as the man who rejected a nuclear option for Germany when it was in effect offered to him." When Kissinger asked the chancellor what nuclear option he was referring to, he replied, "ownership schemes . . . [that] protected Germany in case Israel, India or other small countries acquired nuclear weapons." A stunned Kissinger could not get Erhard to elaborate.[97]

The West German government tried to keep its options open in the face of mounting US pressure. Sacrificing the MLF to the Soviets would not convince "the bloc-free nations that primarily matter for the NPT—India, Israel, Sweden"—that their security would be improved. As one West German official put it, "these would be concessions from the wrong side and to the wrong address."[98] The domestic political stakes for the FRG were high: in the words of one US observer, "if Erhard were to return from America with a signed nonproliferation treaty, 'civil war' would break out within the CDU/CSU [Christian Democratic Union/Christian Social Union Parties]." The normally moderate leader of West Germany's Social Democratic Party, Fritz Erler, stated that a nonproliferation treaty that excluded his country from power sharing would "force all parties to review their attitude toward the Atlantic Alliance."[99] Erhard's successor, Georg Kiesinger, told President de Gaulle in April 1967 that as the nonproliferation treaty was currently written, the FRG would "not sign it." France and Germany had to "take an independent position towards both America and the Soviet Union" to blunt the superpowers' efforts to make arrangements over their heads.[100] Kiesinger told Vice President Humphrey that the nonproliferation treaty was "the most difficult problem that has emerged in a long time" between the United States and Germany, and emphasized "what a serious matter it is for the Federal Republic."[101]

Yet on realizing that nonproliferation held the "utmost importance" for President Johnson, West German officials had little choice but to accept the United States' new, stronger nonproliferation stance: "Everything else is secondary. . . . Nonproliferation concerns the President highly personally."[102] Nor would the West Germans receive any tangible benefits for acceding to the new policy. Secretary of State Rusk was blunt in his conversations with FRG leaders, stating, "I would be unable to support you if you made the question of reunification a condition for progress toward a general nonproliferation arrangement."[103]

The Gilpatric Report and the Shift in US Proliferation Policy

On January 21, 1965, the Gilpatric committee issued its report. The committee recommended that the US government develop stronger nonproliferation policies because "the spread of nuclear weapons poses an increasingly grave threat to the security of the United States." If not stopped or slowed, proliferation would undermine US political and military influence and encourage "a retreat to isolation to avoid the risk of involvement in nuclear war." The committee stated that a case-by-case approach to the proliferation problem was no longer effective because China's atomic test meant that the "world is fast approaching a point of no return in the prospects of controlling the spread of nuclear weapons."

Thus, when US nonproliferation goals clashed with other policy interests, nonproliferation should take precedence. The US government, the committee wrote, must give "nonproliferation policies far greater weight and support than they have received in the past."[104]

The committee's report included a number of controversial proposals. For example, it recommended a full-blown US effort to negotiate a nuclear nonproliferation agreement, a comprehensive test ban treaty, and regional nuclear-free zones. France should be isolated in the nuclear realm, and the United Kingdom should be encouraged to give up its independent deterrent. NATO strategy should begin to de-emphasize the organization's nuclear options. The entirety of US policy toward China should be reexamined in light of its nuclearization (no specifics were offered), and cooperation with the Soviets should be pursued. On the most controversial issue—the fate of the MLF and the German question—the report acknowledged widespread disagreement within both the government and the committee. The committee did agree that the United States should "continue urgent exploration of possible alternatives to an MLF/ANF [Atlantic nuclear force] which would permanently inhibit Germany from acquiring nuclear weapons, but would nevertheless assure that, in the absence of German reunification, West Germany would remain as a real ally on the Western side."[105]

The Gilpatric committee's conclusions elicited strong reactions. Secretary of State Rusk, for example, argued that the report was as "explosive as a nuclear weapon" and worked to keep it secret.[106] An apparent leak of the report's contents to Johnson's political rival, Robert Kennedy, threatened to undermine its credibility with the president. Kennedy, who in his first Senate speech called the "spread of nuclear weapons" the "most vital issue now facing the nation and the world," demanded that the Johnson administration assign "central priority" to crafting a nonproliferation treaty. He declared, "We cannot allow the demands of day-to-day policy to obstruct our efforts to solve the problem of nuclear spread."[107] President Johnson responded angrily in conversation with McGeorge Bundy, "I need, I think, to have a position which would probably be a harder one than they would recommend and we will let the peace lovers get on board with Bobby and we will just not buy the thing. Let Gilpatric go his way. Now Gilpatric has been up to this, it is an old stunt for him to leak stuff. I told you when we put him on that Committee. It was against my better judgment, I did not want to do it but damn it, I just did not have the steel in my spine."[108]

The idea, however, that, as AEC chairman Seaborg claimed, "the standing of the report with the president" was not "helped by the thought that Gilpatric himself was thought to have assisted Kennedy in preparation of his June 23 speech" misses the larger picture.[109] Thomas Schwartz convincingly argues that, as evidenced by a national security action memorandum dated June 28, 1965, President Johnson himself had accepted the thrust of the Gilpatric report's recommendations.[110] In it, Johnson instructed his administration to develop a program to halt the "further spread of nuclear weapons." Most tellingly, he put the ACDA (the department most in favor of Gilpatric's recommendations) and not the State Department (home to the nonproliferation skeptics) in charge of producing the new policy.[111]

The report led to a far more active US nonproliferation policy. On the question of whether the MLF should be traded for a nonproliferation treaty, the administration's judgments proved decisive. And, although the bureaucratic disputes over the price the United States should pay to achieve nonproliferation continued, by 1966 the administration had begun to make an NPT treaty—and arms control in general—a US foreign policy priority. The shift in US nonproliferation policy was not inevitable, and the Johnson administration made the change at great risk and some political cost. Despite the conventional wisdom, the Kennedy administration's policy was, at best, similar to the Gilpatric committee's option two (i.e., the "prudent course"). President Kennedy had offered to help the French with their nuclear program at least three times,[112] displayed occasional ambivalence and confusion toward Israel's nuclear program,[113] and considered helping India with its nuclear program.[114]

The Nixon administration was, if anything, even less committed to nuclear nonproliferation than the Kennedy administration had been. A briefing paper for President Nixon pointed out that "some have argued" that there were cases where an "independent nuclear weapons capability might be desirable," if only to "spread the responsibility for defense or enable the U.S. to reduce involvement in their defense." If it were decided that "the NPT was not in the U.S. interest," a formal disengagement would "have considerable support in the FRG and in some circles in Italy, Japan, India, Brazil, and Israel."[115] An NSC memo argued that the "problems with the FRG are understated."[116] The U.S embassy in Japan cabled Washington seeking clarification of the following quotation by Henry Kissinger, which had appeared in a recent magazine article: "The nuclear nonproliferation treaty may have had the opposite effect: it may have encouraged nuclear proliferation."[117] Nixon himself argued that "treaties don't necessarily get us very much" and that if countries wanted to "make their own weapons" they could "abrogate the treaty without sanction."[118] In the end, while the United States would continue to support the NPT, Nixon made clear that he would "not pressure other nations to follow suit, especially the Federal Republic of Germany."[119]

So why were the Gilpatric committee and President Johnson willing to take great risks on what McCloy and other key architects of the United

States' containment strategy believed was the most important question of the Cold War, the political and military status of Germany? The most important reason was their recognition that the United States had entered a new era. The great power competition that in October 1962 had brought the United States and the Soviet Union to the brink of nuclear war had eased considerably. Even critics of the new policy—such as former ambassador to the Soviet Union Thompson, who did not think the Soviets were serious about nonproliferation and did not want to run risks with Germany finding out—acknowledged that the United States was now living in a far different world in terms of security.[120] While criticizing the Gilpatric committee, Thompson also argued that the idea of a Soviet attack in Central Europe was a scenario "so remote that it is scarcely worth considering."[121] Given this assessment, it is no surprise that more farsighted analysts would seek to update the United States' strategic priorities.

Détente and great power stability in Central Europe would wax and wane over the next few decades, but it was clear that the proliferation of weapons of mass destruction had become a permanent fixture in world politics. Proliferation and the transition from a bipolar to a more multilateral world that accompanied it—what US ambassador to the United Nations Adlai Stevenson called the "revival of global polycentrism"—meant that US "policies which were triumphs in 1950 have become barely adequate by the mid-60's and are likely to be obsolete and in some cases counterproductive before 1970." While the actions of countries such Iran, Iraq, Libya, North Korea, and Pakistan were hardly on the minds of most policymakers in the mid-1960s, Stevenson accurately predicted that proliferation, combined with "instability and radicalism in the underdeveloped world," would become more pressing over time. This new world demanded new policies. The sensitivities of "the Germans," Stevenson argued, "should not be permitted through their excessive nervousness to veto any forward movement in their area to the detriment of the worldwide security of the west."[122]

Policymakers and analysts often gloss over past tensions in the belief that today's problems are unique. When they do look to the past, they "ordinarily use history badly."[123] We should not dismiss the relevance of the 1960s to current US concerns about nuclear proliferation, including the potential nuclear arming of Germany and Japan. In 1999 German chancellor Gerhard Schröder described his country as "a great power in Europe" that would pursue its national interests, warning that NATO's traditional mission as protector "against Germany" no longer had value.[124] In Japan, "talk of acquiring nuclear weapons" is no longer taboo.[125]

Equally important are the lessons from the Johnson administration regarding "rogue" states and nuclear proliferation. Addressing the issue of real or potential proliferation among unsavory states such as Iran, North Korea, and Pakistan is no small challenge. Yet it is no more frightening than what the Johnson administration faced when it contemplated the consequences of a nuclear-armed China under Mao Zedong. Much can be learned from this history.

Scholars and policymakers must begin to think differently about the periodization of nuclear history. Too much has been made of the sharp divide between the Cold War, post–Cold War, and post–September 11 international environments and their influence on nuclear politics. While critics often argue that the world today is far more dangerous, the majority of nuclear powers developed their weapons before the Cold War ended, while several others have disbanded their programs since 1989. Nor are the fundamental motivations for proliferation, such as the need for security and the desire for prestige, vastly different from what they were in the decades following World War II. Nor is there evidence that current "rogue" states would be any less rational or deterrable than authoritarian nuclear states such as Mao's China or the Soviet Union.

Furthermore, the Cold War period was not static. By 1964 the United States and the Soviet Union had become status quo powers whose political conflicts were unlikely to lead to nuclear war. China, on the other hand, had become an aggressive foe whose behavior worried both superpowers. At the same time, pressure on West Germany and Japan to develop nuclear weapons left countries in both the Eastern and Western blocs deeply unsettled. Many new and potential nuclear powers no longer saw the Cold War as their most important concern and believed that nuclear weapons could guarantee their security in an uncertain world. This nascent multipolar world was more similar to today's international environment than has been suggested in contemporary policy and strategy assessments.

The history of the 1960s reveals important lessons for those seeking to craft an effective, long-term nuclear nonproliferation policy. In the early 1960s, many US policymakers believed that nuclear proliferation was inevitable and that the United States could gain political currency by managing, and in some cases aiding, the efforts of would-be proliferators. In its efforts to retard proliferation, the Johnson administration faced difficult choices with potentially contradictory outcomes. Achieving nonproliferation required the United States to cooperate with an enemy—the Soviet Union—to hinder friends. Preemption carried grave risks, but so did appeasement. Arms control might be welcomed by nonaligned states, but it could weaken extended deterrence and lower the bar for new nuclear powers. A no-first-use strategy could delegitimize nuclear weapons but undermine the United States' commitments to nonnuclear powers. Additional military commitments could pull the United States into dangerous regional conflicts that had little connection to its national interests. Missile defense could deter nuclear aspirants or fuel further atomic spread. It does not appear that post–Cold War administrations have grappled with these complex issues with the same rigor as the Johnson administration did.

A final lesson of this chapter is to reveal how an effective policymaking process can lead to better policy decisions. Through its thoughtful and intensive deliberations, the Gilpatric committee initiated a reconceptualization of the nuclear proliferation question; it analyzed the painful trade-offs that were necessary to implement a more active nonproliferation policy. Before focusing on specific questions and problems, the committee laid out four broad proliferation scenarios and identified the assumptions behind each before calculating how its adoption would affect US interests. Aware of the bureaucratic politics involved, the committee took great care to seriously consider the interests of various government stakeholders.

President Johnson took substantial risks when he ordered the implementation of the Gilpatric committee's recommendations. By abandoning the MLF proposal and cooperating with the Soviets at the expense of West Germany, he overruled the "proliferation pessimists" in the State Department and "wise men" such as John McCloy and Dean Acheson, who did not believe that nuclear proliferation was either bad or inevitable. Overcoming political obstacles, the Johnson administration succeeded in negotiating the Nuclear Nonproliferation Treaty, which established an increasingly powerful international consensus against proliferation. This norm, which had been weak in the mid-1960s, acted as a powerful constraint against would-be proliferators. Johnson's policies paved the way for countries such as Germany and Japan to achieve a certain "virtuous" status by not joining the nuclear club, a status that brought domestic pride and a measure of international standing.

This process led to the adoption of thoughtful, less reactive policies that were in the long-term interests of the United States. Consider US policy toward China, the ultimate "rogue" state. Before the Gilpatric committee's deliberations, US policymakers had contemplated an attack, either alone or with the Russians, against China's nuclear facilities. Mao's regime did not appear "rational" or deterrable, and some analysts argued that a preventive strike would deter other states from developing nuclear weapons. After thoughtful consideration, the Gilpatric committee and the Johnson administration wisely rejected preemption, both for China and in general. China has not, as was once feared, used its nuclear weapons. Nor has it been reckless or undeterrable. By 1969 China and the United States had begun a dialogue that flourished into a tacit anti-Soviet alliance by 1972, a mere eight years after the PRC acquired a nuclear capability. This relationship played an important role in ending the Cold War on terms favorable to the United States.

In some ways, the Kennedy and Johnson administrations' early analysis of China mirrored the Bush administration's public portrayal of Iraq in the lead-up to the war. Insofar as Iraq was surrounded by potential nuclear adversaries (Iran and Israel) and threatened with regime change by the most powerful country in the world, Saddam Hussein's desire to develop nuclear weapons may have been understandable. Indeed, since the US war against Iraq, North Korea and Iran have increased the pace of their nuclear weapons programs. Additionally, Iran has exploited the current regional power vacuum to increase its standing in the region. A more thoughtful policy process, similar to the Gilpatric committee's efforts, might have produced policies that better served long-term US interests.

[5]

Nuclear Nixon

In the nuclear field, the Nixon presidency has long been known for, above all else, the landmark Antiballistic Missile Treaty and the Strategic Arms Limitation Treaty, both negotiated with the Soviet Union and signed in 1972. Arms control advocates hailed these treaties as the cornerstone of strategic stability that formally recognized that nuclear weapons offered no military and scant political utility in a world of superpower parity and mutually assured destruction. For those analysts who saw the nuclear arms race as one of the leading causes of tension during the Cold War, Nixon's arms control policies removed the major irritant in US-Soviet relations, recognized the equality of the superpowers, and ushered in a period of cooperative relations often referred to as détente.

This focus on ABM and SALT, however, has obscured other key arms control events during the Nixon administration, including a treaty to ban biological weapons and the beginning of negotiations with the USSR aimed at mutual reduction of conventional forces. In addition, the administration signed a treaty with the Soviets aimed at preventing nuclear war, and its officials were among the first to recognize the dangers of nuclear terrorism. Two other key policies in the nuclear realm proved even more important: the 1968 ratification of the Nuclear Nonproliferation Treaty and a transformation of US nuclear strategy. Taken as a whole, these Nixon era policies were impressive. When viewed through the widely shared perspective that saw arms control as the best (and only) option to curtail the instabilities and dangers of the nuclear arms race, Nixon's presidency was, despite other failings, a great success.

This view, however, suffers from a fatal flaw: Nixon and his powerful foreign policy adviser, Henry Kissinger, did not accept the worldview of the arms control community, nor did they share the enthusiasm of the previous two administrations for limiting the vertical and horizontal spread of nuclear weapons. Neither saw the nuclear arms race as the cause or key factor in the Cold War with the Soviet Union. For Nixon and Kissinger, geopolitical competition, and not the arms race, remained the core driver of international politics, much as it had been viewed in the time of Metternich and Bismarck. They believed that treaties would be violated if it were in a state's interest to do so. Despite some overheated rhetoric, Nixon and Kissinger had a coherent, if controversial, set of theories about the nuclear age. They did not, as has often been portrayed, simply rely on the "madman" theory or desire to subsume all policy to political expedience. Their framework was based on years of experience participating in and observing US national security policy, and it provided a credible, if at times harrowing, alternative to the more conventional views of those in the arms control community.

What was the substance of their philosophy? Neither accepted many of the core ideas surrounding the so-called nuclear revolution. In the first place, neither Nixon nor Kissinger thought that nuclear weapons transformed the way people think and the way nations behave. While these fearsome weapons were extraordinarily important, they did not fundamentally alter more powerful political forces. Second, nuclear weapons had value far beyond simply deterrence, offering military and political utility, even in an age of superpower parity. Nixon and Kissinger believed strategic nuclear superiority mattered and that it should be regained if at all possible. If it was not possible to reclaim numerical advantage, other tactics, including flexible nuclear options and strategies based on what Thomas Schelling had called "manipulation of risk" and threats that left something to chance, could be employed to gain advantage. Third, given their political and military utility, they believed that other nations would want these powerful weapons. Neither Nixon nor Kissinger thought halting nuclear proliferation merited sacrificing other geopolitical goals. That more states would obtain nuclear weapons was not only inevitable but also potentially desirable. In sum, this was a strategy built on the puzzles and ironies of making policy in the nuclear age. "And we've got to play it recklessly. That's the safest course."[1]

Why did Nixon and Kissinger pursue arms control arrangements that appeared to contradict their core beliefs about the world? Nixon and Kissinger had ambitious geopolitical goals at a time of declining US power, shrinking military budgets, and decreased domestic support for US engagement in the world. US prospects in the global order were dim: the administration inherited a disastrous war in Southeast Asia and pressure for retrenchment in East Asia; conflict and Soviet encroachment in the Middle East; and malaise and drift among America's closest

European allies. These issues shaped the Nixon administration's views on nuclear questions. In order to reverse these trends, arms control was considered to be a useful tool but not an end in itself. At the same time, Nixon and Kissinger believed that—in the absence of strategic superiority—nuclear threats, and the strategies that gave them credibility, could be deployed to advance US interests. And, in a dangerous world, neither Nixon nor Kissinger saw much to gain by spending valuable political capital trying to prevent states that were not superpowers from acquiring their own nuclear weapons.

Before exploring Nixon and Kissinger's nuclear philosophy, it is important to lay out how most other analysts, policymakers, and arms control participants viewed the influence of nuclear weapons on international politics and the importance of arms control. As remarkable as the ABM and SALT treaties were, many believed their negotiation was not only necessary but also practically inevitable. Since the beginning of the atomic age, strategists puzzled over the influence of these fearsome weapons on international politics. Nuclear weapons presented an obvious dilemma—their terrifying power, if used, could kill tens of millions and destroy civilized life. It was this very feature, however, that strategists believed could prevent a third world war. If two adversaries both possessed these weapons, they might think twice before initiating hostilities. This idea—that nuclear weapons could make war between great powers less likely—was at the heart of the concepts of deterrence and the nuclear revolution.[2]

As strategists puzzled over the dynamics of nuclear weapons, they soon recognized that mere possession of a handful of atomic bombs might not be enough to achieve deterrence, which required two additional characteristics. First, a state had to be able to deliver their weapons against its adversaries. In many ways, developing the technology to deliver nuclear weapons became as important as developing the weapons themselves. As a result, the Soviet Union and the United States spent billions on long-range bombers, land-based intercontinental ballistic missiles, and submarine-launched weapons. Second, a state's nuclear force had to be robust enough, or invulnerable enough, to withstand a surprise attack, with enough weapons left over to threaten the attacker with unacceptable damage. For nuclear deterrence to be effective there had to be strategic stability; in other words, both the Soviet Union and the United States had to possess secure "second-strike" forces. If one side's nuclear forces were in any way vulnerable, if they could be wiped out by a surprise attack, the balance would be unstable and dangerous. The policy goal of both superpowers, according to strategists and arms control advocates, should be to construct nuclear forces and strategies that accepted mutual vulnerability and did not seek a first-strike advantage.

Would the United States and the Soviet Union accept the logic of nuclear deterrence and the profound effect it would have on world politics? Looking to the past, strategists noted the natural tendency of rival states to accumulate more and more weapons, ostensibly for defensive purposes. They believed this often unleashed a dangerous competition for arms between rival states that could spiral out of control and lead to war. Plans for disarmament were naive and overlooked the deterrent benefits a stable nuclear order might bring. According to this view, these dangerous arms races could only be stopped by mutually agreed on restraints, in other words, arms control. The arms controllers and strategists found a policy champion in Robert McNamara, the secretary of defense from 1961 until 1968. He eschewed the search for nuclear superiority and embraced the idea of "mutual assured destruction," or MAD. He belittled defensive forces, arguing that cheaper offensive forces could easily overwhelm proposed antiballistic missile systems. And he became a forceful advocate of negotiating treaties with the Soviet Union to stem an arms race in both defensive and offensive nuclear weapons.

These views dominated the policy landscape that Nixon and Kissinger inhabited, and it has long been assumed that they reluctantly accepted them as reality. One of the key arms control officials of the period has argued that "Nixon surprised both critics and supporters by vigorously pursuing Johnson's initiatives on capping strategic nuclear arms and nuclear proliferation."[3] Another scholar claims that "these [SALT and ABM treaties] were given enormous importance in American thinking and were the legacy of Richard Nixon and Henry Kissinger."[4] These arms control treaties have been accorded enormous historical importance, even by analysts inclined to dislike both Nixon and Kissinger. Even a critic like McGeorge Bundy applauded the Nixon administration for "arms control arrangements . . . [that] were by far the largest achieved in the nuclear age" and that laid the foundation for a "bilateral rhetoric of détente that had worldwide appeal."[5] Sidney Drell, a prominent scientist and arms control advocate, summed up the conventional wisdom when he declared that he considered the ABM treaty negotiated by the Nixon administration "to be our most important arms control achievement to date."[6] Nixon biographer Joan Hoff contends that "in the areas of arms control, Nixinger détente policy contained the potential not only to substitute for containment" but to transcend the "procrustean ideological constraints" that animated the Cold War.[7] Judging from their memoirs written after they had left office, the president and his national security advisor appeared to share these views. Nixon stated: "The ABM treaty stopped what inevitably would have become a defensive arms race, with untold billions of dollars being spent on each side." The treaty made "permanent the concept of deterrence through 'mutual terror.'"[8]

Kissinger claimed: "The fundamental achievement was to sketch the outline on which coexistence between the democracies and the Soviet system must be based. SALT embodied our conviction that a wildly spiraling nuclear arms race was in no country's interest and enhanced no one's security."[9]

The documents, however, reveal that Kissinger and, especially, Nixon had a different notion of how nuclear weapons affected international relations. Nixon and Kissinger did not share the view of the arms controllers or liberal internationalists, who put their faith in global organizations, international law, and treaties. Theirs was a realist view—they believed that world politics was driven, as it had been for centuries, by geopolitical competition between great powers. The "nuclear revolution" had not changed this core feature of the international system. In relations with the Soviets, the message to their opponents was clear: "Look we'll divide up the world, but by God you're going to respect our side or we won't respect your side."[10]

Their belief in the supremacy of geopolitics influenced Nixon and Kissinger's skepticism of arms control. There was to be no rush to negotiations with the Soviet Union, and, in fact, the SALT discussions were shelved during the first months of the administration. For the president and his national security adviser, the subject of armaments could not be separated from the question of their political use. Arms races did not lead to war. According to Kissinger, "Our reading of history indicates that all crises have been caused by political conditions, not by the arms race as such."[11] In his first official meeting with Soviet ambassador to the United States Anatoly Dobrynin, Nixon cautioned that "there is no guarantee that freezing strategic weapons" would bring about peace. He added: "History makes it clear that wars result from political differences and problems."[12] Just as in the age of Metternich and Bismarck, hard-nosed personal diplomacy mattered far more than treaties or idealism. In Nixon's words: "Finally, it comes down to the men involved. It is the will of the men rather than the treaties. We have had treaties such as the Hitler-Stalin pact—but all wars have started with broken treaties, World War I and World War II. I approach Soviet-American relations in a totally pragmatic fashion."[13]

Nixon and Kissinger actually feared that arms control, in certain circumstances, could be a bad thing. During a briefing for the president, Kissinger stated that the prevailing view among US policymakers and intellectuals was that the Soviet Union and the United States shared a common interest in survival and the prevention of war. This led to the belief that "every effort should be made to engage the Soviets in negotiations wherever common interests occur and especially arms control."

Even if unsuccessful, these analysts believed arms control talks could "serve as a firebreak to prevent confrontations from getting out of hand." Kissinger disagreed with this view. "Arms per se rarely cause wars," he said, and narrowly focusing on these issues risked "the danger that the Soviets will use the bait of progress in one area in order to neutralize our resistance to pressure elsewhere."[14] Nixon cautioned his secretary of state, William Rogers, that arms control was not simply a matter of "purely technical and military matters" and that he needed to be wary that the Soviets did not use "talks on arms as a safety valve on intransigence elsewhere." The president reminded Rogers that "the invasion of Czechoslovakia was preceded by the exploration of a summit conference."[15]

Nixon and Kissinger were always suspicious the Soviets were trying to dupe them into an arms control agreement that would tie down the United States while Russia made aggressive moves elsewhere. Right before the Moscow summit, Kissinger told the president he believed the Soviets "were determined to hit China next year" and that they wanted to sign SALT so that they could "get their rear cleared."[16] On many occasions, they lamented the attention arms control received over what they considered more important issues. During the US bombing of Cambodia, Nixon said, "Looking back over the past year we have been praised for all the wrong things: Okinawa, SALT, germs, Nixon Doctrine. Now [we are] finally doing the right thing."[17] Neither saw any value in arms control for its own sake. With the Vietnam War still unresolved, Nixon told Kissinger, "I don't give a damn about SALT; I just couldn't care less about it."[18] The president was regularly dismissive of his negotiating team: "The arms control people will support anything."[19] Nixon was uninterested in discussions that focused on the technical minutiae of arms control. On the controversial question of the number and performance of Soviet radars, Nixon told Kissinger that "[as] you and I both know, it doesn't make a hell of a lot of difference."[20] Both agreed a debate over the number of missile interceptors was "just of no consequence." As Nixon said to Kissinger: "I don't think it makes a hell of a lot of difference."[21] Nixon also told Kissinger to "do the best you can," because it would not do to have an arms control treaty that "looks as if we got took. They're going to analyze that son-of-a-bitch right down to its wire teeth."

The president adamantly opposed having an ABM site protect the capital with the purpose of preventing a "decapitating" nuclear strike against US command, control, communications, and intelligence centers, a contingency arms controllers greatly feared. He said: "I don't want Washington. I don't like the feel of Washington. I don't like that goddamn command airplane or any of this. I don't believe in all that crap I think the idea of building a new system around Washington is stupid."[22] At the end of the day, Nixon thought that none of these technical issues or treaty agreements had any worth if the core underlying geopolitical tensions remained unresolved. As the president pointed out, "What sense does it make to sit there with the Soviet Ambassador at a time they're raiding South Vietnam and say that they made a great contribution to peace by signing the silly biological warfare thing, which doesn't mean anything? Now, you know it and I know it."[23]

So why pursue the arms control negotiations and treaties with the Soviet Union in the first place? The president told his General Advisory Committee on Arms Control that, while the public message was "let us curb the arms race and prevent nuclear war," the real reasons for negotiation could be found elsewhere. From the Soviet side, Nixon thought the motivations were at best temporary: "The arms race is burdensome, the Soviet economy has been flat, their neighbor to the East could be a big problem in 20 years, so that may be a good opportunity to deal with the U.S." Other more sinister motives might also be involved. Arms control might help the Soviets "break up NATO" by coupling "SALT with a European Security Conference." It could also help them keep "Eastern Europe under control."[24] The Soviets were not to be trusted. Kissinger told the president, "If the Soviets believe they have strategic predominance then, of course, this document will be meaningless."[25] As Nixon put it, "If the balance shifts, we are all in deep trouble."[26]

US motivations proved equally complex. Nixon and Kissinger wanted a return to nuclear superiority, but because of domestic politics and the world situation, it was simply not in the cards. According to Nixon, "the possibility of our going into a massive arms build-up is no longer what is was." Perhaps they could "frighten the U.S. people" into something, but "time was running out." The Soviets and Americans were now equal, but the United States was no longer "credible" when it threatened to keep up with further Soviet increases. Nixon reminded his advisory committee that "in this room we know—and Soviet intelligence knows—that we have weaknesses."[27] The president told his deputy national security advisor, Alexander Haig, that, while he shared the right-wing's aversion to arms control, he understood that "we simply can't get from the Congress the additional funds needed to continue the arms race with the Soviets in either the defensive or offensive missile category."[28] Nixon recognized that after more than two decades of an expensive commitment to the Cold War, and years of a bloody, failing war in Southeast Asia, Americans did not have the stomach for escalating the strategic arms race with the Soviets. He said: "We face the reality of a change in strategic relations. We face the reality of a complex domestic situation."[29] The Nixon administration had its hands full simply staving off isolationism. According to

Nixon, "The real question is whether the Americans give a damn any more. Americans don't care about Cambodia, Laos, Thailand and the Philippines. No President could risk New York to save Tel Aviv or Bonn."[30]

Kissinger and, especially, Nixon believed nuclear weapons had powerful military and political utility beyond simple deterrence and that the strategic nuclear balance mattered. US nuclear superiority was not, as the arms controllers would have it, either useless or even dangerous. To them, America's numerical advantage had held the Soviets at bay and allowed earlier administrations to prevail during crises in the past. Time and time again, they lamented the conditions of nuclear parity and highlighted how much more freedom the United States had during the earlier period. The new strategic balance explained what Kissinger labeled "the aggressiveness" of Soviet foreign policy. Nixon was obsessed with the strategic superiority the United States had during the Cuban missile crisis and the leverage it provided President Kennedy: "Kennedy saw 5–1 in 1962, had confidence. We can't do this today. . . . We may have reached a balance of terror."[31] Three years later, Nixon stated: "In 1962, at the time of the Cuban missile crisis, it had been 'no contest,' because we had a ten to one superiority."[32] At a meeting with NATO ambassadors over a year later, Nixon again brought up how different the US situation was eleven years after Kennedy's showdown with the Russians: "We also have had to consider that we are conducting foreign policy under extremely difficult circumstances. We did not invent the new strategic balance. We inherited a changed strategic relationship. Whereas the Kennedy administration dealt with the Soviet Union when the Soviets had 80 ICBMs that were liquid fueled and took ten minutes to prepare, we face over 1,000 ICBMs that can be fired immediately."[33]

Nixon and Kissinger would have preferred to recapture US nuclear superiority, but the obstacles were simply too great. Kissinger, in a briefing paper on nuclear options early in Nixon's first term, pointed out, "Now we have no first strike capability (like we had in 1962) [and that it would be] hard to recapture 5 to 1 superiority."[34] During the same meeting, the chair of the Joint Chiefs of Staff, Earle Wheeler, stated if the US could develop an ABM system that "gave first strike capability, I would advocate it, destabilizing or not. . . . Wouldn't bother me." Nixon agreed: "Wouldn't bother me either." Nixon pushed the point on his arms control chief Gerard Smith and undersecretary of defense David Packard:

> Nixon: Suppose you could defend cities. Really means credible threat of first strike would be much greater if they are screwing with Allies.
>
> Packard: Wouldn't really give you first strike.

Smith: Population protection is historically a signal of going for first strike. Would be more threatening.

Nixon: We say glibly we will fire on warning. Who's sure? As soon as you do, you are risking great destruction.[35]

Nixon and Kissinger recognized what the arms control community often chose to ignore: that the US commitment to defend Western Europe and other allies was only really credible if the United States had nuclear superiority. In an age of parity, the president declared the "nuclear umbrella in NATO a lot of crap." As Kissinger recognized, "Europeans don't realize American nuclear umbrella depended on first strike. No longer true." The administration had to undertake a review of nuclear options, as they believed the strategy they inherited from Kennedy and Johnson was bankrupt. "Flexible response is baloney. They have possibility of conventional options, greater options. We remember our massive retaliation, gave us freedom to act. This has changed." The age of parity meant that the Soviets' "assured destruction edge affects their willingness to be aggressive." This might push the Soviets to more "local aggression." The president thought that with the nuclear umbrella diminished, the US "bargaining position has shifted. We must face facts."[36]

Neither Nixon nor Kissinger wanted to accept either the logic or reality of MAD, and both sought ways out of the limitations imposed by strategic nuclear parity. This effort had two parts. First, the administration sought changes in nuclear strategy that would provide more flexible, "useable" options. Second, they wanted to pursue what Nixon, his aides, and scholars have called the "madman" strategy, which was in fact a variation on Thomas Schelling's idea of the manipulation of risk.[37] Both Nixon and Kissinger saw great political utility in engaging in nuclear brinkmanship in order to prevail in a crisis. With the American public unwilling to support the increased spending necessary to support a strategy of nuclear superiority, Nixon and Kissinger had to find other ways to exploit what they saw as the military and political utility of nuclear weapons to advance US interests.

Scholars William Burr and Terry Terriff have admirably chronicled the Nixon administration's efforts to create more flexible nuclear war plans that gave the president more options in a crisis.[38] Nixon and Kissinger were stunned by their strategic nuclear inheritance from previous Democratic administrations. McNamara had, with great fanfare, announced the Kennedy administration's ambition to construct a more supple strategy in 1962. This new doctrine, "flexible response," was supposedly a reaction to Eisenhower's "massive retaliation" plan. Massive retaliation, it was argued, relied exclusively on a large, preordained strategic nuclear response against thousands of targets throughout the Communist world in the event of Soviet aggression. In a crisis, critics argued, the plan's inflexibility gave the president only two options—capitulation or launching a nuclear attack that would leave tens of millions of people dead. Flexible response was supposed to provide US decision makers with an array of less extreme options and the ability to deploy effective forces on any rung of the so-called escalation ladder.

In retrospect, it is clear that the strategy of flexible response was a rhetorical policy and nothing more.[39] Under McNamara, there was some minor tinkering with the nuclear war plan, but the general thrust of the strategy—massive, preprogrammed, inflexible strategic nuclear strikes against thousands of targets—remained in place. Nixon and Kissinger demanded changes that would give the president politically plausible options that did not involve appalling outcomes. Not only was a strategy that relied on killing tens of millions of Russians immoral—even the realist Kissinger said that to "have only the option of killing 80 million people is the height of immorality"—it was of questionable credibility.

The administration pushed the military establishment to dramatically revise its war plans and provide more options. Kissinger demanded to know if "all-out thermonuclear war became too dangerous, would limited applications of nuclear forces still be feasible?"[40] The military bureaucracy, however, presented enormous resistance to deviations from the large, preprogrammed attacks.[41] The Defense Department, led by Melvyn Laird, did not begin a serious effort to alter the war plans until January 1972, when a committee led by the director of defense research and engineering, John Foster, was tasked with producing a policy for nuclear attack and targeting to guide the Joint Chiefs of Staff. While much of the background of the report remains classified, it appears that the committee did go some way toward recommending the flexibility that Nixon and Kissinger desired. An aide to Kissinger at the time described the recommendations as a "radical departure" from the current war plan. Instead of trying to "win the war through the destruction of the enemy's forces and military capability," the new plan would aim to control escalation and "re-establish mutual deterrence."[42] In addition to the major general war attacks, the plan called for selected, regional, and limited attack options. President Nixon took almost two years to sign National Security Action Memorandum 242, authorizing the military to make the changes the Foster panel recommended. Despite the national security decision memorandums and the public pronouncements of Laird's successor, James Schlesinger, that the US sought flexible nuclear options, evidence indicates that the new "single integrated operational plan" or SIOP was only marginally different than those that preceded it.[43]

The other aspect of Nixon and Kissinger's nuclear strategy has been called the "madman" strategy. The idea—which has been previously laid out by policy participants, such as H. R. Haldeman, and scholars, such as Jeffrey Kimball—was to convey the impression that the administration was willing, in a crisis, to use "excessive" force and to threaten, often implicitly, that nuclear weapons might be used.[44] As Kissinger told the National Security Council during the first month of the new administration, "for deterrence, what the other side thinks is as important as what we think" because in the nuclear age a "bluff [is] taken seriously."[45] What is perhaps more interesting is that conversations between Nixon and Kissinger indicate that these may have been more than threats and that the use of nuclear weapons was not completely off the table.

Excellent research by Jeremi Suri, Scott Sagan, Jeffrey Kimball, and William Burr has made clear that one of the first and most important tests of the "madman" theory occurred in fall 1969. Nixon ordered an increase in US nuclear readiness to signal to the Soviets the possibility that he might use extreme force to bring the Vietnam conflict to an end.[46] These scholars argue that Nixon and Kissinger hoped to convey the possibility that the president might not be entirely rational in his application of force. No evidence exists that the Soviets made any changes in policy as a result of this worldwide alert.

Nixon and Kissinger engaged in veiled or explicit brinkmanship in several other cases. In late 1971, India intervened in Pakistan's bloody civil war that saw East Pakistan become an independent country, Bangladesh. The administration feared India would destroy West Pakistan, humiliating a US ally and providing what Nixon and Kissinger believed would be an unacceptable victory to their Cold War rival, the USSR. Less than half a year later, Nixon and Kissinger appeared willing to scuttle the Moscow summit and end any possibility of SALT by threatening massive escalation after a spring offensive by North Vietnam into the south.[47] Kissinger claimed that during the dispute over the Soviet submarine base at Cienfuegos in 1970, the Nixon administration "used more or less the same tactics [as Kennedy used in 1962] and we achieved more or less the same result."[48] The most explicit case of nuclear brinkmanship occurred in October 1973. After Israel had reversed its initial losses from Egypt and Syria's surprise attack, the Soviet Union pressed the United States to jointly deploy a peacekeeping force to prevent the Israeli military from destroying Arab military forces. After Kissinger rejected this suggestion, the Soviets appeared as if they might intervene unilaterally. With Nixon supposedly in a debilitated physical and emotional state due to Watergate and the aftermath of the "Saturday night massacre," when he fired the Watergate special prosecutor, Kissinger ordered US military forces to a high alert, DEFCON 3. While it is unclear how the Soviets interpreted and responded to the alert, they ceased pushing for a joint or unilateral superpower military intervention in the conflict.[49]

Kissinger and, especially, Nixon had developed this "madman" idea based on their view of the past. Nixon may have believed Eisenhower's claim that nuclear threats had brought the Korean conflict to an end in 1953 and allowed the United States to protect Nationalist China's interests during the crises in the Taiwan Strait. Even more impressive to Nixon was Khrushchev's use of brinkmanship during the Suez Crisis and the Berlin Crisis when the Soviets were in a position of strategic nuclear inferiority. Regardless of the historical precedent, both Kissinger and Nixon believed nuclear threats could be effective. Kissinger believed these threats were "how we broke the India-Pakistan situation last year."[50] And Nixon argued that brinkmanship in October 1973 had been successful: "The Soviets had a hard choice to our alert—to go back to the Cold War and risk the United States relationship, or to back off. They joined us in the UN and called for a cease-fire."[51] Or consider this exchange, in which Kissinger and Nixon explicitly refer to the "Dulles strategy" of threatening nuclear use in situations where the use of such excessive force seemed out of line with the interests engaged:

Kissinger: But one thing we might consider, Mr. President—it just occurred to me this week—as long as we're playing it this way—

Nixon: Yeah.

Kissinger: —whether it—depending—if they don't accept it, or if they keep it in abeyance—if, at the end of the meeting, I don't tell Xuan Thuy to talk to me alone for five minutes with just his interpreter present.

Nixon: Good.

Kissinger: If I tell him, "Now, look, this President is extremely tough. You've been wrong every time. If you think you're going to defeat him, if you don't accept this, he will stop at nothing."

Nixon: That's right.

Kissinger: And imply that you might do it—

Nixon: That's right.

Kissinger: Use nuclear weapons—

Nixon: And then you could say—

Kissinger: Do—do the Dulles ploy—

Nixon: You can say that. You can say, "I cannot control him." Put it that way.

Kissinger: Yeah. And imply that you might use nuclear weapons.

Nixon: Yes, sir. "He will. I just want you to know he is not going to cave."

Kissinger: If—if they, then, charge us with it, I'll deny it.
Nixon: Oh, sure.[52]

More interesting than the threats to manipulate risk during crises are the examples in which Nixon appeared at least willing to contemplate employing nuclear weapons. Consider this remarkable exchange between Nixon and Kissinger at the height of the 1971 India-Pakistan conflict. When Kissinger argued, "[If] the Soviets move against them and we don't do anything, we'll be finished," the president asked, "So what do we do if the Soviets move against them? Start lobbing nuclear weapons?" While not answering the question, Kissinger suggested that if "Pakistan is swallowed by India, China is destroyed, defeated, humiliated by the Soviet Union, it will be a change in the world balance of power of such magnitude that the security of the United States may be forever [weakened], certainly for decades."[53] During the 1972 North Vietnamese spring offensive, weeks before the scheduled Moscow summit, Nixon fumed: "We're going to do it. I'm going to destroy the goddamn country, believe me, I mean destroy it if necessary. And let me say, even the nuclear weapons if necessary. It isn't necessary. But, you know, what I mean is, that shows you the extent to which I'm willing to go. By a nuclear weapon, I mean that we will bomb the living bejeezus out of North Vietnam and then if anybody interferes we will threaten the nuclear weapons."[54] A week later, Nixon repeated the threat: "I'd rather use a nuclear bomb. Have you got that ready?" When Kissinger appeared to protest, Nixon asked, "A nuclear bomb, does that bother you? . . . I just want you to think big, Henry, for Christ's sake!"[55]

How did Nixon and Kissinger's theories about nuclear weapons affect their attitudes toward the atomic aspirations of other powers? While the primary focus of arms control experts and US officials was on the strategic nuclear balance between the United States and the Soviet Union, a new concern arose in the 1960s. States other than the superpowers were expressing an interest in acquiring their own atomic weapons. How would this issue of new nuclear powers—the Nth country problem, in the parlance of the day—affect international politics? Once again, Nixon and Kissinger had much different views than most.

The Kennedy and Johnson administrations recognized the need for policies to slow the threat of nuclear proliferation. China's detonation of a nuclear device in October 1964 led to concerns about a "chain reaction" of nuclear proliferation. India, Japan, Pakistan, Taiwan, Indonesia, and Australia, it was feared, would acquire atomic weapons. East Asia was not the only region where the administration was worried about nuclear proliferation. In the Middle East, Israel was suspected of developing nuclear weapons. And in Europe, there was great concern that West Germany, at the frontline of the Cold War, would want to defend itself with the same weapons its closest allies, the United States, Great Britain, and France possessed. A nuclear-armed Bundeswehr, however, worried all of West Germany's neighbors, allies and adversaries alike.[56]

Nixon's predecessors saw promising opportunities for cooperation with their Cold War enemy, the Soviet Union, to slow the spread of nuclear weapons. In the summer of 1968, the two sides completed over two years of intense, detailed negotiations and announced the signing of the Nuclear Nonproliferation Treaty. The NPT forbade signatories that already had nuclear weapons from helping states acquire these weapons; it also committed nuclear states to reducing and eventually eliminating their nuclear stockpiles. Nonnuclear signatories waived their rights to these weapons. Although the treaty was considered a great success, the Soviet invasion of Czechoslovakia prevented Johnson from sending it to the US Senate for approval.

What was the attitude of the new Nixon administration to nuclear nonproliferation? Nixon opposed the treaty during his election campaign. Neither Nixon nor Kissinger believed proliferation could be halted if states really wanted to go nuclear. As early as 1957, Kissinger argued that a nonproliferation treaty would be unenforceable.[57] The president himself argued that "treaties don't necessarily get us very much" and that if a country wanted to "make their own weapons" they could "abrogate the treaty without sanction."[58] Some in the administration actually argued that the United States should help friendly states acquire atomic weapons. If it were decided that "the NPT was not in the US interest," a formal disengagement would "have considerable support in the FRG and in some circles in Italy, Japan, India, Brazil, and Israel."[59] When Nixon did finally send the NPT to the Senate for ratification, he told his staff to downplay its importance, and that the United States should not pressure other countries, especially the Federal Republic of Germany, to ratify it.[60]

The ambivalence the Nixon administration displayed to broader nuclear nonproliferation policy became outright hostility in specific cases. Soon after de Gaulle left office as president of France, the Nixon administration decided they would "like to give assistance" to France's nuclear program.[61] Kissinger told the French ambassador, "It is too dangerous to have one country as the repository of nuclear weapons. We would like France to be a possessor."[62] The United States also stopped pressuring Israel to get rid of its nuclear weapons. This policy change emerged after an apparently unrecorded, undocumented meeting between Nixon and Israeli prime minister Golda Meir led to a secret, mutual, and as yet unrevealed understanding on Israel's nuclear weapons program.[63]

Time and time again, Nixon and Kissinger placed geopolitical goals ahead of nuclear nonproliferation. When Secretary of State Rogers argued that the NPT required the United States to pursue nuclear arms reductions, Nixon rejected this view.[64] When Winston Lord, a Kissinger National Security Council staffer, asked of the Nixon Doctrine, "[Which] is the lesser of two evils—nuclear proliferation or the extension of more concrete America nuclear assurance?" the answer was clear. In regard to Asia, Lord asked, Would Japan going nuclear "necessarily be against our long range interests?"[65]

The Nixon administration pursued other policies that, intentionally or not, increased the incentives and opportunities for nuclear proliferation. According to Raymond Garthoff, the administration's tilt toward Pakistan in 1971 "may have had one critical effect—it may have influenced India to develop nuclear weapons."[66] Furthermore, Nixon's opening to China, which gave the United States new leverage in its conflict with the Soviets, set America's East Asian allies on edge. Taiwan, in particular, stepped up its efforts to acquire nuclear weapons. Attempting to stop development of weapons programs in South Africa, Brazil, and Argentina was given relatively low priority. Finally, Nixon's crusade to privatize the nuclear power industry diluted US control over world nuclear fuel production and led countries to replace US agreements with ones less focused on preventing nuclear proliferation.

It is perhaps not unexpected that Nixon and his close adviser Kissinger disagreed with the views of the Democratic administrations that preceded them, nor with the ideas espoused by academic strategists and arms controllers. What is surprising, however, is that they had a broad, consistent, and intellectually defensible (if controversial) view of the influence of nuclear weapons on modern statecraft. Scholars have not seen it this way, choosing instead to emphasize Nixon and Kissinger's expediency and personalities. The historian Robert Dallek, for example, argues that during the SALT negotiations Nixon was most concerned about "personal credit and domestic politics."[67] Jeffrey Kimball, an important scholar of Nixon's decision making in the Vietnam War and particularly the "madman" strategy, emphasizes Nixon's "peculiar psychology" and his "odd relationship" with Kissinger.[68] While these assessments—and many others like them—contain a certain amount of truth, they underestimate the coherence and validity of a philosophy of the nuclear age that had been developed during their years as policymakers and observers. Nixon and Kissinger's theories about statecraft in a nuclear age, and how they were manifested in their policy choices, should be taken seriously and judged on their merits.

Consider their views on nuclear strategy. Nixon and Kissinger believed strategic nuclear superiority mattered and that President Kennedy was able to prevail in his showdown with the Soviets because the United States had what almost amounted to a first-strike capability in October 1962. Members of Kennedy's inner circle have vigorously denied that nuclear superiority, if it even existed, played any role in the outcome of the Cuban missile crisis. Who was right? The answer is not as clear-cut as many proponents of the nuclear revolution thesis would suggest.[69] While Nixon and Kissinger recognized that neither the domestic nor the international political factors they faced in office would allow for the massive strategic buildup necessary to recapture their vision of "nuclear superiority," it does not mean they would not have pursued such a strategy if circumstances had allowed it.

When judged on their merits, Nixon and Kissinger's nonconventional views are at least credible. No conclusive evidence exists that arms races cause wars, and the strategic studies literature can be justly criticized for emphasizing autonomous military factors over more important developments in global politics.[70] The massive *History of the Strategic Arms Competition*, 1945–1972, written by scholars commissioned by the Office of the Secretary of Defense, concluded the "facts will not support the proposition that either the Soviet Union or the United States developed strategic forces only in direct immediate reaction to each other."[71] Nixon and Kissinger's policies certainly cast doubt on the widely held belief that the possession of nuclear weapons diminished "the tendency of nations to take risks."[72] And there is certainly an intellectually credible case that the United States should not sacrifice core political interests in the world in order to vigorously impede nuclear proliferation.[73]

This is not to justify Nixon and Kissinger's nuclear philosophies or praise their statecraft. While assessing the results for each crisis remains difficult, the Nixon administration's attempts to manipulate risk (or employ the "madman" strategy) often proved ineffective and, at times, reckless. Nixon's discussions of actually using nuclear weapons were irresponsible. For those who consider nuclear proliferation the greatest threat to US interests, the Nixon period represents lost years, years that did great damage. The case for and against Nixon and Kissinger's worldview and policies can be argued in many ways. But before doing so, it is important to recognize their worldview for what it was. Before the Nixon period can be analyzed correctly, it is important to note that Nixon and Kissinger had distinct ideas that were well thought-out about how international politics functioned in a world with nuclear weapons, views that stood in sharp contrast to the beliefs of most other policymakers and analysts of their day.

[6]

That Seventies Show

The Consequences of Parity Revisited

> Parity in this sense cannot be objectively measured; it is essentially a state of mind.
>
> —National Intelligence Estimate, November 24, 1970

What would be the consequences of, and the appropriate response to, nuclear parity between the Cold War superpowers—the Soviet Union and the United States? American policymakers and strategists had anticipated and worried about this development since the Soviet Union detonated its first nuclear device on August 29, 1949. There had been much debate during the 1950s and 1960s about when the moment of parity would arrive, but by the 1970s its existence was accepted. The effects and reaction to this new condition, however, were widely disputed.

Intense debate over the meaning, consequences, and appropriate response to nuclear parity with the Soviets dominated US strategic discourse throughout the 1970s. The answers to these questions drove some of the most important foreign and military policies of the decade, from arms control negotiations to alliance relations to multibillion dollar weapon systems deployments. The ensuing, increasingly bitter disputes over these issues helped shape, and in many ways calcified, domestic political divisions in the United States, bringing a final end to the remnants of the "Cold War consensus" that had not already been sacrificed in the quagmire of Southeast Asia.

In retrospect, these disagreements seem esoteric and even bizarre. Dig a little deeper, however, and it becomes clear that these debates had important meanings and consequences that went beyond nuclear strategy. Arguments that appeared to focus on obscure technical terms such as "throw-weight" and "single-shot kill probability" often masked divergent views of international relations and the place of the United States in global politics during the Cold War. In other words, competing visions of the US role in the world, differing interpretations of the nature of the international system, and contested metrics for what constituted power and influence in world affairs were at stake in the fight over nuclear parity.

This chapter identifies three different responses to nuclear parity that emerged during the 1970s. The best-known school of thought accepted and even embraced nuclear parity. Mutual vulnerability, it was argued, prevented war and ensured "strategic stability" by guaranteeing that a first strike by either side would be suicidal, as it risked a devastating response from the surviving forces of the adversary. While variations of this worldview existed, it made achieving arms control with the Soviet Union a priority and linked the military balance to what proponents saw as a promising "détente" between the superpowers.

The second response rejected the inevitability and desirability of parity and doubted the concept of strategic stability. Critics from what might be called the "nuclear superiority" school ranged from those who believed parity with the Soviets undermined US ability to fulfill its commitments to defend its allies to those who thought a nuclear war could be fought and won. As a whole, this group was uncomfortable with the moral and strategic consequences of parity and détente with the Soviet Union. These first two worldviews engaged in a passionate and often bitter political struggle over the future of US nuclear doctrine, military procurement, and grand strategy.

The third response—or set of responses—was very different from either of these other two. From a variety of sources and in a variety of ways, nuclear weapons came to be seen in many circles as far less relevant to international politics than either the mutual vulnerability/strategic stability or nuclear superiority school contended. These responses ran the gamut from nuclear abolitionism to focusing on what we now call "soft power," and had as many internal differences as similarities. All, however, were connected by the belief that nuclear deterrence was not the cornerstone of international relations and that the great shifts in world politics were driven by fundamental changes that went beyond the nuclear revolution. While this set of ideas was diffuse and had no obvious policy champion during the 1970s, these nascent ideas and forces would come to define the post–Cold War era of globalization.

A Church Divided—Mutual Vulnerability vs. Nuclear Superiority

From the first atomic detonation, strategists wrestled with the implications nuclear weapons had for statecraft and military competition. Among these analysts within the United States, there were many disagreements, but, in essence, the debate revolved around a basic question: Did these fearsome weapons have any other purpose than to deter an adversary from attacking the United States (or its allies)? While more traditional thinkers accepted the profound implications of nuclear weapons, they did not believe it possible or wise to preclude the possibility they might actually be used, and they sought to develop strategies that could help the United States prevail or at least limit damage should deterrence fail. Naturally, this entailed having more and better weapons than the Soviet Union. A different group—one that came to be seen as more intellectually sophisticated and influential in policy circles—argued vehemently that nuclear weapons had no other utility than to deter others from a nuclear attack and that strategies that sought to accomplish more were foolish and often dangerous. Weapons and strategies that provided for stability, not superiority, was the goal.

These debates and discussions—which began in universities and think tanks like RAND in the 1950s before moving to more public forums in the 1960s and 1970s—are among the most well chronicled in modern strategic and political history.[1] Most accounts portray a remarkable and rare time when wise and important policymakers implemented the ideas produced by cutting-edge intellectuals. There is reason to question, however, how good these ideas were and, more important, how influential they were in the making of policy.[2] And, while advocates on each side spoke from the platform of "social science" assuming their ideas were generalizable over space and time, neither the "nuclear superiority/damage limitation" school nor the "mutual vulnerability/strategic stability" view found much acceptance outside of the United States. Another unusual feature was that the "mutual vulnerability/strategic stability" school appeared to triumph in the intellectual debate—and make real headway in policy circles—at the moment of greatest US nuclear strength. Despite constant public fears during the first two decades of the atomic era that the USSR would catch up and surpass the Unites States in the number of weapons, bombers, or missiles, at the time of the greatest nuclear tension—during the Berlin Crisis and the Cuban missile crisis—the United States had, by many measures, significant nuclear superiority.

What did it actually mean to have nuclear superiority, however, and how did it translate into world politics? The question exposed the key divide within the strategy community in the United States. Many American (as opposed to Soviet) veterans of the superpower standoff concluded that US nuclear superiority had little or no influence on the outcome of confrontations, and that by itself it was dangerous. Looking back on the crisis years, former national security advisor McGeorge

Bundy claimed, "It is sometimes argued that in the past nuclear superiority . . . has had a decisive influence on events. I find this a very doubtful proposition."[3] One of the most important participants in the nuclear standoff, Secretary of Defense McNamara, advocated a US defense policy in which mutual vulnerability and strategic stability were the most important ends of a grand strategy. This led to cancellations in nuclear delivery systems and, after years of increases, a ceiling on strategic nuclear-delivery vehicles. Combined with a massive surge in the number of Soviet strategic nuclear weapons—an increase largely unforeseen by analysts and US intelligence agencies—the nuclear superiority of the early 1960s gave way to parity by the end of the decade.

Oddly, this dramatic shift in the balance of military power was not lamented. In fact, within mainstream policy circles, there was a strong consensus that parity was inevitable, nuclear superiority useless, and that mutual vulnerability should be embraced. Writing in early 1971, foreign policy analysts Paul Warnke and Leslie Gelb summed up the conventional wisdom: "The United States and the Soviet Union are now in a constellation of parity, both sides possessing a secure second strike capability. . . . As long as neither pursues an unreachable quest for 'superiority' in the form of knock-out first strike capability, there will be continued strategic stability."[4] In what must have been a first in the history of great power politics, the analysts of the leading power welcomed the passing of its quantitative advantage, secure in the belief that its adversary would see the benefits of nuclear equality.

And why would either side reach for this superiority? To the mutual vulnerability/strategic stability school, the logic of parity was less a policy choice than an inescapable fact of international political life. This attitude is borne out in the title of a chapter—"MAD Is a Fact, Not a Policy"—in Robert Jervis's influential book on the nuclear revolution.[5] Any attempt to return to a mythical world of superiority was pointless. As William Foster, who directed the Arms Control and Disarmament Agency throughout the 1960s, claimed, "whatever index of strategic nuclear power is used, it would seem rather fruitless for either side to claim superiority, when, no matter what it does, the other side will still have the capability to inflict unacceptable damage."[6]

This view—that mutual vulnerability was a fact of life that could not be overcome—exposed a troubling paradox. If seeking superiority was "fruitless," there was little anyone could or should do to affect the nuclear balance. Wouldn't the best idea be to let nature—in this case, the laws of international politics—take its course? This was not, however, the policy recommendation of the mutual vulnerability/strategic stability school. While the efforts to overcome mutual vulnerability were bound to fail, they were also destabilizing. According to Alton Frye, "one of those realities is that the attempt by either side to alter the stability of deterrence by overcoming its own vulnerabilities is bound to be dangerous. A unilateral quest for escape from the paradox of deterrence is a reckless and counterproductive gesture calculated only to jeopardize both countries' security."[7] In other words, strategic behavior that once was considered normal and expected—trying to have more useable firepower than your enemy—was now to be avoided at all costs.

This paradox got to the heart of how the mutual vulnerability/strategic stability school understood the world. To them, international politics were driven by what strategists called the security dilemma. In a dangerous world, states did what they could to protect themselves. Adversaries, however, could easily misunderstand these defensive measures. A strategy or weapon system deployed to protect a country could be seen as aggressive and offense oriented by a nervous neighbor. The threatened nation would undertake its own defensive countermeasures that could be similarly misperceived. In other words, in a world where states did not trust each other, defensive efforts could spiral into an unwanted arms race or even a conflict.[8]

This dangerous dynamic was heightened in a world of nuclear weapons, where the side that launched weapons first could have tremendous advantages, particularly if it was not vulnerable to a devastating second strike. Things could not be allowed to develop "naturally," instead, policymakers had to intervene to retard or halt the security dilemma process. Only mutually negotiated arms controls that maintained each side's vulnerability could slow the arms race and reduce instability. The mutual vulnerability school's recommendations were a strange brew of realism and international law, two approaches not typically associated with each other. The world was a scary, unpredictable place, but instead of seeking as much military power as possible, self-restraint and treaties could make the world safer.

This view of parity and mutual vulnerability engendered a fierce resistance from a vocal and influential minority. For them, the idea of self-restraint in an uncertain world was dangerous and even bizarre. Targeting civilian populations seemed immoral. Arms control skeptic Fred Iklé charged that the "jargon of American strategic analysis works like a narcotic. . . . It blinds us to the fact that our method of preventing nuclear war rests on a form of warfare universally condemned since the Dark Ages—the mass killing of hostages."[9] The notion of constructing a strategy that had no concept of victory—only deterrence—seemed beyond the pale for many who viewed nuclear weapons through a traditional political-military lens. Critics such as Paul Nitze understood the arguments about parity but were dismayed by the willingness of the mutual vulnerability crowd to embrace arms control as an end in itself, naive to the possibility the Soviets would exploit any advantage. He wrote, "There is every prospect that under the terms of the SALT agreements the Soviet Union will continue to pursue a nuclear superiority that is not merely quantitative but designed to produce a theoretical war-winning capability."[10] Even if the agreements were fair, could the Soviets be trusted to keep their word?

The sharpest criticism came from those who believed that the Soviet Union simply did not buy the logic behind mutual vulnerability and strategic stability. Russia expert Richard Pipes argued: "There is something innately destabilizing in the very fact that we consider nuclear war unfeasible and suicidal for both, and our chief adversary views it as feasible and winnable for himself."[11] Some went even further, arguing that arms control gave away the United States' greatest advantage—a powerful economy and strong technological base that would allow it to win an arms race with the Soviets. As defense intellectual Colin Gray argued, "the instability arguments that are leveled against those who urge an American response (functionally) in kind are somewhat fragile . . . there is good reason to believe that the Soviet Union would be profoundly discouraged by the prospect of having to wage an arms competition against an American opponent no longer severely inhibited by its long-familiar stability theory."[12]

Did the nuclear superiority/damage limitation school offer ideas and policies that were any more logical and appealing? The ideas of the more extreme critics of mutual vulnerability—those who argued that one had to think about fighting and winning a nuclear war—seemed unsound and dangerous. And while it is easy to assume in retrospect that arms racing exposed weaknesses in the Soviet system, it was hard for anyone looking at US economic performance during the 1970s to think the United States had the wherewithal to excel in such a competition. The arguments that superiority was needed to "limit damage" in any nuclear exchange were hardly more convincing. Was it wise, or even rational, for the United States to spend hundreds of billions of dollars on complex, exotic nuclear systems to reduce, at best, American fatalities in a nuclear exchange to, say, thirty or forty million from over one hundred million?

The nuclear superiority arguments were driven, one suspects, more by political than technical arguments, namely, by a deep unease with the so-called détente that was associated with an acceptance of parity and support for arms control. Was the Soviet Union a responsible status quo power willing to obey international law and adopt Western norms? Or was it an aggressive, authoritarian state interested in world revolution and willing to engage in nuclear diplomacy in order to dupe naive

American policy elites? And, even if the Soviets were responsible and interested in maintaining the status quo, was the stability of détente, parity, and arms control worth dividing the world, particularly Europe, between free and unfree? Did the United States—seen by many as an exceptional nation and beacon to the world—have a moral if not military responsibility to expand freedom and fight tyranny? These arguments found mixed domestic support within the United States. Polls showed backing for both arms control and increases in military expenditures as well as support for détente and unease with Soviet behavior on the world stage. Members of the "nuclear superiority" school displayed similar inconsistency and even incoherence, as if some of the more important advocates were themselves unsure what to believe. Policymakers such as Henry Kissinger and Paul Nitze switched sides more than once.

Was it possible that the mutual vulnerability/strategic stability crowd underestimated the political, if not military, utility of nuclear superiority?[13] In the years following the Cuban missile showdown, US participants argued that it was the vast conventional edge and not the nuclear superiority of the United States that determined the outcome.[14] If true, shouldn't the same logic have applied to West Berlin, where NATO and, in particular, the United States resisted Soviet ultimatums and pressure despite an insurmountable inferiority in conventional forces? There is at least some reason to think that nuclear superiority played some role.[15] Even if there was no military utility in nuclear superiority, there was certainly a political and even a psychological advantage. President Nixon, for example, lamented the loss of nuclear superiority and its perceived geopolitical advantages, even as his official doctrine accepted parity and his administration pursued strategic arms control.[16] And, while nuclear equality may have been enough to ensure an adversary did not attack, was it enough to guarantee the same adversary did not attack one's allies? In other words, could the United States "extend" deterrence to its friends and allies in an age of parity?

This pointed to a second flaw. The mutual vulnerability/strategic stability school, in their obsession with the US-Soviet strategic arms rivalry, paid very little attention to nuclear dynamics outside of the superpower rivalry. Their focus was on vertical, not horizontal, arms races, and as such they tended to overlook the arguably bigger long-term threat to global security from nuclear proliferation. This lack of awareness manifested itself in two ways. First, by accepting parity, they risked "decoupling" US nuclear forces from the security of their nonnuclear allies, tempting them to acquire their own atomic weapons. In retrospect, it is striking how some members of the mutual vulnerability/strategic stability school failed to appreciate how their positions—on issues ranging from arms control to no first use to the neutron bomb, Pershing II missiles, and even missile defense—ignored or discounted the security concerns of nonnuclear allies such as West Germany and Japan.

There was an even larger proliferation issue. Advocates of strategic stability rarely realized that their arguments endorsed the virtues of nuclear weapons. If nuclear weapons stabilized relations between the superpowers and prevented war, why wouldn't they do the same thing for other countries and regions? Is it any wonder that while the 1970s witnessed the greatest strides in vertical arms control, proliferation worries increased. Israel, India, Pakistan, South Africa, Brazil, Argentina, Taiwan, and South Korea, among others, flirted with and in some cases moved forward with nuclear weapons programs.

The third weakness in the mutual vulnerability/strategic stability school involved their understanding of what factors drove international politics. For most strategists, the bipolar military competition was the ultimate example of how an uncontrolled arms race, driven by the security dilemma, could lead to instability and, without arms control, potentially war. If the nuclear arms race could be controlled or even suspended, international politics would stabilize and the threat of global conflagration would dissipate.

Arguing that the Cold War was a product of the security dilemma, however, drained it of its political and even ideological or moral content. Would the United States and Soviet Union have avoided bitter disputes over important matters, such as the military and political status of Germany, in a world of mutual vulnerability and arms control? Would there have been no ideological competition? By focusing almost exclusively on the interaction between rival militaries, the mutual vulnerability advocates tended to underplay the importance of geopolitics, ideology, and diplomacy. In fact, it is difficult to find a clear-cut case of a modern war unambiguously caused by the security dilemma or an arms race.[17]

Arguably the most authoritative study on the question—a 1,000-plus page top secret scholarly study commissioned in the 1970s by the secretary of defense James Schlesinger—revealed that the military competition between the superpowers was not driven by the security dilemma: "The facts will not support the proposition that either the Soviet Union or the United States developed strategic forces only in direct immediate access to each other."[18] There were other, more rational reasons for each side to increase its number of nuclear weapons: "Surges in strategic force deployments sprang from interaction between a scientific community producing basic technical developments and political leaders affected by immediate crisis events."[19] Furthermore, acquiring and deploying arms often acted as an effective way to signal unhappiness or aggressive intent between adversaries. Arms control—by limiting this signaling device—could increase the possibility of misperception.

Looking back at the pages of the leading US academic and policy journals during the 1970s, one would think that these debates surrounding nuclear arms control and strategy were the pivot on which world politics turned. In fact, we now know that the global order during the 1970s was driven by complex and fundamental changes in international relations that may have included, but certainly went well beyond, the choices of either mutual vulnerability or nuclear superiority. Were there reactions to nuclear parity that went beyond the narrow perspective of the leading strategists?

Beyond Deterrence?

A third response to the nuclear equality between the Soviet Union and the United States emerged from diffuse sources and with few champions within the strategic studies community. In fact, to label it a "response" to parity, similar to mutual vulnerability and nuclear superiority, is misleading. It is perhaps better described as a sensibility, animated by the notion that that there was something not quite right about the debate within the strategy community. In other words, the rift in the strategy "church" seemed somewhat unreal and disconnected from how the world actually worked. The four strands of this sensibility—nuclear abolitionism, the rise of a nuclear taboo, the notion that major war was obsolete, and the emergence of "softer" forms of power—shared a common trait: skepticism about nuclear deterrence and arms control as the cornerstone of international politics in the coming decades. Often disregarded by contemporaries during the 1970s, these responses to the emergence of nuclear parity may have, in the long run, provided a better understanding of the profound transformation of international relations in the past four decades than the more traditional insights of the strategy community.

Nuclear Abolitionism

The nuclear age did not just produce weapons, it also produced the world's largest grassroots transnational peace movement, fostered by nongovernmental organizations. While strategies differed among the myriad groups, they shared a common belief that eliminating nuclear weapons from the planet—not strengthening nuclear deterrence—was the key to global peace and stability.

Because these views were so at odds with those of most strategists and mainstream scholars, the influence of abolitionism on nuclear history has been understated. Worldwide pressure from nuclear abolitionists played a key role in any number of nuclear and arms control policies, from the crafting of the partial test ban treaty to the decision not to deploy the "neutron bomb." It is important to note, however, that the view that there was something problematic about basing world peace on nuclear deterrence was not just held by so-called peaceniks. Unlike some of their national security staff and cabinet officers, most presidents (with the possible exception of Nixon) during the postwar period felt a deep ambivalence about nuclear weapons. During the 1976 presidential campaign, Jimmy Carter "proclaimed a goal of abolishing nuclear weapons, albeit one step at a time," and as early as January 26, 1977, he informed Soviet leader Brezhnev that "my solid objective is to liquidate nuclear weapons completely."[20] More surprisingly (and controversially), there may have been abolitionist tendencies in Carter's successor, Ronald Reagan. According to scholar Paul Lettow, "Reagan's nuclear abolitionism, which grew out of his deeply rooted personal beliefs and religious views, resulted in some of the most significant—and least understood aspects of his presidency." Even Reagan's call for arms increases were in accord with his belief, which he had enunciated since the early 1960s, that "the aim of his arms buildup was to attain deep cuts in nuclear weapons."[21]

Nuclear abolitionism found wider public support than many other peace movements because of a widespread abhorrence of the effects of atomic weapons and the sense that nuclear deterrence was a problematic solution at best. The absurdity of mutual vulnerability—that idea that security depended on leaving a nation open to destruction—was matched by skepticism about spending tens of billions of dollars on additional weapons systems that would only improve security at the margins, if at all. The emergence of parity highlighted long-standing fears and concerns about the nuclear age; if these weapons no longer had any conceivable political or military use, perhaps it was time to purge them from the planet.

Nuclear Taboo

A related critique of the mutual vulnerability and nuclear superiority responses to parity is that deterrence cannot, by itself, explain the nonuse of nuclear weapons after they were first used by the United States against Japan in August 1945. For one thing, the United States did not use nuclear weapons against its adversaries after the end of World War II. It possessed a nuclear monopoly against the Soviets during the Berlin blockade but abstained from using them. It enjoyed a nuclear superiority throughout the 1950s and into the early 1960s, an edge that by some estimates gave the United States a first-strike capability. After the attack on Japan, however, neither the United States nor any other nuclear power used its weapons against nonnuclear adversaries. This was not due to a lack of opportunity or support for such actions at the highest policy levels. During the bloody Korean War, talk on the US side of using nuclear weapons produced concern and even outrage at home and abroad; the 1953 armistice was signed before such threats could be carried out. During the Vietnam War, the United States at times considered, but eventually turned away from, using nuclear weapons, despite the military advantages it could have brought.

Political scientist Nina Tannenwald has argued that moral revulsion of using nuclear weapons among the wider public restrained policymakers in ways that supplemented, and even went beyond, deterrence.[22] This emerging taboo against using nuclear weapons ever again arguably crystallized in the age of nuclear parity, when the ideas of taboo and mutual vulnerability came together to make nuclear use among "civilized" nations inconceivable. Parity only highlighted the absurdity of any responsible leader advocating the use of these weapons.

Obsolescence of War

War, according to the international affairs scholar John Mueller, is nothing more than an idea.[23] And, like all ideas, it is created in a cultural, political, and sociological context that can change over time. During the second part of the twentieth century, the idea of great power war was increasingly seen in Europe and other parts of the developed world as obsolete. Similar to dueling and slavery a century earlier, an institution or practice that had been seen as beneficial and important increasingly came to be seen as anachronistic and even repulsive. In this explanation, it was not nuclear weapons that kept the peace: the peace would have been maintained even in a nonnuclear world. Furthermore, the status and prestige that was previously accorded to war was now given to economic success.

According to this analysis, the endless, divisive debates over the minutiae of arms control negotiations were a waste of time. Neither the United States nor the Soviet Union had the stomach for a conventional war with each other, to say nothing of a nuclear war. While these ideological rivals might trade insults and fight limited proxy wars in the developing world, by the 1970s there was almost no conceivable scenario that might lead to a nuclear exchange. There was simply nothing to be gained from great power war; the real action in international politics was now elsewhere.

The Rise of Globalization

The fourth response was the most inchoate and least noticed, with the least policy exposure during the 1970s. In the long run, however, it had the most significant consequences for US global policy. Coinciding with the emergence of parity—a condition that many argued rendered nuclear weapons militarily useless and politically impotent—was the rise of a new international system, with new actors, new norms, and, most important, new metrics for power. According to this view of the world, ideas, innovation, technology, and culture were more likely to shape world politics than arms control agreements or the nuclear balance between the superpowers. What happened in Wall Street, Hollywood, Silicon Valley, or even Napa Valley was as important, and sometimes even more important, to America's position in the world than decisions made in Washington, D.C. What Harvard professor Joseph Nye termed "soft power," in other words, was more likely than nuclear armaments to determine the outcome of the struggle with the Soviet Union.

The increasing reach of global capital markets, the spread of popular culture via Hollywood, the popularity of consumer-oriented capitalism, and the power of new innovations and technology were just some of the "soft power" phenomena that transformed the world economy after the 1970s, and with it the political landscape. These phenomena, more than nuclear weapons, were game changers for states looking to improve their global political position after the 1970s. Nations that had flirted with nuclear weapons in the past—among them Taiwan, South Korea, Brazil, Argentina, and Indonesia—now focused on spurring economic growth and integrating into the world economy. Under the new metrics of power, the economic dynamism of a "Pacific tiger" counted for a lot more than simply possessing a weapon that translated into little useable power on the world stage.

The much-anticipated arrival of nuclear parity between the United States and the Soviet Union during the 1970s unleashed a furious and often vitriolic debate over US grand strategy during the Cold War. The battlegrounds for these fights seem esoteric and strange from our current perspective. They were often dominated by technical questions concerning specific weapons systems. Should the Soviet fighter-bomber Backfire be classified as a tactical or strategic weapon? Were cruise missiles that were fired from airplanes qualitatively different than those fired from the sea or ground? Was Washington and its command-and-control facilities vulnerable to a decapitating first strike? Should hundreds of billions of dollars be spent on strategic nuclear weapons, not to achieve superiority but to enhance the stability of deterrence? Would strategic defenses undermine this stability, even if there was some question as to whether they would work? Perhaps the most fascinating aspect of this period is that so much time and intellectual energy of some of our most esteemed policymakers and strategists was consumed by these questions.

It is not even clear that these were the most important nuclear policy issues at the time. As nuclear parity was achieved and then institutionalized by a remarkable series of arms control treaties between the United States and the Soviet Union during the 1970s, the decade witnessed increasing pressure on the global nonproliferation regime. India detonated a "peaceful" nuclear device, and, in response, Pakistan responded with a crash program that also spawned the A. Q. Khan black market in nuclear technology. Iran and Iraq both flirted with weapons programs, as did many other countries, including Argentina, Brazil, South Korea, North Korea, and Taiwan. It is not that this issue, which dominates our current policy landscape, received no policy or scholarly attention at the time. It is striking, however, how much more attention was paid to strategic arms issues between the United States and the Soviet Union.

What then are we to make of the reactions to nuclear parity? These debates are less interesting for their assessments of specific questions than for what they say about how leading thinkers and statesmen thought about how the world worked and what America's role should be. The mutual vulnerability school argued that the nuclear revolution had fundamentally altered the laws of great power politics and statecraft. Unlike the past, the state could no longer depend on its most powerful and innovative weapons to pursue its goals in the world. The new landscape of international relations demanded a new response: self-restraint, respect for the interests of one's adversaries, and devotion to international treaties. This viewpoint sought to freeze the status quo, both militarily and politically, in order to avoid the risks of nuclear war. Most radically, the stability of the new system demanded accepting and even embracing openness to catastrophic destruction. This set of ideas became so enmeshed in conventional wisdom that it is easy to forget how novel and counterintuitive this framework for understanding world politics actually was.

The superiority school did not dispute that the nuclear revolution had changed international politics in important ways. In their view, however, this did not include suspending the laws of world politics or what many saw as a moral, political, and ideological duty to challenge the Soviet

Union. While many intellectuals dismissed this view, there is a strong argument to be made that policymakers on both sides of the rivalry never abandoned their search for nuclear primacy.

Who was right? This questions turns on what brought about the peaceful end of the Cold War, largely to the advantage of the United States. The mutual vulnerability school argues that the stability of deterrence allowed Gorbachev's Soviet Union to transform itself without fear that the United States would militarily exploit the situation. The nuclear superiority school argues that the arms race exposed weaknesses in the Soviet economy that eventually bankrupted their empire. Both views have some merit, but both may have missed the larger, more profound changes in international politics that have marked the past four decades.

The third set of responses—the idea that tectonic forces beyond nuclear deterrence were shaping the global order—may be the most compelling. Consider behavior in the nuclear field. First, despite the pressures on the nonproliferation regime during the 1970s, what is striking is how few eligible states did develop nuclear weapons. And those that did eschewed either local nuclear superiority or even secure second-strike strategies. Several embraced minimal deterrence, believing that simply possessing a few nuclear weapons would be enough to keep their adversaries from attacking. Even China and India, which could build far larger and more sophisticated nuclear forces if they chose to, maintain relatively small forces and have not been drawn into either regional nuclear arms races or a nuclear arms race with the United States. How might strategists from the 1970s view the embrace by policymakers of nuclear abolitionism—an idea that was considered fringe in polite mutual vulnerability and nuclear superiority circles?[24]

Understanding the responses to nuclear parity within the United States during the 1970s is important for more than just academic purposes. Advocates and disciples of both the mutual vulnerability and nuclear superiority schools continue to play a large, even dominating, role in debates about US global policy. It is important to recognize the role the earlier debates over parity and deterrence had on their grand strategies and worldview. It is even more important to recognize that there were alternative frameworks even then with which to analyze the emergence of parity, views that may have been more effective at explaining the great changes that began to transform global politics during the 1970s and that shape our world today.

[7]

Same as It Ever Was?

Nuclear Weapons in the Twenty-First Century

Many scholars and practitioners share the view that nuclear proliferation and its effect on US national security constitutes the gravest threat facing the United States, that it is worse than ever before, and that new, more effective policies are needed to confront the problem. At the same time, the history of nuclear proliferation—in particular, the history of the Cold War—has little to tell us about contemporary nuclear dangers and possible policy solutions. According to this view, the so-called Long Peace offers few meaningful lessons that can be applied to the complex and dangerous world we face today.

This view, which I term "nuclear alarmism," transcends partisan differences. During their 2004 presidential debates, for example, candidates John Kerry and George W. Bush agreed on one point: that "nuclear proliferation" was "the most serious threat" to US security.[1] Four years later, Republican presidential candidate John McCain declared: "No problem we face poses a greater threat to us and the world than nuclear proliferation."[2] Candidate Barack Obama called it "the most significant foreign policy issue that we confront."[3] During a presidential debate before the New Hampshire primary, moderator Charles Gibson asserted, "The next president of the United States may have to deal with a nuclear attack on an American city. . . . The best nuclear experts in the world say there's a 30 percent chance in the next 10 years . . . Graham Allison at Harvard says it's over 50 percent."[4] In a nonscientific poll of leading security experts conducted by Republican Senator Richard Lugar of Indiana in 2005, 62 percent of the respondents (49 of 79) said that the chance of a nuclear attack somewhere in the world over the next ten years was between 10 and 50 percent. Only one respondent put the probability at 0 percent.[5] As William Potter and Gaukhar Mukhatzhanova observe, "today it is hard to find an analyst or commentator on nuclear proliferation who is not pessimistic about the future."[6]

Many experts contend that this terrifying new world bears little resemblance to that of the past. In the words of expert David Von Drehle, "During the Cold War, the world's security was built on a handful of interlocking truths that were dreadful to contemplate, but blessedly stable . . . every brick of that deterrent edifice is now crumbling."[7] The success of Cold War deterrence is less relevant today, however, because "the world is no longer a stand-off of the titans."[8] Or, as one expert claims, "these are really twenty-first-century nuclear challenges that we're attempting to address using twentieth-century post–World War II international agreements."[9] In 2007 four prominent former policymakers, two Republicans and two Democrats, warned that "unless urgent new actions are taken, the U.S. soon will be compelled to enter a new nuclear era that will be more precarious, psychologically disorienting, and economically costly than Cold War deterrence."[10] Writer David Ignatius observes, "We inhabit a world that makes the Cold War seem like the good old days."[11]

Should nuclear alarmism be accepted at face value? In my view, the answer is no: its claims are overstated and, in some cases, wrong, emerging from a poor understanding of the history of nuclear proliferation and nonproliferation. Nuclear alarmism is based on four myths. The first myth is that today's nuclear threats are new and more dangerous than those of the past. They are not. The second myth is that, unlike today, during the Cold War nuclear weapons stabilized international politics. In fact the record was mixed. The third myth conflates the history of the nuclear arms race with the geopolitical and ideological competition between the Soviet Union and the United States. This is an oversimplified portrayal of the Cold War. The fourth myth is that the bipolar military rivalry during the Cold War was the only force driving nuclear proliferation in the decades following the end of World War II. This ignores other important drivers of postwar international relations, such as decolonization, questions surrounding the political status of postwar Germany, and regional security issues.

My argument is not based on Kenneth Waltz's contention that "more may be better," nor do I suggest that nuclear proliferation is not an important policy challenge.[12] By overreacting to current dangers while mischaracterizing those of the past, however, nuclear alarmists drive misguided policies that could threaten international stability and US interests today and in the future. The world was far more dangerous in the decades following the end of World War II than it is today, and the challenges presented by nuclear weapons were more complex. There are important lessons to be learned from this history. Current proliferation challenges have deep roots in the past, and for US policies to be successful, an understanding of this history is vital.

This chapter is divided into three sections. The first section presents the nuclear alarmists' main argument. The second section debunks the four myths perpetuated by nuclear alarmists and offers a history of postwar nuclear politics that is more nuanced. The conclusion considers some of the lessons of this new interpretation and suggests changes in how the scholarly and policymaking communities might think about nuclear nonproliferation policy today and in the future.

Nuclear Alarmism and the Second Nuclear Age

Nuclear alarmists argue that (1) the spread of atomic weapons has become more likely and more dangerous, and (2) that it is the greatest threat to both US national security and international security. Nuclear proliferation, in what has been labeled the "second nuclear age," is more likely for two reasons: the end of bipolarity and the emergence of so-called tipping points.[13] During the Cold War, international politics were dominated by two superpowers of nearly equal military strength, the United States and the Soviet Union. Both constructed large alliance systems and offered security guarantees to their client states, in some cases backed by a promise to use nuclear weapons if the client was attacked. Given the bipolar structure of the international system and the relatively equal strength of each side's alliances, small or medium powers had little incentive to develop or acquire nuclear forces.

The end of the Cold War and bipolarity following the collapse of the Soviet Union in 1989 increased states' incentives to acquire nuclear weapons. As David Ignatius writes, "the moment of maximum danger, [Herman] Kahn warned, would be in moving from a bipolar to a multipolar world."[14] According to political scientist Benjamin Frankel, "bipolarity inhibits the spread of nuclear weapons while multipolarity induces their proliferation." Frankel predicted that in the post–Cold War era "nuclear arms proliferation will likely intensify" and "the owners of these weapons will likely brandish them more openly to advance their political objectives." He warned that their "inherent complexity . . . dooms multipolar systems to instability, making them susceptible to crisis and war." Thus, the "end of bipolarity means that superpower guarantees—the most effective instrument to moderate the effects of systemic characteristics—will be reduced and weakened."[15]

Although the predictions of Kahn, Frankel, and others have yet to materialize, many observers believe that it is only a matter of time before the disappearance of bipolarity leads to more states having nuclear weapons. As scholar Stephen Rosen notes, the future could lead to "multipolar nuclear interactions," a phenomena that "we're totally unfamiliar with. We're used to dealing with a bipolar U.S.-Soviet nuclear deterrent relationship which was stable over a number of decades."[16] Many experts believe this change will be disastrous. According to a senior US Defense Department official from the George W. Bush administration, "we know how nukes worked in a two-player situation (the US and Russia), or even on the Indian subcontinent. But we don't know how it works in a multiplayer situation. . . . The risk of catastrophic misuse rises dramatically. I don't think the international community has addressed it with sufficient urgency."[17]

The second reason nuclear alarmists believe that proliferation is more likely is because the world has reached a potential nuclear tipping point. Changes in the international environment, starting with the end of the Cold War and accelerating after the September 11, 2001, terrorist attacks, have tempted nations that once foreswore nuclear weapons to reconsider their utility. These alarmists fear that even democratic states and signatories to the NPT might begin to pursue "hedging" strategies including developing nuclear weapons capability.[18]

Many nuclear alarmists assert that a nuclear "chain reaction" is imminent. Former US State Department director of policy planning Mitchell Reiss claims, "In ways both fast and slow, we may very soon be approaching a nuclear 'tipping point,' where many countries may decide to acquire nuclear arsenals on short notice, thereby triggering a proliferation epidemic."[19] A leading group of nonproliferation experts agrees, also arguing that "the world has arrived at a nuclear tipping point."[20] Says former senator and current chair of the non-profit Nuclear Threat Initiative Sam Nunn, "We are at the tipping point. . . . And we are headed in the wrong direction."[21] In other words, actual or threatened proliferation, particularly by one or two states within an unstable region such as East Asia or the Middle East, might cause governments that previously eschewed nuclear weapons to reconsider their decisions. If North Korea's nuclear program is not eliminated, for example, policymakers in Japan, South Korea, and Taiwan might feel little choice but to develop a nuclear capability. Australia, Indonesia, and Malaysia might then feel a need to do so as well. A nuclear Iran might drive Egypt, Saudi Arabia, and Turkey into the nuclear club.

Nuclear alarmists also contend that proliferation is a greater threat to US interests than it was in the past and that it therefore demands a more vigorous US response. The first nuclear age, according to nuclear alarmists, was a challenging but ultimately predictable period in history. As dangerous as the Soviet Union was, its rulers were rational. Its weapons of choice were bombs delivered by airplanes, submarines, or missiles.

Most important, the Soviets and the Americans were constrained by their mutual vulnerability to devastating nuclear attacks. Both sides understood that pushing too far risked a catastrophic war.

According to nuclear alarmists, the second nuclear age is less predictable, involves more complex and dangerous rivalries, and includes new and far more terrifying actors than existed during the Cold War. According to one commentator, "in the first nuclear age, centered on Europe and the cold war, we were on familiar ground. The second, though, is happening across a swath of Asia and is steeped in historic grudges, suppressed national pride and regional ambitions that the West poorly understands, let alone controls."[22] To many observers, the Cold War—with its stable list of players and its known conventional and nuclear arsenals—has little relevance to today's nuclear world, and offers few, if any, lessons for the future.

During the first nuclear age, concerns about nuclear proliferation were secondary to other strategic and political issues. Controlling vertical proliferation, or the strategic arms competition between the Soviet Union and the United States, was seen as more important. And even though nuclear proliferation was officially frowned on by the United States, policymakers did not go to great lengths to force Cold War allies (including France, Great Britain, Israel, Pakistan, and South Africa) out of the nuclear business. On balance, the support these states provided in the geopolitical struggle against the Soviet Union outweighed US concerns about nuclear proliferation. This approach, according to nuclear alarmists, is no longer acceptable.

The Cold War, to these observers, was a Long Peace.[23] As author Michael Dobbs writes, "while U.S. leaders hated the idea of their communist adversaries possessing the bomb, Washington at least trusted Moscow and Beijing to act in their own self-interest and refrain from blowing up the entire planet."[24] Nuclear weapons stabilized international politics during the Cold War, preventing political disagreements between the United States and the Soviet Union from escalating into armed conflict; few (if any) political goals were worth the risk of mutual annihilation. Since the "cold-war world was a bipolar world, stabilized by a nuclear balance between two superpowers," columnist Thomas Friedman has opined, it was far less frightening than today's nuclear environment.[25]

Today's "rogue" states and terrorist organizations, the nuclear alarmists argue, may not be as deterrable as the Soviets and the Americans were during the first nuclear age. Their leaders may not be rational; they might value human life so little that they would be willing to use nuclear weapons despite the threat of retaliation; or they could develop nonconventional and nontraceable ways of delivering nuclear weapons.

Dobbs argues, "Four decades later, the world is in an infinitely more complicated—and in some ways more dangerous—place than it was during the Cuban missile crisis. Back then we knew who the enemy was and where he would be most likely to strike. These days, we cannot be sure who the enemy is or who possesses the power to destroy worlds."[26]

Nuclear Alarmism: Four Myths

In this section I examine the four myths on which nuclear alarmism is grounded. In addition, I demonstrate that the alarmists' mischaracterization of the nuclear past leads them to advocate policies that potentially threaten not only international stability but US national interests.

Old Threats in New Clothing

The three threats alarmists focus on—rogue regimes, tipping points, and nuclear terrorism—are not new problems and are often overstated, especially compared with the apocalyptic challenges confronting the world following the atomic bombing of Japan in 1945. In addition, alarmists often mischaracterize the past, especially the so-called Long Peace, while conflating nuclear history with Cold War history and Cold War history with post–World War II history.

Rogue States

Rogue states are seen as those that participate in unsavory behavior: violating international norms, threatening violence against their neighbors, supporting terrorist organizations, and committing human rights violations against their citizens. Before the 2003 US invasion, Saddam Hussein's Iraq was identified by the Bush administration as a rogue state, a definition that is still applied to Iran and North Korea.

Nuclear alarmists assert that the threats posed by rogue states are unprecedented. Consider this assessment of the likely consequences of a nuclear Iran: "Its leaders are theologically motivated and believe Israel should be wiped off the map. It is the chief global sponsor of terrorism through groups such as Hezbollah and Hamas. Middle East experts believe a nuclear-armed Iran would soon be followed by Egypt, Saudi Arabia, and Turkey, and perhaps others as well."[27] In this view, rogue states do not adhere to the logic of nuclear deterrence that kept the Cold War from becoming "hot." As the scholar and former Bust administration deputy assistant secretary of defense Keith Payne has claimed, "we believed we had great insight into the thinking of the Soviet leadership, could communicate well with its officials, and that those leaders ultimately would behave in well-informed and predictable ways. Consequently, we could be wholly confident deterrence would 'work.' But today, there is no basis for comparable faith with regard to rogue regimes."[28] To some nuclear alarmists, this perceived unpredictability justifies the use of preemptive strikes against rogue states seeking atomic weapons. Democratic Defense Department officials Ashton Carter and William Perry have written, "Should the United States allow a country openly hostile to it and armed with nuclear weapons to perfect an intercontinental ballistic missile capable of delivering nuclear weapons to U.S. soil? We think not."[29]

Neither the existence of rogue regimes nor the fear they inspire, however, is new. Analysts have been deeply worried about nuclear weapons falling into the hands of noxious regimes since the start of the atomic age. Fred Iklé expressed this concern in 1965: "People fanatically dedicated to some revolutionary cause may have no concern for the survival of their country. . . . To carry out such 'nuclear anarchism' or acts of personal revenge, modern delivery systems would not be needed; it would suffice if the weapons could be sneaked close enough to a target clandestinely."[30]

Throughout the post–World War II period, analysts worried that proliferation among small or unstable countries could increase the "likelihood of nuclear war."[31] Such "deterministic" assessments rested on the assumption that these countries "would act less maturely with nuclear weapons under their belt, thus inevitably leading to regional, and in turn global, instability."[32] Yet no nuclear crisis involving a small country has remotely approached the danger and risk levels seen during confrontations between the superpowers during the Cold War.

More important, contemporary analysts often forget that two of the United States' Communist adversaries, whose rogue status by current definitions was unparalleled in the atomic age, pursued nuclear weapons: the Soviet Union and the People's Republic of China. The United States dreaded the Soviet Union's acquisition of the bomb. Stalin's Soviet Union was both a murderous and secretive regime: it violated international norms and pursued aggressive foreign policies even before it tested an atomic bomb. The Soviet Union's behavior after its August 1949 atomic test seemed to realize the worst fears of the Harry S. Truman administration when Moscow's client, North Korea, attacked South Korea without any apparent concern over the US response. During the winter of 1950–51, the United States was convinced that nuclear weapons had so emboldened the Soviet Union that a third world war might be unavoidable.[33] In 1953, however, fighting on the Korean Peninsula ended and tensions with the Soviets eased. Although the Soviet Union's nuclearization would remain a serious threat, in time the United States developed policies to cope with this challenge.

In 1964, when the PRC tested its first nuclear device, China was perhaps the most "rogue" state in modern history. Mao Zedong's domestic policies caused the death of tens of millions of China's citizens. Moreover, he had pursued an aggressive foreign policy before the atomic test. Examples include: attacking India, fighting the United States directly in Korea and by proxy in Vietnam (where it armed a nonstate actor, the Viet Cong), and threatening war over Taiwan. Mao made a series of highly irresponsible statements about the PRC surviving and even thriving in a nuclear war. No country in the post–World War II period—not Iraq, Iran, or even North Korea—has given US policymakers more reason to fear its nuclearization than China.[34]

Within five years of the PRC's nuclear test, however, the United States and China initiated a covert dialogue. In less than a decade, they began an anti-Soviet alliance that put great pressure on the USSR and helped to bring the Cold War to an end. Nuclear weapons did not make China more hostile. If anything, its foreign policies became less aggressive and more mature over time. Today China has one of the most restrained and responsible nuclear-force postures and deployment policies of any nuclear power; it maintains a minimal deterrent under tight command and control while eschewing a first-use doctrine.[35]

That Iran—surrounded by rivals with nuclear ambitions and singled out by the United States, the largest military power in the world—has an interest in nuclear weapons is not surprising. Even assessments that view Iranian behavior as a challenge to US interests in the Middle East do not consider the regime as being as threatening as the PRC was during the 1960s. As analyst Shahram Chubin writes, "[Iran] is not overtly confrontational or given to wild swings in behavior or to delusional goals; it has not denounced arms control treaties to which it formally adheres; and there is evidence of pluralism and some debate within the country."[36] Nuclear weapons could make Iran more aggressive. Or, as with China, they could provide international legitimacy and security, making Iran less aggressive than it has been. As one analyst put it in 2009, "if anything, Iran might find that possession of a nuclear weapon actually diminishes its options in the Middle East and forces it to act with greater restraint."[37] A deeper understanding of nuclear history and the underlying geopolitical circumstances Iran faces makes the prospect that it would take actions (such as supplying Hamas or Hezbollah with nuclear weapons) that could invite its own destruction highly unlikely.[38]

Nuclear weapons are often seen as particularly desirable to countries that are located in unstable regions or that acquired statehood in ways that make them feel vulnerable to claims against their legitimacy. Before acquiring nuclear weapons, many nuclear powers faced strong challenges to their security and legitimacy. These states include India and Pakistan, born of a violent civil war and bitter partition; the PRC, unrecognized by the United States until 1979; Israel; apartheid-era South Africa; and, of course, an artificially divided Korea. US regional security dynamics and the historical origins of the state in question may be more important than regime type in determining whether a state will want nuclear weapons and how it might behave once it acquires them. For example, the nuclearization by Germany, Japan, or especially Taiwan—all open, tolerant, market-oriented liberal democracies—might destabilize regional and world politics and undermine US interests more than Iran's or North Korea's nuclear weapons programs.

Tipping Points

One of the greatest fears of nuclear alarmists is that if a key state acquires nuclear weapons others will follow. This idea of a nuclear tipping point, chain reaction, or "domino" effect, however, is by no means new. Consider this headline—"Many Nations Ready to Break into Nuclear Club"—from a front-page article in the *Washington Post* in June 1981.[39] Articles with similar titles can be found from almost every year since at least the early 1960s.

Fears of a tipping point were especially acute in the aftermath of China's 1964 detonation of their first atomic bomb: it was predicted that India, Indonesia, and Japan might follow, with consequences worldwide, as "Israel, Sweden, Germany, and other potential nuclear countries far from China and India would be affected by proliferation in Asia."[40] A US government document identified "at least eleven nations (India, Japan, Israel, Sweden, West Germany, Italy, Canada, Czechoslovakia, East Germany, Rumania, and Yugoslavia)" with the capacity to go nuclear, a number that would soon "grow substantially" to include "South Africa, the United Arab Republic, Spain, Brazil and Mexico."[41] A top secret, blue-ribbon committee established to craft the US response contended that "the [1964] Chinese nuclear explosion has increased the urgency and complexity of this problem by creating strong pressures to develop independent nuclear forces, which, in turn, could strongly influence the plans of other potential nuclear powers."[42]

These predictions were largely wrong. In 1985 the National Intelligence Council noted that for "almost thirty years the Intelligence Community has been writing about which nations might next get the bomb." All of these estimates based their largely pessimistic and ultimately incorrect estimates on factors such as the increased "access to fissile materials," improved technical capabilities, the likelihood of "chain reactions," or a "scramble" to proliferation when "even one additional state demonstrates a nuclear capability." The 1985 report goes on: "The most striking characteristic of the present-day nuclear proliferation scene is that, despite the alarms rung by past Estimates, no additional overt proliferation of nuclear weapons has actually occurred since China tested its bomb in 1964." Although "some proliferation of nuclear explosive capabilities and other major proliferation-related developments have taken place in the past two decades," they did not have "the damaging, system-wide impacts that the Intelligence community generally anticipated they would."[43]

In his analysis of more than sixty years of failed efforts to accurately predict nuclear proliferation, Moeed Yusuf concludes that "the pace of proliferation has been much slower than anticipated by most." The majority of countries suspected of trying to obtain nuclear weapons "never even came close to crossing the threshold. In fact, most did not even initiate a weapons program." If all the countries that were considered prime suspects over the past sixty years had developed nuclear weapons, "the world would have at least 19 nuclear powers today."[44] As Potter and Mukhatzhanova argue, government and academic experts frequently "exaggerated the scope and pace of nuclear weapons proliferation."[45]

Nor is there compelling evidence that a nuclear proliferation chain reaction will ever occur. Rather, the pool of potential proliferators has been shrinking. Proliferation pressures were far greater during the Cold War. In the 1960s, at least twenty-one countries either had or were considering nuclear weapons research programs. Today only nine countries are known to have nuclear weapons. Belarus, Brazil, Kazakhstan, Libya, South Africa, Sweden, and Ukraine have dismantled their weapons programs. Rogue states that are/were a great concern to US policymakers—Iran, Iraq, Libya, and North Korea—began their nuclear weapons programs before the Cold War ended.[46] Syria is perhaps the only nation that may have begun a new nuclear weapons program since the demise of the Soviet Union in 1991.[47] Ironically, by focusing on the threat of rogue states, policymakers may have underestimated the potentially far more destabilizing effect of proliferation in "respectable" states such as Germany, Japan, South Korea, and Taiwan.

Nuclear Terrorism

The possibility of a terrorist nuclear attack on the United States is widely believed to be a grave, even apocalyptic, threat and a likely possibility, a belief supported by numerous statements by public officials. Since the collapse of the Soviet Union, "the inevitability of the spread of nuclear terrorism" and of a "successful terrorist attack" have been taken for granted.[48]

There is no doubt that we should develop well-thought out and coherent policies to reduce the risk of a nonstate actor using nuclear weapons. In particular, the rise of the A. Q. Khan nuclear technology network should give pause.[49] But again, the news is not as grim as nuclear alarmists would suggest. Much has already been done to secure the supply of nuclear materials, and relatively simple steps can produce further improvements. Moreover, there are reasons to doubt both the capabilities and even the interest many terrorist groups have in detonating a nuclear device on US soil. As Adam Garfinkle writes, "the threat of nuclear terrorism is very remote."[50]

Experts disagree on whether nonstate actors have the scientific, engineering, financial, natural resource, security, and logistical capacities to build a nuclear bomb from scratch. According to terrorism expert Robin Frost, the danger of a "nuclear black market" and loose nukes from Russia may be overstated. Even if a terrorist group did acquire a nuclear weapon, delivering and detonating it against a US target would present tremendous technical and logistical difficulties.[51] Finally, the feared nexus between terrorists and rogue regimes may be exaggerated. As nuclear proliferation expert Joseph Cirincione argues, states such as Iran and North Korea are "not the most likely sources for terrorists since their stockpiles, if any, are small and exceedingly precious, and hence well-guarded."[52] Chubin states that there "is no reason to believe that Iran today, any more than Sadaam Hussein earlier, would transfer WMD [weapons of mass destruction] technology to terrorist groups like al-Qaida or Hezbollah."[53]

Nuclear expert Michael Levi demonstrates that effective planning can prevent catastrophe. For nuclear terrorists, what "can go wrong might go wrong, and when it comes to nuclear terrorism, a broader, integrated defense, just like controls at the source of weapons and materials, can multiply, intensify, and compound the possibilities of terrorist failure, possibly driving terrorist groups to reject nuclear terrorism altogether." The dangers from a terrorist acquiring a nuclear weapon are based on an inaccurate image of an "infallible ten-foot-tall enemy." This type of alarmism, writes Levi, impedes the development of thoughtful strategies that could deter, prevent, or mitigate a terrorist attack: "Worst-case estimates have their place, but the possible failure-averse, conservative, resource-limited five-foot-tall nuclear terrorist, who is subject not only to the laws of physics but also to Murphy's law of nuclear terrorism, needs to become just as central to our evaluations of strategies."[54]

A 2008 study by terrorism expert Anne Stenersen contends that al-Qaida's interest in acquiring and using nuclear weapons may be overstated. Stenersen claims that "looking at statements and activities at various levels within the al-Qaida network, it becomes clear that the network's interest in using unconventional means is in fact much lower than commonly thought."[55] She further states that "CBRN [chemical, biological, radiological, and nuclear] weapons do not play a central part in al-Qaida's strategy."[56] In the 1990s, members of al-Qaida debated whether to obtain a nuclear device. Those in favor sought the weapons primarily to deter a US attack on al-Qaida's bases in Afghanistan. This assessment reveals an organization unlike that envisioned by nuclear alarmists who imagine terrorists obsessed with using nuclear weapons against the United States regardless of the consequences. Stenersen asserts, "Although there have been various reports stating that al-Qaida attempted to buy nuclear material in the nineties, and possibly recruited skilled scientists, it appears that al-Qaida central have not dedicated a lot of time or effort to developing a high-end CBRN capability. . . . Al-Qaida central never had a coherent strategy to obtain CBRN: instead, its members were divided on the issue, and there was an awareness that militarily effective weapons were extremely difficult to obtain."[57] Most terrorist groups "assess nuclear terrorism through the lens of their political goals and may judge that it does not advance their interests."[58] Frost has written that "the risk of nuclear terrorism, especially true nuclear terrorism employing bombs powered by nuclear fission, is overstated, and that popular wisdom on the topic is significantly flawed."[59]

US officials have worried about nuclear terrorism, the unconventional delivery of nuclear weapons, and the problem of "no return address," since the dawn of the atomic age. As early as 1946, Edward Condon, a prominent US nuclear scientist, warned, "In any room where a file case can be stored, in any district of a great city, near any key building or installation, a determined effort can secrete a bomb capable of killing a hundred thousand people and laying waste to every ordinary structure within a mile."[60] The Central Intelligence Agency began warning about the danger of a nuclear weapon being smuggled into the United States only months after the Soviets detonated a nuclear device.[61]

An October 1962 US government study suggested that the future would hold complex and unforeseen nuclear threats, including those from rogue states and nonstate actors: "Nuclear weapons will become increasingly economical" and may become available by "theft, commercial purchase, or diplomatic trading." New nuclear powers would not need sophisticated strategic forces or ballistic missiles: "A fishing boat or a cheap airplane might have been an adequate means of delivery for, say, the Algerian Nationalists against Marseilles, or Castro's Cuba against Baltimore or Miami."[62] An aide to National Security Advisor Kissinger wrote, "Nuclear raw materials . . . if captured by terrorists, can be made into crude atomic bombs or exploded to cause contamination. (This is a real threat, not science fiction.)"[63] In 1970 the National Security Council warned of "terrorist actions against nuclear installations, or involving nuclear material," emphasizing the psychological effects of the "panic" that would follow such an attack, and arguing that "we are not in a very strong position" to deal with these situations.[64] At the time, worries over nuclear terrorism, dirty bombs, and covert weapons did not receive more prominence because the potential of a nuclear war with the Soviets or the PRC was considered far greater and more likely to be devastating.

Even some of the current fears surrounding a nuclear explosion with "no return address" are similar to those from the Cold War. During the 1960s, for example, US policymakers worried that France might use its nuclear weapons against the Soviet Union—which might not be able to determine the origin of the attack—as a trigger to force the United States to launch a retaliatory strategic nuclear weapons attack in support of its ally.[65] Eisenhower's administration even exploited elements of this logic to its advantage, as its "massive retaliation" strategy would have held the Soviet Union responsible for any nuclear attack emerging from the Communist world, including China. This may have forced the Soviets to try to rein in their more aggressive neighbors, alienating China's leaders and fostering the Sino-Soviet rift.[66] Today a similar strategy might be effective against Iran; that is, by letting the Iranians know that if they develop nuclear weapons, they would be held responsible for any suspicious atomic detonation against the United States or its allies anytime or anywhere.

Nuclear Weapons and the Long Peace

The so-called Long Peace was not as peaceful or stable as nuclear alarmists claim. During the Cold War, the United States, the Soviet Union, and their allies spent trillions of dollars on their rivalry, fought proxy wars and overthrew governments, and dramatically transformed their domestic institutions for five decades, in what many considered a life-and-death struggle. The competition was not predictable or free of crisis. To give just a few examples: between 1950 and 1953, a civil war in an area of questionable geopolitical significance to the United Sates, the Korean Peninsula, threatened to escalate into a global conflagration, in large measure because of the acquisition of nuclear weapons by the Soviet Union. In the 1950s the Soviets issued nuclear threats against the British and the French during the Suez Crisis, and the United States threatened the PRC over disputes in the Taiwan Strait. Between 1958 and 1962, the United States and the Soviet Union engaged in a standoff over the isolated city of Berlin, culminating in the Cuban missile crisis.

Even after the emergence of mutual vulnerability during the 1960s, there were periods of marked instability, uncertainty, and danger. Wars in Vietnam and Afghanistan killed hundreds of thousands and threatened to escalate into broader conflicts. In 1963 the United States approached the Soviet Union about a preemptive nuclear attack on the PRC; in 1969 the Soviets approached the Americans with the same proposal. Richard Nixon's administration issued nuclear threats on several occasions. At different times, each superpower received false information—as late as 1979 for the United States and 1983 for the Soviet Union—that its adversary was planning a nuclear attack.

To be sure, the rivalry between the Soviet Union and the United States did not lead to world war. If, however, one defines stability as the absence of crisis, uncertainty, and risk-taking behavior that could lead to war, then this rivalry looks different indeed.[67] On close historical inspection, it can be seen that nuclear weapons often caused and exacerbated dangerous Cold War crises between the superpowers. There were two basic reasons: nuclear weapons affected statecraft in ways that often undermined international stability, and the particular strategies employed by the United States were often the cause of crises that would never have occurred in the prenuclear world.[68]

Nuclear weapons destabilized international politics in several ways during the Cold War that are often overlooked by contemporary alarmists. They nullified the influence of other, more traditional forms of power, such as conventional forces and economic strength, allowing the Soviet Union to minimize the United States' enormous economic, technological, and even "soft power" advantages.[69] Nuclear weapons also changed military calculations in potentially dangerous ways. It has long been understood that in a nuclear environment, the side that strikes first gains an overwhelming military advantage. This meant that strategies of preemption, and even preventive war, were enormously appealing. It was for this reason that both the United States and the Soviet Union considered attacking China's nuclear weapons program before China could deploy a strategic nuclear force.[70] Throughout the 1950s, NATO explicitly grounded its strategy on the advantages of preemption.[71] A military strategy based on a rapid, forceful preemptive strike affords diplomats little time or leeway to end a crisis. Even after the establishment of parity, analysts in both the United States and the Soviet Union supported nuclear-force structures and strategies grounded in maintaining a first-strike capability.[72]

The most destabilizing aspect of nuclear weapons during the Cold War, however, was how the dynamics of a nuclear crisis often emphasized balance-of-resolve considerations over balance-of-power concerns. As Marc Trachtenberg argues, in the prenuclear world, "more or less objective factors—above all, the balance of military power"—helped to determine the outcome of political conflicts. "The weak tended to give way to the strong," and "the military balance gave some indication as to how a dispute would be worked out." In the nuclear world, the likelihood of a state risking the use of nuclear weapons may be more important than the number or types of weapons it possesses. "The side with the greater resolve, the side more willing to run the risk of nuclear war, has the upper hand and will prevail in a showdown," writes Trachtenberg. In such a world, there would be a "great premium on resolve, on risk-taking, and perhaps ultimately on recklessness."[73] Measuring resolve is a more subjective exercise than measuring capabilities, making it easier for either or both sides to miscalculate in a crisis; it also encourages each side to be more rigid than it might otherwise be. As Thomas Schelling put it, one or, more dangerously, both sides might decide to manipulate the risk inherent in a nuclear confrontation to accomplish important political goals.[74] Such a conflict might become a dangerous contest in risk taking that could easily lead to war.

The Berlin Crisis and the Cuban missile crises reveal the importance of balance-of-resolve considerations in understanding how the crises both began and ended. Khrushchev generated four years of crisis by pushing Soviet demands over Berlin's status between 1958 and 1962, despite a strategic balance that overwhelmingly favored the United States.[75] Throughout this period, the Soviet premier believed that "so long as the Soviet Union was the weaker superpower, it had to practice brinkmanship to keep its adversary off balance."[76] In 1961, for example, some believed the United States could carry out a devastating first strike against the Soviets without incurring much damage.[77] Yet, according to Khrushchev, the Soviet Union did not need to fear such an attack because the United States would not risk even one or two Soviet weapons hitting US territory.[78] But US plans, like those of Khrushchev, also counted on the other side backing down. As Secretary of State Rusk stated, "One of the quickest ways to have a nuclear war is to have the two sides persuaded that neither will fight."[79]

Khrushchev's gambits, conceivable only in the nuclear age, nearly forced the stronger and less reckless power to initiate military actions that could have led to either a nuclear war or accepting an overwhelming geopolitical defeat.[80] As Aleksandr Fursenko and Timothy Naftali claim, Khrushchev's brinksmanship would have been a "dangerous strategy at any time in history, but in the nuclear age this approach was potentially suicidal."[81] The Nixon administration also employed nuclear brinksmanship on multiple occasions to achieve policy goals in crises in Vietnam, South Asia, and the Middle East that were far from vital to US national security interests.[82]

This emphasis on resolve and the credibility of commitments often distorted geopolitical calculations in unusual and destabilizing ways. Consider how different the United States' Cold War policy might have been in a wide range of situations in a nonnuclear world. Based on traditional calculations of the balance of power, losing South Korea, Vietnam, or even Berlin may not have been considered disastrous to the United States in a nonnuclear world.[83] None of these entities added much to the United States' material strength, nor would they have augmented the strength of the Communist bloc if they had been lost to the Soviet Union.[84] In each of these crises, however, US policymakers were determined to demonstrate resolve to prove that the United States' commitments to geopolitically important regions were credible.[85] A struggle dominated by resolve rather than capabilities is far more prone to blackmail, miscalculation, and overcommitment. What would a Berlin or Cuban crisis have looked like in a world without nuclear weapons—assuming such a crisis had occurred at all?[86]

The need to demonstrate resolve—the most valued currency of the nuclear age—not only expanded US military commitments, but it also shaped the types of nuclear strategies the United States embraced during the Cold War. To demonstrate the credibility of its commitment to defend its allies, the United States sought nuclear superiority and eschewed (and still does) promises not to use nuclear weapons first. In the absence of this commitment and the strategy that backed it, countries such as Japan, South Korea, Taiwan, and West Germany might have obtained nuclear weapons to guarantee their security. Ensuring that these states remained nonnuclear was an important US objective, as their nuclearization would have deeply unsettled international politics.[87]

This history of the Cold War demonstrates the importance of understanding the particular nuclear strategies that states employ before one can assess the influence of nuclear weapons on world politics. If a state seeks only to protect its homeland, where there is little question of its resolve and interest, its nuclear force requirements may be small and its strategies nonprovocative. A state that seeks to extend its nuclear shield to defend far-flung commitments faces a different calculus. To convince Japan and South Korea to remain nonnuclear, or to protect an allied city deep in enemy territory against superior conventional forces, the United States employed strikingly different forces and strategies. To demonstrate resolve and credibility in places and in situations where it was not obvious its survival was at stake, the United States sought nuclear superiority and embraced strategies that called for the early, massive use of atomic weapons. Not only were these potentially destabilizing and expensive choices, but they encouraged proliferation among nations outside the United States' extended deterrence umbrella.

Politics, Not Weapons

Too often, alarmists focus on how the nature and qualities of nuclear weapons shape the international environment, as if the possession of nuclear bombs, absent political intent, diplomacy, motivations, or particular strategies, drives world politics. For example, nuclear alarmists often fail to fully explore the underlying political and security interests that make Iran and North Korea willing to take extraordinary political risks to acquire the bomb. Much of their analysis emerges from a view of the past that conflates nuclear history with the history of the Cold War.

A widely held view portrays the US-Soviet rivalry largely through the lens of the nuclear arms race. According to this analysis, the Cold War presented a classic security dilemma. In a dangerous world, the United States and the Soviet Union took steps to protect themselves, but each side easily misunderstood the defensive measures taken by the other. Strategies and weapon systems deployed for defensive purposes were frequently seen by a nervous adversary as aggressive and offense oriented, which led to a dangerous, unnecessary, and largely unwanted arms race.[88] Nuclear weapons heightened the security dilemma, because the side that launched weapons first could have tremendous advantages.

In this reading, the Cold War was a tragedy, born from the anarchic nature of international relations that drove a military competition that increased the likelihood of an unwanted and potentially catastrophic war.[89] The only way to dampen this competition was to negotiate arms control treaties that allowed both sides to restrain the deployment of particularly destabilizing weapons without fear that the other side might take advantage.[90] Other observers believe that the anarchic nature of the international system and the intense pressures for survival made it impossible to end this competition, as states would continue to seek ways to achieve military advantage.[91]

Shifting power balances, highlighted by dramatic changes in military technology, no doubt strongly influenced US and Soviet policies and their outcomes.[92] Nuclear weapons changed the international environment, often in profound ways. But the core issues driving Cold War crises were explicit geopolitical (and ideological) clashes of interest between the Soviet Union and the United States, clashes that might have been as sharp in a nonnuclear environment.

Focusing solely or even largely on nuclear weapons to the exclusion of geopolitics, ideology, and diplomacy caricatures both the Cold War and international politics today by draining them of important political and diplomatic components. Even in a nonnuclear world, the superpowers would have disagreed about such important and unresolved geopolitical questions as the postwar status of Germany and Japan or influence in the Middle East. Arms control treaties resulted from improved political conditions between the United States and the Soviet Union. These treaties were motivated as much by a desire to settle outstanding geopolitical questions as to limit arms.[93]

Consider, again, arguably the most dangerous period of the Cold War—the four years that began with Khrushchev's November 1958 ultimatum on Berlin and ended with the Cuban missile crisis in October 1962. Khrushchev was ready to take risks and to exploit balance-of-resolve considerations in a nuclear environment, despite the Soviet Union's strategic inferiority. But to what end? The Soviet Union believed that its vital national interests were threatened by the rise of West Germany's military power, its potential possession of nuclear weapons, and its unwillingness to accept the division of Germany. Combined with related concerns, including a desire to redress the strategic balance, thwart a Chinese challenge to Soviet leadership of the world Communist revolution, and desire to stabilize East Germany, West Germany's emerging power made the Soviets willing to initiate crises and even risk war.[94] Initially, the United States was neither well aware of the intensity of Soviet concerns nor willing to alleviate Soviet worries by taking steps it feared would weaken NATO.[95] Over time, however, the Kennedy administration came to appreciate and even share the Soviet Union's concerns and, as such, to move to guarantee West Germany's nonnuclear status and stabilize the political status quo.[96]

The core geopolitical clash of interests generating hostility between the Soviet Union and the United States was, if not fully resolved, greatly eased, leading to a relaxation of tensions by 1963. The danger of nuclear war decreased dramatically, and despite ongoing differences and conflicts, the superpowers even managed to recognize areas of mutual interest, including slowing nuclear proliferation. This "détente" began well before the two countries achieved strategic parity and almost a decade before the ABM and SALT treaties were signed.[97] Politics, not weapons, were the key drivers of the conflict and its amelioration.

A simplified and misleading view of the Cold War distorts much scholarly analysis of nuclear issues today. Building on Cold War assumptions, both the academic and intelligence communities have long predicted massive increases in the quality and quantity of China's nuclear forces, with one analyst suggesting that the PRC would develop "3,000–5,000 warheads by 2010" and another forecasting the "aggressive deployment of upwards of 1,000 thermonuclear warheads on ICBMs by

2015."[98] As nuclear expert Jeffrey Lewis points out, however, "none of the U.S. intelligence community's dire predictions have come to pass." China's nuclear forces "today look remarkably like they have for decades."[99] India, Israel, and Pakistan have also built and deployed their nuclear forces in a more modest and less aggressive way than most analysts had predicted.[100]

China chose nuclear policies far different from those that the arms race/security dilemma model would have predicted, because a minimal deterrent in a nonready posture under centralized control meets its political and strategic interests. Might Iran pursue a similar path? Not unlike China in the 1960s and 1970s, Iran finds itself in an extraordinarily difficult security situation, surrounded by enemies and nuclear powers. Understanding and perhaps alleviating these pressures might go further toward making the region and the world safer than demanding that Iran cease its nuclear activities.

Postwar Is More Than Cold War

In the midst of the Cuban missile crisis, the most dangerous nuclear event of the Cold War, the authors of a top secret US study reflected on the uncertainties and dangers in the world that had little to do with the bipolar military clash: "A useful exercise is to speculate on the strategic problems the United States would face if the Soviet Union quietly disappeared. . . . It won't; but thinking about it helps to remind us that taming the Soviets in the years to come (or defeating them militarily) would not end our strategic problems. It can also quicken our appreciation that many latent problems are suppressed by the main East-West antagonism, and some may be tardily recognized because of our preoccupation with the central threat."[101]

Scholars and practitioners often assume that the Cold War was the most important factor shaping world politics during the decades following World War II. From a military perspective, it was: from the end of that conflict until the late 1980s two states possessing the most fearsome military power in history confronted each other with varying degrees of intensity and in nearly every part of the world. This conflict, understandably, dominated the concerns of leaders and citizens in both countries, and it casts an enormous shadow over the second half of the twentieth century. It was not the only issue animating international relations, however, nor was it the only factor driving nuclear proliferation.

The United States and the Soviet Union developed nuclear weapons and their ensuing strategies in large part because of their geopolitical rivalry. This fact has prompted many US strategists, policymakers, and scholars to view the entire post–World War II period solely through a Cold

War lens.[102] However, the remaining seven states that developed nuclear weapons as a result of programs begun during the Cold War—France, Great Britain, India, Israel, Pakistan, the People's Republic of China, and South Africa—did so for reasons that went beyond, and at many times had little to do with, the US-Soviet rivalry. Robert Jervis, for example, notes, "The most important change in world politics—decolonization—was one that neither offended nor was engineered by either superpower."[103] The unwinding of empires, European integration, tensions in the Middle East, and the changing balance of power in East Asia and South Asia, while connected to the Cold War, were phenomena that were also important drivers of nuclear proliferation. This assessment supports the position of those who argue that "countries by in large acquire nuclear weapons because of local problems and local threats."[104]

Why, for example, did France and Great Britain develop nuclear weapons when they were under the US nuclear security umbrella? To be sure, they feared the Soviet threat to Western Europe. But they had other security concerns as well.[105] Both countries worried that the United States might abandon Western Europe after World II, leaving them to defend themselves. Moreover, both were concerned about the future political orientation of Germany and wanted to protect themselves against the reemergence of an aggressive regime in Central Europe. Could either state be certain that, at some future time, another expansionist Germany would not emerge, this time armed with nuclear weapons? Both France and Great Britain began their nuclear programs before World War II, possessed empires entailing worldwide security commitments, and perceived themselves as great powers. Both underwent a painful and at times dangerous decolonization process that dominated the concerns of their policymakers as much as, and at times more than, fears of the Soviet Union. Nuclear weapons, French and British policymakers hoped, might preserve their countries' great power status, or at least slow their decline, and provide a measure of independence from the superpowers.

India and Israel, as new states with uncertain legitimacy, unresolved territorial disputes, and troubling regional security problems that would have existed in some form or another even if there had been no Cold War, felt compelled to explore nuclear weapons programs almost from the start of their nationhood. For India, nuclear weapons not only provided security against China and Pakistan, they also allowed it to resist pressure to ally with either the United States or the Soviet Union and to become a leader of the nonaligned world. For Israel, nuclear weapons provided security in the face of hostile, larger neighbors in a world where it had few reliable allies. Largely because India's and Israel's interests in nuclear weapons fell outside a narrowly defined Cold War framework, the United States was unable to offer meaningful security guarantees or persuade either country, despite great efforts, to abandon its weapons programs.

Other states developed nuclear weapons for reasons only tangentially related to the Cold War. Pakistan's weapons program was developed in response to India's. South Africa developed nuclear weapons because, among other things, it was worried about a "possible race war between the apartheid regime and black African nations."[106] Other near-nuclear programs, including those of Argentina, Australia, South Korea, and Taiwan, were motivated as much by regional security issues as by the superpower rivalry. Even states with weapons programs of most concern after the end of the Cold War—Iran, North Korea, and pre-invasion Iraq—began developing them during the Cold War. Few would argue, however, that Cold War logic drove these states toward proliferation.

Even the United States had reasons beyond competing with the Soviet Union for how it deployed nuclear weapons and developed its strategies. At various moments during the postwar decades, Japan, South Korea, Taiwan, and West Germany wanted their own nuclear weapons. Each had unresolved territorial disputes and uneasy relations with its neighbors. Acquisition of nuclear weapons by any of these countries would have been deeply unsettling to friends and foes alike, with potentially troubling consequences for US interests. By providing security commitments (often backed by a promise to use nuclear weapons if necessary), the United States dampened these proliferation pressures.

Distinguishing Cold War history from the larger post–World War II history offers a better understanding of the forces driving proliferation today. Looking back, it does not appear that regime type or the structure of the international system was the most important factor determining who acquired weapons, when they acquired them, and what their strategies were. Nor did the NPT or the emergence of nuclear parity and mutual assured destruction between the superpowers halt proliferation, as might have been expected: the 1970s witnessed intense nuclear proliferation pressures in many regions.

It is always useful to understand the political and security environment in which a state finds itself when attempting to understand the strategies it might employ. In considering contemporary Iran, for example, Tehran's calculations about developing nuclear weapons may have more in common with Brazil, France, India, or Japan than analysts recognize.[107] As a state in a dangerous neighborhood surrounded by nuclear adversaries, Iran understandably has attempted over a long period to provide for its security. Iran began its nuclear program under the shah, restarted it under the ayatollahs, and might continue it even if it one day becomes a democracy. Despite the claims of the nuclear alarmists, Iran may want these weapons purely for deterrent purposes. If so, it is unlikely to pose a threat to the United States greater than that of the medium-sized states that acquired weapons during the Cold War.

Nuclear alarmists exaggerate and oversimplify contemporary nuclear threats while underplaying those of the past. Terrorists, rogue states, and the fear of tipping points did not suddenly appear or become more dangerous after the September 11 terrorist attacks. Understanding nuclear proliferation during a far more dangerous period—the Cold War—provides useful insights into the nuclear dilemmas and challenges states currently confront. The most important lesson of this rich, complex, and at times contradictory history is the value of humility, as it highlights how little scholars and practitioners know about how nuclear weapons affect international relations. Although this should give any commentator pause, there are at least four other lessons from our nuclear history that policymakers would be wise to heed.

First, the idea of a Long Peace based on nuclear stability during the Cold War is misleading, if not belied outright by the facts. The bipolar period witnessed greater proliferation pressures than theorists predicted, and forces only indirectly related to the Cold War—such as decolonization—were more significant than have been acknowledged. During the Cold War itself, extraordinarily dangerous great power crises occurred, even after the United States and the Soviet Union entered the era of mutual vulnerability. Does this mean that more nuclear weapons will automatically destabilize contemporary international politics? Not necessarily, because it was the purposes to which these weapons were used during the Cold War (e.g., protecting Berlin from superior conventional forces), the strategies employed (massive preemption), and the forces required (e.g., nuclear superiority, hard-target counterforce) that made these superpower crises more likely and more dangerous.

Absent these types of higher-risk strategies (or the underlying geopolitical circumstances that fuel them), a nuclearized environment need not be more dangerous. It would seem that most nuclear powers—even "rogue" states such as Iran and North Korea—seek these weapons to deter attacks on their homelands. Arguably, it has been the United States, more than any other state, that has pursued aggressive strategies by offering extended deterrence, seeking nuclear superiority, eschewing no-first-use promises, and even making nuclear threats. As Richard Betts reminds us, "Washington had a more frequent interest in nuclear blackmail than Moscow did."[108]

The second lesson is that nonproliferation policies can be costly and overreaction can be as dangerous as inaction.[109] Preventing states from pursuing weapons they consider vital to their security may actually increase the chance of their use. As Betts notes, "there is an inherent tension between striking a threat at its source, and that action eventually contributing to the very source of the threat."[110] Likewise, making security commitments to prevent states from acquiring nuclear weapons can be expensive, exposing the protector—invariably the United States—to the possibility of being pulled into unwanted conflicts and leaving it vulnerable to manipulation by its client states. The trade-offs and costs of nonproliferation policies are rarely rigorously calculated.

Third, nuclear weapons have not upended the basic tenets of international politics. For example, identifying the nuclear arms race as the driving force behind the Cold War—instead of the geopolitical and ideological conflicts between the Soviet Union and the United States—has led many analysts to overstate the importance of arms control treaties and regimes, both in the past and today. Although the nuclear balance played an important role in shaping superpower crises, Cold War tensions eased considerably well before the United States and the Soviet Union reached nuclear parity, as important geopolitical issues were resolved. When Cold War tensions reemerged, the cause was more political than technological. To paraphrase a National Rifle Association slogan: Weapons don't cause wars, states do. US foreign policy might be better served if it downplayed its often singular and obsessive focus on nuclear proliferation and instead paid more attention to the political and security circumstances in which potential proliferators find themselves.

Fourth, attempting to predict proliferation or nuclear attacks by terrorists is not only difficult but often counterproductive, particularly when it produces alarmist forecasts. As Yusuf concludes that from the beginning of the atomic age, "overall estimates from the intelligence community and, even more so, from academic sources exaggerated concerns regarding nuclear weapons."[111] Alarmist language and predictions of catastrophe are often irresponsible. For example, in April 1999, al-Qaida's number-two leader, Ayman al-Zawahiri, wrote to another senior al-Qaida leader, Mohammed Atef, about the possibility of using chemical weapons: "The enemy started thinking about these weapons before WWI. Despite their extreme danger, we only became aware of them when the enemy drew our attention to them by repeatedly expressing concerns that they can be produced simply with easily available materials."[112]

I do not want to propagate a Pollyannaish view of nuclear weapons. Their potential to cause unthinkable devastation is beyond dispute. This reality requires that the scholarly and foreign policy communities think clearly and soberly about the causes and consequences of nuclear proliferation. Alarmism is not a strategy: nuclear threats are not new or more dangerous than those of the past, and ignoring the continuities and lessons from the past is foolish. Understanding the history of nuclear proliferation and nonproliferation and, in particular, how and why the international community escaped calamity during a far more dangerous time is more relevant than ever.

[8]

Global Zero, History, and the "Nuclear Revolution"

On April 5, 2009, in a speech in Prague, President Barack Obama laid out a bold vision that appeared to be a sharp break with America's past nuclear policies. He said: "So today, I state clearly and with conviction America's commitment to seek the peace and security of a world without nuclear weapons."[1] This was not mere rhetoric; the administration moved vigorously with a number of policies, including a START agreement with Russia, a revised nuclear posture deemphasizing nuclear weapons, and a range of nonproliferation initiatives oriented toward someday achieving what has been called "global zero." This shift is all the more remarkable given than only a few years ago, complete nuclear disarmament was a fringe position, not part of the mainstream dialogue.

This began to change when four prominent former policymakers—Henry Kissinger, Sam Nunn, William Perry, and George Schultz—published a widely read piece in the *Wall Street Journal* in January 2007 that declared: "We endorse setting the goal of a world free of nuclear weapons and working energetically on the actions required to achieve that goal."[2] Other prominent personalities also signed on, new programs and organizations were launched to promote the goal, and several widely viewed documentary films were released. The Stanley Foundation, for example, held a conference in 2009 that included UN officials and foreign policy experts where there was "general agreement that complete and eventual disarmament, or global zero, is the objective."[3] The goal of global zero has become popular with the general public; one poll of twenty-one nations found that "people in every country favor an international agreement for eliminating all nuclear weapons . . . On average across all countries 76 percent favor such an agreement, with 50 percent favoring it strongly."[4]

There are others, however, who see the goal of nuclear abolition as illusory at best and dangerous at worst. Two former senior policymakers, Harold Brown and John Deutch, argue that the goal of "eliminating all nuclear weapons is counterproductive. It will not advance substantive progress on nonproliferation; and it risks compromising the value that nuclear weapons continue to contribute, through deterrence, to US security and international stability."[5] Former secretary of defense James Schlesinger has been even more critical: "The notion that we can abolish nuclear weapons reflects on a combination of American utopianism and American parochialism. . . . It's like the [1929] Kellogg-Briand Pact renouncing war as an instrument of national policy. . . . It's not based upon an understanding of reality." Schlesinger argues that a "world without nukes would be even more dangerous than a world with them."[6] The father of the study of nuclear strategy, Thomas Schelling, points out that nowhere in the global zero debate is it explained "why we should expect a world without nuclear weapons to be safer than one with (some) nuclear weapons."[7] And Charles Glaser reminds us that nuclear weapons helped the world avoid world war for almost seven decades: "Nuclear disarmament might reduce the prospects for preserving such near-perfect major power relations."[8]

Who is right? To get an answer, we must dig deep beneath the surface of these views and identify the underlying assumptions that inform these beliefs. At heart, the debate over global zero emerges from a far bigger quandary: How do nuclear weapons affect international security? Do they make the world safer or more dangerous, and in what ways? Answering these questions is not easy. One way to get some traction on these issues, as we have seen, is to look at the past and examine, not only the role nuclear weapons have played in international politics over the past seven decades, but what various people *believe* their role has been. Many of the advocates in this debate base their arguments, both explicitly and implicitly, on a particular understanding of nuclear history and its relevance (or irrelevance) to our contemporary world. Unfortunately, they do not always use history well.

Nuclear Agonists vs. Sanguinists

The concept of the nuclear revolution—that the extraordinary destructive power of these weapons has fundamentally and forever altered statecraft and calculations about war and peace—is widely accepted.[9] The consequences of this revolution, however, and what it means for US strategy, are hotly disputed. Although there is overlap, contradictions, and people who move back and forth from one camp to another, there are two broadly defined schools of thought about the effects of the nuclear revolution and the appropriate US policy responses. I label these groups the nuclear sanguinists and the nuclear agonists.

In general terms, sanguinists are skeptical of the ability of states, international organizations, or international law to radically alter the basic laws of global politics. Power, not ideals or norms, is what matters. While a sanguinist recognizes the world as a dangerous place, he or she does not become overly alarmed when confronted by new or strange phenomena. In policy terms, a sanguinist might allow events to take their natural course and avoid dramatic government intervention in matters. An agonist, on the other hand, is a "struggler" or combatant. He or she is also often an advocate. In policy terms, agonists may believe it is foolish and irresponsible to allow important matters to simply take their course and will want to use all the tools at their disposal to intervene early to halt processes that could lead to disaster. An agonist wants to see the world changed and believes that with great effort it can be made safer. Such people see international organizations, laws, and norms as powerful tools to make statecraft more peaceful.

In the nuclear world, someone identified as a sanguinist would quickly acknowledge the devastating capabilities of atomic and, especially, thermonuclear bombs. Paradoxically, sanguinists believe this enormous destructive power is precisely what allows nuclear weapons to stabilize international relations and dampen the possibilities of great power war. As a weapon, nuclear bombs are defensive in nature and are most useful for deterring others from action. In other words, nuclear weapons are not very helpful if a state wants to conquer a rival, not in the way that tanks or infantry divisions can be used offensively to take the enemy's territory. Nuclear weapons can, however, convince others not to try to conquer a state; any threat to the homeland can be met with a promise to utterly destroy the adversary. As Bernard Brodie, the father of nuclear sanguinism, recognized only weeks after the nuclear attack on Hiroshima: it was "precisely the weapon's incredible destructiveness" that would serve as a "powerful inhibitor to aggression" and thus "an unexpected asset to peace."[10]

The awesome power of nuclear weapons induces great caution; few foreign policy goals are worth risking a nuclear attack. Nuclear sanguinists believe that despite—or rather, because of—their horrifying might, these weapons have largely eased the most vexing international political problem of modern history, great power war, by creating a stable and self-reinforcing deterrence system. Our leading nuclear sanguinist, the international relations theorist Kenneth Waltz, neatly summarizes this view when he declares: "Those who like peace should love nuclear weapons."[11] Importantly, sanguinists do not believe the nuclear revolution can somehow be reversed, even if it were a desirable goal. The atomic genie cannot be put back in the bottle. As Thomas Schelling once said, "Short of universal brain surgery, nothing can erase the memory of weapons and how to build them."[12]

Nuclear agonists, on the other hand, think sheer luck is an important reason we have avoided a nuclear catastrophe over the past seven decades. It would be foolish, they argue, to expect such good fortune to continue indefinitely. Nor do they believe that deterrence is either self-reinforcing or sufficient to provide international peace and stability, particularly in the post 9/11 world.[13] Instead, they see a fragile system where peace and stability are largely maintained through arms control treaties, global norms, complex alliances, and international institutions. At the heart of this order is something they call "the NPT system," which goes beyond the 1968 Nuclear Nonproliferation Treaty to include things like the Nuclear Suppliers Group and the Additional Protocol, which agonists fear is under threat of collapsing.

Agonists worry about a world with aggressive and potentially nonrational actors, such as rogue states and terrorists groups, who would not hesitate to use nuclear weapons against the United States if they had a chance. Even within the confines of a rational state system, nuclear tipping points, terrorist transfers, regional arms races, accidents, and crisis instability make a world with nuclear weapons far more dangerous than one without.[14] Bombs may not be able to conquer territory, but they can be used to coerce, terrorize, and blackmail. Agonists acknowledge that abolition will not be easy, but they believe ridding the world of nuclear weapons is both a shared global interest and a moral imperative. According to a leading agonist, Scott Sagan, the sanguinist view as presented by people like Waltz "exaggerates the peace-inducing effect of nuclear weapons" while completely ignoring "the risks of nuclear terrorism."[15]

These contrasting views of the consequences of the nuclear revolution generate different predictions about the future and drive divergent policy prescriptions. American agonists want to see a world with far fewer and eventually no nuclear weapons. Any effort to increase or improve nuclear systems or embrace strategies that emphasize the early use of nuclear weapons is looked at with scorn; at the same time many agonists are skeptical of missile defense. For agonists, the nuclear question is far and away the most important global policy concern, and they are willing to pay a very high price to prevent proliferation, including the use of security commitments, sanctions, coercion, and even preventive force. They put great faith in arms control and international institutions to reduce the danger of war.

Sanguinists are skeptical about both the prospects for and the desirability of a world free of nuclear weapons. In their view, nuclear deterrence has done a remarkable job of keeping the world safe, and they do not see any reason it will not do so in the future. Nuclear weapons have also allowed the United States to extend its security umbrella to spread deterrence and cement alliances. Many of the positions held by agonists, particularly that of global zero, strike many sanguinists as naive and even dangerous. Nuclear deterrence requires careful thought about the numbers and types of nuclear weapons and the strategies developed for their use. Most (though not all) sanguinists prefer to see proliferation slowed but without too high a price, and certainly not at the cost of preventive military attacks.[16]

Agonists and sanguinists both accept the profound and transformative nature of the "absolute weapon," but they understand the effects of the nuclear revolution in fundamentally different ways. The consequences of one side or the other prevailing in these debates about the future of US nuclear and nonproliferation policy are enormous. There are very smart people with powerful arguments on both sides of the question, and choosing sides is difficult. Which view is correct? What might we learn from our nuclear history to provide insight into these debates?

Which Nuclear Revolution?

Not everyone agrees that looking to our nuclear history is useful or relevant for understanding the world we live in today. Many agonists believe we live in a second nuclear age, which began when the certainties of the Cold War—two rational, predictable superpowers who disliked each other but were not crazy enough to risk thermonuclear destruction—was replaced by a far messier, more complex world where not only states but also nonstate actors seek nuclear weapons.[17] Any doubt about this new world gave way after the 9/11 attacks. Rogue states, regional arms races, nuclear terrorism, and tipping points, not superpower rivalry, threaten global peace and stability. This new world, the agonists contend, bears little resemblance to the past, which holds few lessons for us today. They believe it would be a grave mistake to apply Cold War strategies to twenty-first-century problems. Many agonists argue that it was sheer luck, rather than deterrence, that allowed the world to avoid a catastrophe during the Cold War.[18]

Sanguinists also divide the past into two distinct eras, although they believe the power of nuclear deterrence largely transcends periodization. They think of the Cold War as the Long Peace, emphasizing the role nuclear weapons played, along with bipolarity, in preventing a third world war. While there were some scary moments, nuclear weapons played a salutary role in world politics because they injected caution and common sense into the ideological and geopolitical rivalry between the superpowers. Given how bloody such disputes had been during the first part of the twentieth century, sanguinists consider this a remarkable achievement. Nuclear deterrence is such a powerful force that it should be able to keep the peace in the post–Cold War world, even if the structure of international politics has changed.

Is the history of almost seven decades of nuclear statecraft relevant to today's concerns? A key point to make is that many of the phenomena described by agonists are not new. As we have seen, US policymakers worried about nuclear terrorism from the first days of the nuclear age.[19] Tipping points, or what were then called nuclear dominoes, were a constant concern.[20] And it is hard to imagine a contemporary definition of "rogue regime" that would not describe the Soviet Union and certainly Mao's China during the Cold War.

This does not mean the sanguinists' framework for viewing our nuclear past—which focuses almost entirely on the nuclear arms race between the United States and the Soviet Union—is completely accurate either. As the documents have been declassified in recent decades, archival work reveals a postwar nuclear history at some odds with the sanguinist narrative that is dominated by superpower rivalry. Much of the world's nuclear past is only tangentially related to the Cold War.

Think about the motivations and policies of nuclear powers other than the United States and the Soviet Union. France and Great Britain sought atomic weapons not only to deter the Soviets but also to defend against a resurgent Germany, to reclaim their status as great powers, and to reduce their dependence on the United States for their security. Both countries may have been more concerned with decolonization and European integration than the Cold War. Similarly, non–Cold War factors help explain the nuclear aspirations of other states. China was motivated by ideology, security threats from both superpowers, the dangers of a renascent Japan, and the opportunity to lead the nonaligned world. Israel was surrounded by hostile Arab neighbors and had no reliable ally in the world. India and Pakistan retained bitter grievances against each other from their violent breakup in 1947. South Africa was driven to preserve its apartheid regime. Even Iran and North Korea began their programs under the shadow of the bipolar system, though for reasons that had little to do with the Cold War. They lived in tough neighborhoods populated by hostile rivals.

The bottom line is that there is a lot of continuity between our nuclear past and our contemporary nuclear world. Both the agonist and sanguinist histories may have overemphasized the importance of the Cold

War—especially when it is narrowly defined as the nuclear arms race between the Soviet Union and the United States—at the expense of other factors and historical forces shaping the world since 1945. This broader, more complex nuclear history is the foundation of and has important continuities with today's nuclear environment. The bottom line is that we have had one nuclear revolution, not two, and we are still coming to terms with it.

Competing Histories

Both agonists and sanguinists derive many of their ideas about the contemporary scene from their version of the nuclear past. Much of this book has been animated by the question, what should we expect to find in the historical record of US policy if one or the other view of the world was correct? For example, what would each school of thought have predicted about the role of nuclear weapons in creating and resolving crises since 1945? What sort of decisions would we have expected to see about US nuclear strategy and weapons deployment? And what would each school of thought have predicted about US attitudes toward nuclear nonproliferation and how vigorous American efforts to prevent the spread of nuclear weapons would have been?

The agonist perspective is problematic for three reasons. First, as we have seen, the threats identified by agonists have been overstated.[21] Second, agonists often discount our ability to manage and control nuclear weapons. They ignore or underplay that we have created numerous policies, institutions, and strategies to dampen the more terrifying aspects of nuclear weapons over the past seven decades, with arguably great success. Despite widespread predictions to the contrary, nuclear weapons have not been used for aggression since 1945. There is little reason to think we will not continue to maintain this exemplary record. Third, agonists have discounted how nuclear weapons, and in particular nuclear strategies that sought superiority, allowed the United States to extend deterrence and dampen proliferation pressures. In the process, agonists have overrated the role played by the NPT system. Finally, the deterrent power of nuclear weapons may have played a far more important role in reducing interstate war than agonists allow.

Agonists often overinflate the likelihood that nuclear weapons will be used. Alarmist predictions of nuclear terrorism have not come true. Nuclear terrorism is far more difficult, the nuclear black market less dangerous, and the phenomena of rogue scientists less of a threat than agonists suggest. Tipping points, a constant worry of the agonists, have not emerged. For example, Egypt and Saudi Arabia did not develop nuclear weapons after Israel did. Japan stayed nonnuclear after China's 1964 atomic test. Even states with advanced weapons efforts, such as South Korea, Taiwan, Sweden, Australia, and Argentina, did not cross the threshold.

Nor did the so-called NPT regime appear to have much to do with particular decisions about whether or not to develop nuclear weapons. In most cases, states lacked either the financial or the technical wherewithal or were provided superpower reassurances in exchange for their abstinence. The latter point is most important—by extending the nuclear umbrella over West Germany, Japan, South Korea, and Taiwan, the United States prevented these potentially "revisionist" states from acquiring their own nuclear weapons, and in the process underwrote regional and global stability. To maintain this extended deterrent and dampen proliferation, the United States had to pursue policies agonists dislike, including missile defense, nuclear superiority, and strategies that relied on the first use of nuclear weapons.

And contrary to the assumption of many agonists, regime type did not seem to matter all that much in how states behaved with nuclear weapons. The democracies France, Israel, and the United States were as bad as the Soviet Union and China when it came to sharing nuclear technologies. The United States probably has issued more nuclear threats than any other atomic power since 1945, and it has asked nuclear weapons to do more than simply deter attacks on the American homeland.

The most important argument against the agonist position, however, may be the absence of great power war during the nuclear age. It is easy to forget the horrors of two world wars that took place in the first part of the twentieth century, when conflict between the great powers killed tens of millions of people, undermined the global economy, destroyed empires, and bankrupted states. There are many reasons why the threat of great power war has receded since 1945, but surely the deterrent power of nuclear weapons has played some role. Agonists reveal their ahistorical bias when they fail to acknowledge the relevance of this past nor explain why we should not expect a return of the horrors of great power war should nuclear weapons be eliminated.

The sanguinist framework also has problems when held up to our nuclear history. First, preventing the spread of nuclear weapons has been a far higher priority of US policymakers since 1945 than sanguinists recognize. Second, US nuclear strategies—such as missile defense and nuclear superiority—reveal that policymakers never fully embraced mutual deterrence, as sanguinists often believe and certainly recommend. Finally, while nuclear weapons may have played a role in preventing great power war, they also caused and/or made worse many dangerous crises.

When thinking about nuclear weapons, sanguinists have overemphasized concerns over horizontal proliferation, that is, the strategic arms competition between the Soviet Union and the United States, while overlooking the fact that dampening horizontal proliferation was always a high priority for US policymakers. Less than a year after the Cuban missile crisis, the United States and the Soviet Union cooperated to craft a partial test ban treaty aimed at slowing global proliferation.[22] Even more remarkable, this treaty and other efforts were aimed at the allies of both superpowers. In other words, these bitter enemies worked together to keep nuclear weapons out of the hands of their friends, including West Germany, Japan, and the People's Republic of China. Both even went so far as to approach the other at different times about supporting preventive attacks against China's nuclear facilities.

Sanguinists also do not have a satisfying explanation for US nuclear strategies and policies since the end of World War II. If the United States wanted weapons only for deterrence, it would not have pursued the number or types of weapons it did. The United States has never fully eschewed efforts to achieve nuclear superiority, nor has it abandoned asserting a right to use them first.[23] These policies are, in some measure, responsible for another problem with the sanguinist narrative—the nuclear age, and particularly the rivalry between the United States and Soviet Union, was far more dangerous than any Long Peace argument would have us believe.

As we have seen, US policymakers cared about the nuclear balance and were emboldened to take risks when they thought they had the upper hand. The most dangerous period of the Cold War—1958–62—was directly related to US efforts to extend deterrence over an area—West Berlin—that would have been indefensible in a nonnuclear environment. The Cuban missile crisis was, by definition, a crisis that would not have happened in a nonnuclear world. And we have also seen that presidents from Eisenhower to Nixon were willing to demonstrate greater resolve to use nuclear weapons than their adversary in order to prevail in crises. As Dale Copeland and others have pointed out, the Long Peace was less stable and secure than we often remember.[24]

Even allowing for these competing histories, there are still things we would need to know before we could properly assess the merits of global zero and understand the influence of nuclear weapons on international relations. If these weapons are so revolutionary, why haven't there been *more* states with nuclear weapons? There is no doubting that the costs of these weapons are high. If, however, they virtually guarantee homeland protection against invasion, as well as according other benefits (like prestige), these costs should be well worth paying. Given these weapons' terrifying power, acknowledged by agonists and sanguinists alike, shouldn't the real historical puzzle be why there has been *so little* nuclear proliferation since 1945? There are literally dozens of states that have the financial, scientific, and technical ability to build a nuclear bomb. In a world where security is supposedly scarce and conventional armaments useless against atomic weapons, and with a state's most important duty being to protect itself, it is hard to see how the NPT, all by itself, could have kept the number of nuclear-armed nations to single digits. Why do nuclear forces appear to matter *far less* in international politics now than they did forty or fifty years ago?

If the benefits of possessing nuclear weapons are as profound as advocates of the nuclear revolution of all stripes proclaim, then a second historical question presents itself: Has some entity been dampening proliferation pressures, and if so, why has it been willing to pay such a high price? An obvious candidate for this role is the United States. It has offered its nuclear umbrella to several obvious candidates for proliferation and succeeded in keeping them nonnuclear. It has sought nuclear superiority and preemptive strategies while resisting a non-first-use pledge. It has not hesitated to use threats of sanctions and even force to keep states from becoming nuclear. These policies have come at an extraordinarily high cost, financially, militarily, and diplomatically. Both agonists and sanguinists need to look to the past and reconstruct the reasons why the United States has been willing to pay this cost in the past and how this relates to global zero.

It is clear that our nuclear history is far more complicated than either the agonist or sanguinist framework allows. So what does this mean for contemporary debates over nuclear policy and, in particular, the global zero movement? Who is right—the sanguinists or the agonists? Does the past offer clues as to whether we should enthusiastically support or be wary of the effort to eliminate all nuclear weapons? Behind all the high-minded rhetoric and sharp public debate, the answer to this question depends, in the end, on how one balances three different sets of issues and concerns.

The first issue is how to assess the role of nuclear weapons in preventing interstate/great power war. This is a hard question to answer, but it is easy to forget that we have had seven decades of great power peace since 1945. It is even easier to forget the horrendous bloodletting that great power war produced in thirty-one years before the development of the atomic bomb. There are many reasons why the United States and Soviet Union did not go to war during the Cold War, just as there are many reasons why the rivalry between the United States and China seems unlikely to become a hot war anytime in the future. Is it a coincidence that great power war has receded at the same time as nuclear weapons have become part of the international system? Twenty years ago, John Mueller argued that a combination of industrialization and developing abhorrence of war after decades of bloodletting would have kept the peace even if nuclear weapons had never been invented. But most of the historical evidence indicates that the overwhelming deterrent effect of nuclear weapons certainly has played a peacekeeping role.

Are we willing to forego this salve to great power war? One counterargument is that other forces have emerged to make great power war less likely. In the first half of the twentieth century, demographic pressures, the ease of conquest and empire, and the great power value of land and territory, combined with fervent ideologies, intense racism, and hypernationalism to create a dangerous and unstable international system. Few contemporary powers are feeling the strain of population increases, and if anything the greater concern in much of the developed world is aging and contracting populations. The wars in Iraq and Afghanistan, among others, have revealed that conquest and empire is a much more expensive project than in the past. Perhaps more important, the fundamental sources of power may be much different in the twenty-first century than they were in 1950 or 1930. A case can be made for wealth and power emerging more from innovation and technology than from land and armies. In other words, a nation's power may be measured more by the number of patents and PhDs it has than the number of tanks and battleships. And while the world is not (nor is it ever likely to be) free of extremism, there does not appear to be an existential threat to the liberal capitalist order that fascism, Nazism, and communism represented in the twentieth century.

These are still largely untested propositions, however. And part of this assessment has to do with what can potentially be gained by eliminating nuclear weapons. And this gets to the second set of concerns that must be balanced: How worrisome is the possibility that nuclear weapons will fall into the hands of those who are not deterrable? This is probably the most prominent of the agonists' concerns, yet also the weakest—that we live in an age of new, unprecedented, and potentially apocalyptic nuclear threats. This is simply not true. As we have seen, rogue states have been no more likely to use or even to threaten to use nuclear weapons than other countries. When top US officials argue that a nuclear Iran "would have an utterly catastrophic effect," they are, at best, speaking carelessly.[25] The issues of loose nuclear materials, rogue scientists, and the ability of terrorists groups to acquire, assemble, deliver, and detonate a nuclear weapon (assuming they want to) have been vastly overstated.[26] Tipping points have been nonexistent in our nuclear past. The fears of the agonists have been overstated.

So if the dilemma is that of giving up nuclear deterrence to reduce great power war versus the possibility of nuclear materials falling into the wrong hands, the historical record is pretty clear. Even if a terrorist group did manage the difficult feat of getting its hands on a nuclear weapon, delivering it, and detonating it, such an event, while horrific, would likely be significantly less awful and destructive than a world war.[27] Furthermore, it is not clear that major powers giving up nuclear weapons is necessary or even related to the core concerns of the agonists. Measures to secure fissile materials and prevent and/or mitigate nuclear terrorism can and have been accomplished on their own, absent global zero. Isn't this part of an agonist pattern of underestimating the effectiveness of both US and global policy responses to the problems of nuclear weapons? Finally, a push toward global zero could make the states that rely on the US extended deterrent—most of NATO Europe, Japan, South Korea, and Taiwan—insecure. These states might feel the need to build up their conventional forces, or worse, seek their own nuclear weapons.

In considering these two issues, it might seem that global zero is a bad bet. There is, however, a third issue to assess, and that is the issue of when nuclear weapons actually create or worsen crises between states. As we have seen, there is often a temptation to do *more* with nuclear weapons than simply deter attacks on one's homeland. Whether it was protecting West Berlin or Nixon's efforts to manipulate risk, US nuclear statecraft has arguably been, at times, destabilizing. The same strategies of preemption and nuclear superiority that were necessary to extend deterrence and dampen proliferation, for example, also increased danger in the system. This statecraft often undermined the very predictability sanguinists argue was the key benefit of a nuclearized world: Russia and China had no doubt that the United States would use nuclear weapons if attacked. But did they have reason to believe we would use them if they attacked West Berlin or Taiwan?

There are other areas of concern as well. Have nuclear weapons stabilized relations between India and Pakistan? Are we confident they will prevent an all-out war in the future? Would a nuclear Taiwan or Japan increase or decrease the chance of war in Asia? Deterrence is a powerful force, but so, potentially, is misperception or the temptation to coerce. The US persistence in considering preventive war against emergent nuclear powers highlights both America's aggressive attitude and its perception that nuclear weapons in the hands of others may be destabilizing to US interests.

I present a final thought, one that is not part of the agonist or sanguinist positions but that may be the most compelling argument there is for nuclear abolition. Agonists often portray global zero as an ethical issue, whereas sanguinists emphasize realist considerations. But isn't it possible that it is in the interests of the United States as a great power to have a world without nuclear weapons? In every other possible measure of power, from its large economy and technological base to its ideal geography, large educated citizenry, and overwhelming conventional military power, the United States has an overwhelming edge over every other nation, with no plausible rival in sight. The awesome power of nuclear weapons minimizes, if it doesn't cancel, these US advantages. Would the United States fret as much about the erratic leadership of North Korea, the political instability of South Asia, or the intentions of Iran in a world where there were no nuclear weapons? If global zero were realized, America's great power advantages—and the disparity with the rest of the world—would increase dramatically, while its often draining extended deterrent commitments would be eliminated. From a strictly US perspective, the boost to its relative power that global zero could bring about might be worth the increased chance of war. Even if there was cheating in such a world, the depth and breadth of US scientific knowledge and technical capacity to quickly rebuild nuclear weapons would be greater than that of any potential rival.

In the end, in order to debate the merits of global zero, we must have a keener appreciation on how nuclear weapons influence international relations, for bad and for good. And the best way of exploring this difficult issue is to look to our nuclear past, to undertake detailed archival case studies of the critical moments and players engaged in atomic statecraft. There is, however, one fundamental lesson that does emerge from this history, and while it is a basic point, it bears repeating: the mere existence of these weapons does not create the danger, and, in fact, nuclear weapons *can be* a stabilizing force. It is *how* they are deployed, how they are incorporated into a state's strategy, how they are employed in statecraft and to what ends, and even how they are thought about as instruments of national policy that matters most. The policy implication is clear—the key is not to worry so much about *who* possesses them and instead make sure they are never used. What is often lost in the global zero thrust is that these are not goals. Many of the policies that might reduce the number of entities possessing nuclear weapons could, unfortunately, increase the likelihood of their use.

We are still early in these debates, and there is much work to be done. But if we are to get the answer right, we cannot overlook the seven decades of experience we already have with these terrifying weapons. And we owe it to ourselves to understand this history better, even if it means challenging a powerful, and flawed, received wisdom that has provided fewer answers than we realize.

Notes

Introduction

1. The New START treaty was signed in Prague, 8 April 2010, accessed 9 October 2011, http://www.state.gov/t/avc/newstart/c44126.htm.

2. Jill Lepore, "Tea and Sympathy: Who Owns the American Revolution," *New Yorker*, 3 May 2010, accessed 12 December 2011, http://www.newyorker.com/reporting/2010/05/03/100503fa_fact_lepore?currentPage=all.

3. Michael Howard, *The Lessons of History* (New Haven: Yale University Press, 1991), 10.

4. John Lewis Gaddis, *The Long Peace: Inquiries into the History of the Cold War* (New York: Oxford University Press, 1987); Robert Jervis, *The Meaning of the Nuclear Revolution: Statecraft and the Prospect of Armageddon* (Ithaca: Cornell University Press, 1989); and Marc Trachtenberg, *History and Strategy* (Princeton: Princeton University Press, 1991).

5. For popular accounts chronicling the rise and influence of the nuclear strategy community, see Gregg Herken, *Counsels of War* (New York: Alfred A. Knopf, 1985); Fred Kaplan, *The Wizards of Armageddon* (Stanford: Stanford University Press, 1991); and John Newhouse, *War and Peace in the Nuclear Age* (New York: Vintage Books, 1990). For a trenchant critique that challenges both the ideas and influence of this community, see Bruce Kuklick, *Blind Oracles: Intellectuals and War from Kennan to Kissinger* (Princeton: Princeton University Press, 2006).

6. Steven M. Walt, "A Renaissance in Security Studies?" *A Realist in an Ideological Age* (blog), 21 January 2010, accessed 31 March 2010, http://walt.foreignpolicy.com/posts/2010/01/21/a_renaissance_in_nuclear_security_studies.

7. See "Secretary of State John Foster Dulles and the Strategy of Massive Retaliation" (speech), January 1954, *Department of State Bulletin* 30, 17–110, reproduced in Gary Donaldson, *Modern America: A Documentary History of the Nation since 1945* (Armonk, NY: M.E. Sharpe, 2007), 66.

8. John Lewis Gaddis, *Strategies of Containment: A Critical Appraisal of American National Security Policy during the Cold War* (New York: Oxford University Press, 2005), 172–74, 176.

9. For example, the Soviets initiated the 1958 Berlin crisis at a time when the United States possessed impressive strategic nuclear superiority, whereas they did not put serious pressure on West Berlin from the mid-1960s onward, as the strategic balance

moved toward parity. This was because many of the core geopolitical issues that drove the crisis were resolved by the mid 1960s.

10. Lawrence Wittner, *Resisting the Bomb: A History of the World Nuclear Disarmament Movement,* 1954–1970 (Stanford: Stanford University Press, 1997).

11. See William Burr and David Alan Rosenberg "'This God Damn Poker Game': The Nuclear Competition in an Era of Stalemate, 1963–1975"; and James Hershberg, "The Cuban Missile Crisis," both in *Cambridge History of the Cold War,* vol. 2, ed. Melvyn P. Leffler and Odd Arne Westad (Cambridge: Cambridge University Press 2010).

12. "President's News Conference, 21 March 1963," *Public Papers of the President: Kennedy* 1963 (Washington, DC: Office of the Federal Register 1964), 280.

13. "Into the Open," *Time,* 2 January 1961, accessed 29 August 2011, http://www.time.com/time/magazine/article/0,9171,895206,00.html.

14. Fred C. Iklé, "Possible Consequences of a Further Spread of Nuclear Weapons," 2 January 1965, National Security Files, Committee on Nuclear Proliferation, box 7, Lyndon B. Johnson Presidential Library, Austin, Texas (hereafter cited as LBJ Library).

15. Trachtenberg, *Constructed Peace,* 232–38.

16. Burr and Rosenberg, "This God Damn Poker Game," 56.

17. "A Report to the President by the Committee on Nuclear Proliferation," Personal Papers of Roswell Gilpatric (hereafter cited as PPRG), box 10, tab 1, John F. Kennedy Library, Boston, Massachusetts (hereafter cited as JFK Library).

18. "Probable Consequences: All-Out Efforts to Stop Proliferation," PPRG, box 10, collateral documents 1, JFK Library.

19. For an important book that disagrees with my interpretation of the Gilpatric Committee's importance and discounts the shift in US nuclear nonproliferation policy, see Shane J. Maddock, *Nuclear Apartheid: The Quest for American Atomic Supremacy from World War II to the Present* (Chapel Hill: University of North Carolina Press, 2010), 237–44.

20. Hudson Institute, "Measures for Retarding the Spread of Nuclear Weapons: Proposal to the Arms Control and Disarmament Agency," 13 March 1964, National Security File, box 5, LBJ Library.

1. History, Theory, and Statecraft in the Nuclear Age

1. This is a common argument, but for the best versions, see: Paul Kennedy, *The Rise and Fall of Great Powers: Economic Change and Military Conflict from 1500 to 2000* (New York: Random House, 1987); William H. McNeil, *The Pursuit of Power: Technology, Armed Forces, and Society since AD 1000* (Chicago: University of Chicago Press, 1982); and Charles Tilly, *Coercion, Capital, and European States, AD 990–1990* (Cambridge, MA: Blackwell, 1990).

2. The best and most important book making this claim is Robert Jervis, *The Meaning of the Nuclear Revolution: Statecraft and the Prospect of Armageddon* (Ithaca: Cornell University Press, 1989). Of course, Bernard Brodie first made this claim in *The Absolute Weapon: Atomic Power and World Order,* ed. Bernard Brodie (New York: Harcourt, Brace and Company, 1946).

3. One could make a strong case that there is a fourth category of analysis surrounding nuclear statecraft—ethics. Clearly, ethical questions influenced many debates over nuclear policy from the beginning of the Manhattan Project to reactions to the bombing of Hiroshima and Nagasaki to the Baruch plan and questions of the US monopoly on nuclear weapons to debates over tactical use to SDI and domestic politics (LBJ's "Daisy" ad, the 1983 Catholic bishops' letter, the nuclear freeze movement, etc.). One could also argue the ethical category influenced how scholars have both addressed and ignored nuclear issues. I am grateful to Will Inboden for these observations.

4. Although, as Philip Tetlock has demonstrated, much of this confidence is unwarranted, as experts are as apt, and in many cases more apt than the general public, to make poor predictions about political events. This is especially true of what Tetlock calls "hedgehogs," or experts who see the world through the lens of one defining idea. The international relations expert Kenneth Waltz would be a prime example of a hedgehog. Philip E. Tetlock, *Expert Political Judgement: How Good Is It? How Can We Know?* (Princeton: Princeton University Press, 2006).

5. Francis J. Gavin, "History and Policy," *International Journal* 63 (Winter 2007–2008): 162. The essay identifies five types of historical analysis that can be used can to improve policy. The study of: vertical history, horizontal history, unintended consequences, chronological proportionality (my own term for understanding that events that seem very important during our own times may not be "historically" important, while events that seem small today may loom large decades from now), and identifying when policy is less important than large-scale structural forces.

6. Bruce Kuklick, *Blind Oracles: Intellectuals and War from Kennan to Kissinger* (Princeton: Princeton University Press, 2006), 159. Kuklick explicitly criticizes Richard Neustadt and Ernest May for their efforts to use history as an aid to policymakers.

7. Two examples of poor predictions by esteemed international historians can be found in the final parts of Kennedy, *Rise and Fall of the Great Powers;* and Ernest R. May, *"Lessons" of the Past: The Use and Misuse of History in American Foreign Policy* (New York: Oxford University Press, 1975).

8. For example, Kuklick argues that the ideas of US defense policy intellectuals during the Cold War often "served to legitimate but not to energize policies." Often, "fashion was more important than validity," and policy intellectuals who "professed deep understanding" actually "groped in the dark." Kuklick, *Blind Oracles*, 15.

9. What late-1960s event mattered more in the long run: the war in Southeast Asia, the Nuclear Nonproliferation Treaty, or the 1967 Arab-Israeli War? The last event did not receive nearly the contemporary attention as did the Vietnam War, but it may have had far more important long-term consequences for international relations. Or consider unintended consequences of the Vietnam War: if the United States had prevailed, it might have been stuck in a draining commitment and forced the Soviets and Chinese to keep cooperating. Losing exposed the Sino-Soviet split, which the United States exploited to its advantage against the Soviet Union in the later stages of the Cold War.

10. Arthur M. Schlesinger, Jr., "Folly's Antidote," *New York Times*, 1 January 2007, accessed 12 December 2011, http://www.nytimes.com/2007/01/01/opinion/01schlesinger.html.

11. Patricia Cohen, "Great Caesar's Ghost! Are Traditional History Courses Vanishing?" *New York Times*, 10 June 2009, accessed 12 December 2011, http://www.nytimes.com/2009/06/11/books/11hist.html?pagewanted=all.

12. Ibid.

13. Campbell Craig, *Glimmer of a New Leviathan: Total War in the Realism of Niebuhr, Morgenthau, and Waltz* (New York: Columbia University Press, 2003), ix.

14. For a prominent and representative example of focusing on blame, see Maddock, *Nuclear Apartheid* (Chapel Hill, NC: University of North Carolina Press, 2010). Maddock may be right that the United States did seek atomic supremacy, but his otherwise well-researched book reads like an indictment of US policymakers. His argument that such decisions were often based on racial prejudice and ideology as opposed to pure self-interest are unconvincing.

15. Excellent new generation strategists and theorists who do first-rate archival work on nuclear issues include Jacques Hymanns, Daryl Press, and Joshua Rovner, among others. Graduate programs at Columbia, MIT, and the University of Chicago are, for the time being, encouraging students to pursue archival work, although even here the long-term trends in political science are worrisome.

16. For an optimistic view of its possibilities, see Geoffrey Barraclough, *An Introduction to Contemporary History* (New York: Basic Books, 1965).

17. Kuklick, *Blind Oracles*, 157.

18. Robert Jervis, "International Politics and Diplomatic History: Fruitful Differences," published by H-Diplo/ISSF, 12 March 2010, accessed 12 December 2011, www.h-net.org/~diplo/roundtables/PDF/Williams-Jervis-Keynote.pdf. By digging a little deeper, it is not hard to find normative judgments about policy and policymakers in the writings of even the most prominent theorists and strategists, including Jervis himself.

19. For an interesting perspective on the difficulties of doing this, see the chapter "History, Science, and Morality," in E. H. Carr, *What Is History* (New York: Random House, 1961).

20. Kuklick, *Blind Oracles*, 156.

21. Defense Policy: Statement made on Saturday 5 May by Secretary McNamara at the NATO Ministerial Meeting in Athens, C-M(62)5, 5 May 1962, accessed 10 October 2011, http://www.gwu.edu/~nsarchiv/nukevault/ebb236/background%20doc%202.pdf.

22. Notes of National Security Council Meeting, 14 February 1969, 10:40 a.m., Foreign Relations of the United States 1969–1976, vol. 34, National Security Policy, 1969–1972, Department of State, GPO, 20, accessed 12 December 2011, http://static.history.state.gov/frus/frus1969–76v34/pdf/frus1969-76v34.pdf.

23. For my views on the gap between rhetoric and reality in US foreign policy, see Francis J. Gavin, "Acheson, Nixon, and the Politics of Deception," *Orbis* 2 (Spring 1999): 43. For an interesting view from an international relations perspective, see John J. Mearsheimer, *Why Leaders Lie: The Truth about Lying in International Politics* (New York: Oxford University Press, 2011).

24. John Mueller, *Retreat from Doomsday: The Obsolescence of Major War* (Rochester, NY: University of Rochester Press, 1996).

25. Tony Judt, *Postwar: A History of Europe since 1945* (New York: Penguin, 2005).

26. Richard Betts, "Should Strategic Studies Survive?" *World Politics* 50, no. 1 (October 1997): 13.

27. Marc Trachtenberg, *History and Strategy* (Princeton: Princeton University Press, 1991), 44.

28. Campbell Craig exposes the contradictions between Kenneth Waltz's structural theories about the causes of great power war and his nonstructural explanations for the supposedly peace-inducing influence of nuclear weapons in *Glimmer of a New Leviathan*, 117–65.

29. For a compelling version of this argument, see Philip Zelikow, "Some Uses of History," Hertog Global Strategy Lecture Initiative, Public Lecture Series: Nuclear Summer, Columbia University, New York, 8 July 2010, accessed 11 December 2011, http://globalstrategy.columbia.edu/2010-lecture-series/.

30. For a comparison of different national nuclear programs, see McGeorge Bundy, *Danger and Survival: Choices about the Bomb in Its First Fifty Years* (New York: Vintage Books, 1990). For US intelligence assessments of other programs during World War II and beyond, see Jeffrey T. Richelson, *Spying on the Bomb: American Nuclear Intelligence from Nazi Germany to Iran and North Korea* (New York: W. W. Norton, 2006). For the best book on the Soviet nuclear program, see David Holloway, *Stalin and the Bomb: The Soviet Union and Atomic Energy, 1939–1956* (New Haven: Yale University Press, 1994).

31. Craig, *Glimmer of a New Leviathan*, x.

32. Betts, "Should Strategic Studies Survive?," 13.

33. For a critique of the strategists and theorists and their ideas, see Kuklick, *Blind Oracles*. Kuklick does historicize the nuclear strategy and theory-making community and process, although his account is not unproblematic or universally accepted. See the fascinating listserv h-diplo roundtable on the book, "H-Diplo Roundtable—Blind Oracles, Maddux on Kuklick," 7 September 2006, accessed 12 December 2011, http://www.h-net.org/~diplo/roundtables/PDF/Maddux-KuklickRoundtable.pdf.

34. Betts, "Should Strategic Studies Survive?," 14.

35. Curiously, policymakers such as Kennedy administration national security advisor McGeorge Bundy and secretary of defense Robert McNamara made arguments after their time in government service that reflected the views of strategists and theorists, despite the historical record often flatly contradicting their assertions and memories. In addition to chapter 2 of this book, see Kuklick, *Blind Oracles*, 204–20; and chapter 6 in Trachtenberg, "The Influence of Nuclear Weapons in the Cuban Missile Crisis," in *History and Strategy*, 235–60.

36. As Kuklick shows, in perhaps the best part of his provocative and not unproblematic book, a similar process occurred when the theorists/strategists were confronted with the disaster of US policy in Southeast Asia: they blamed, not their theories or the leaders who embraced their ideas, but the bureaucracies that subverted their larger purposes. Kuklick demonstrates the absurdity of heaping praise on those who made decisions during the Cuban missile crisis while giving a pass to many of the same decision makers—and their theories—during the war in Vietnam. See Kuklick, *Blind Oracles*, esp. 156–81. See also Betts, "Should Strategic Studies Survive," 15: "Apart from whatever credit it might claim for helping to prevent World War III, the field's weakness in the first cycle was the overwhelming attention given to the least likely type of war and the late consideration of the most likely. Given the utilitarian rationales for the field, it is hardly surprising that critics saw the Vietnam disaster as a reflection upon it." One wonders if the theorists/strategists were as wrong about nuclear issues as they were about Vietnam, though without the disastrous consequences. In other words, we not have had a nuclear war for reasons that have nothing to do with the arguments of the theorists/strategists.

37. Robert J. Aumann and Thomas C. Schelling, press release, 10 October 2005, accessed 12 December 2011, http://www.nobelprize.org/nobel_prizes/economics/laureates/2005/press.html.

38. Kuklick does this very effectively in *Blind Oracles* for the so-called May group and the rise of the bureaucratic politics school.

39. Trachtenberg, *History and Strategy*, 46.

40. Barry Pavel and Matthew Kroenig "Unilaterally Assured Destruction," *Foreign Policy*, 9 September 2011, accessed 12 December 2011, http://www.foreignpolicy.com/articles/2011/09/09/unilaterally_assured_destruction.

41. Lawrence Freedman, *The Evolution of Nuclear Strategy* (New York: St. Martin's Press, 1997).

42. For the most powerful exposition of this view, see Thomas C. Schelling and Morton H. Halperin, *Strategy and Arms Control* (New York: Twentieth Century Fund, 1961).

43. The theorists/strategists never explained why they believed the Soviets were sure to launch a first strike should the opportunity arise, yet the United States passed not once but twice (in the late 1940s and the late 1950s/early 1960s) on tempting opportunities. This suggests that the theorists/strategists saw Soviet motivations as more aggressive. If the Soviets reacted differently than Americans to nuclear realities, then a study of comparative cultural, ideological, or geopolitical factors would be more appropriate than applying game theoretic models to the strategic arms competition.

44. This is the central theme of Marc Trachtenberg, *A Constructed Peace: The Making of the European Settlement*, 1945–1963 (Princeton: Princeton University Press, 1997).

45. Robert Jervis, the theorist/strategist who highlighted the power and importance of the security dilemma in a famous 1978 article, decades later seems to acknowledge that the Cold War was not the product of a security dilemma. Compare his "Cooperation under the Security Dilemma," *World Politics* 30, no. 2 (1978): 167–214, to "Was the Cold War a Security Dilemma," *Journal of Cold War Studies* 3, no. 1 (Winter 2001): 36–60. If the Cold War, a deep ideological and geopolitical conflict in which information about the other side was scarce and the featured military forces—nuclear weapons—provided enormous incentives to strike first, was not a security dilemma, one wonders what conflict in international history actually was the product of a security dilemma.

46. Trachtenberg, *History and Strategy*, 44.

47. M. Taylor Fravel and Evan S. Medeiros, "China's Search for Assured Retaliation: The Evolution of Chinese Nuclear Strategy and Force Structure," *International Security* 35, no. 2 (Fall 2010): 48–87. The implied message is that absent these suboptimal factors, China would have been free and likely to embrace the most rational strategy—mutual assured destruction.

48. Vipin Narang, "Posturing for Peace? Pakistan's Nuclear Postures and South Asian Stability," *International Security* 34, no. 3 (Winter 2009/10): 38–78. Narang's analysis does make an excellent point: arms control professionals have focused on the number and quality of nuclear weapons when what might matter much more are the strategies, postures, and deployments of weapons. Pakistan's arsenal is dangerous not because of its size or quality but because of how Pakistan deploys and plans to use it.

49. Kier Lieber and Daryl Press, "The End of MAD? The Nuclear Dimension of U.S. Primacy," *International Security* 30, no. 4 (Spring 2006): 7–44. Presumably, the United

States possesses near primacy over every nuclear (and nonnuclear) country in the world. Why aren't France, Israel, and Great Britain more alarmed? One might assume it is because the leaders of those states possess almost no conceivable scenario in which the United States would use its forces against them. It might be that the passing of the intense geopolitical and ideological competition that followed the end of the Cold War has produced similar feelings in Russia. This is not to say there aren't or won't be political disputes, just that it may be hard for decision makers to imagine them rising to the level where the use of nuclear weapons would be likely.

50. It was never clear to Cold War strategist/theorists whether parity, mutual vulnerability, and strategic stability were interchangeable. This helps explain the enormous amount of effort spent by policymakers on defining these concepts in practice. See the discussions and debates throughout the Foreign Relations of the United States volumes dealing with strategic arms limitations and antiballistic missile negotiations during the Nixon period, available at http://history.state.gov/historicaldocuments/frus1969-76v32, but also in the books dealing with US-Soviet relations more broadly at http://history.state.gov/historicaldocuments/nixon-ford.

51. In addition to chapter 4 in this book, see two excellent dissertations: Makreeta Lahti, "Security Cooperation as a Way to Stop the Spread of Nuclear Weapons? Nuclear Nonproliferation Policies of the United States towards the Federal Republic of Germany and Israel, 1945–1968" (PhD diss., Department of Economics and Social Science, University of Potsdam, 2008); and Dane Swango, "The Nuclear Nonproliferation Treaty: Constrainer, Screener, or Enabler?" (PhD diss., University of California—Los Angeles, 2009).

52. This is a theme of Francis J. Gavin, *Gold, Dollars, and Power: The Politics of the International Monetary System,* 1958–1971 (Chapel Hill: University of North Carolina Press, 2004).

53. Michael Howard, *The Lessons of History* (New Haven: Yale University Press, 1992).

2. The Myth of Flexible Response

1. Jane E. Stromseth, *The Origins of Flexible Response: NATO's Debate over Strategy in the* 1960s (New York: St. Martin's Press, 1988), 3.

2. John Lewis Gaddis, *Strategies of Containment: A Critical Appraisal of Postwar American National Security Policy* (Oxford: Oxford University Press, 1982), 216–17.

3. Deborah Shapley, *Promise and Power: The Life and Times of Robert McNamara* (Boston: Little, Brown, 1993), 88.

4. Aaron L. Friedberg, *In the Shadow of the Garrison State: America's Anti-Statism and Its Cold War Grand Strategy* (Princeton: Princeton University Press, 2000), 71.

5. Lawrence Freedman, *The Evolution of Nuclear Strategy,* 2nd ed. (New York: St. Martin's Press, 1997), 230.

6. Fred Kaplan, *The Wizards of Armageddon* (New York: Simon and Schuster, 1983), 250.

7. A list of the most important works on the origins and impact of the flexible response doctrine during the 1960s would include Desmond Ball, *Politics and Force Levels: The Strategic Missile Program of the Kennedy Administration* (Berkeley:

University of California Press, 1980); Campbell Craig, *Destroying the Village: Eisenhower and Thermonuclear War* (New York: Columbia University Press, 1998), esp. 150–62; Saki Dockrill, *Eisenhower's New-Look National Security Policy,* 1953–61 (New York: St. Martin's Press, 1996), esp. 274 and 279; John S. Duffield, *Power Rules: The Evolution of NATO's Conventional Force Posture* (Palo Alto: Stanford University Press, 1995), esp. 112–93; Helga Haftendorn, *NATO and the Nuclear Revolution: A Crisis of Credibility,* 1966–67 (Oxford: Clarendon Press, 1996), esp. 25–109; Michael Mandelbaum, *The Nuclear Question: The United States and Nuclear Weapons,* 1946–1976 (Cambridge: Cambridge University Press, 1979), esp. 90–98; John Newhouse, *War and Peace in the Nuclear Age* (New York: Vintage Books, 1990), 161–65; Scott D. Sagan, *Moving Targets: Nuclear Strategy and National Security* (Princeton: Princeton University Press, 1989), esp. 36–37; David N. Schwartz, *NATO's Nuclear Dilemmas* (Washington, DC: Brookings Institution Press, 1983), esp. 136–92; Georges-Henri Soutou, *L'alliance incertaine: Les rapports politico-strategiques franco-allemands,* 1954–1996 (Paris: Fayard, 1996), 214–29; and Andreas Wenger, *Living with Peril: Eisenhower, Kennedy, and Nuclear Weapons* (New York: Rowman and Littlefield, 1997). For the supposed impact of a new breed of strategists on Kennedy's national security policy, see, in addition to Kaplan, Greg Herken, *Counsels of War* (New York: Alfred A. Knopf, 1985). Not surprisingly, the participants emphasize their role. For the two most important examples, see William W. Kaufmann, *The McNamara Strategy* (New York: Harper and Row, 1964); and Alain C. Enthoven and K. Wayne Smith, *How Much Is Enough: Shaping the Defense Program,* 1961–1969 (New York: Harper and Row, 1971).

There are exceptions to the conventional wisdom. On the nonnuclear side, John Duffield has written an excellent article that downplays the shift between NATO's 1957 MC 14/2 and the 1967 MC 14/3. See, "The Evolution of NATO's Strategy of Flexible Response: A Reinterpretation," *Security Studies* 1, no. 1 (Autumn 1991): 132–56. On the nuclear side, Desmond Ball and, especially, David Rosenberg have captured many of the inconsistencies and failures to implement "flexible nuclear options" during the 1960s. See David Alan Rosenberg, "Reality and Responsibility: Power and Process in Making of United States Nuclear Strategy, 1945–1968," *Journal of Strategic Studies* 9, no. 1 (March 1986): 35–52; Desmond Ball, "The Development of the SIOP, 1960–1983," in *Strategic Nuclear Targeting,* ed. Desmond Ball and Jeffrey Richelson (Ithaca: Cornell University Press, 1986), 35–56. Marc Trachtenberg has demonstrated the political, as opposed to strategic, motivations of both the nuclear and nonnuclear elements of the flexible response strategy in *A Constructed Peace: The Making of a European Settlement,* 1945–1963 (Princeton: Princeton University Press, 1999).

8. Robert Cohen, "A New German Assertiveness on its Foreign Policy Stance," *New York Times,* 12 September 1999, 8.

9. Bundy to Rostow, 13 April 1962, *Foreign Relations of the United States,* 1961–1963, vol. 8 (Washington, DC: U.S. Government Printing Office, 1975), 263 (hereafter cited as *FRUS,* with appropriate year, volume, and page numbers).

10. This was cited in editorial note 127 concerning a White House daily staff meeting held on 4 February 1963. See Colonel Lawrence J. Legere, Assistant to the President's Military Representative, 4 February 1963, *FRUS:* 1961–1963, vol. 8, 463.

11. Interview with General Lemnitzer, Supreme Allied Commander in Europe (1963–69), 11 February 1970, 6–7.

12. L. Wainstein, Project Leader "The Evolution of U.S. Strategic Command and Control and Warning, 1945–1972," Institute for Defense Analyses, June 1975, DOD-FOIA, 287.

13. It is now recognized that Eisenhower's nuclear strategy has also been mischaracterized and that NATO strategy moved away from massive retaliation in 1957 when it adopted the strategy laid out in Document MC 14/2. See Andrew Erdmann, "The Eisenhower Administration, Flexible Response, and the Strategies of Containment," unpublished manuscript, June 1999 (in author's possession); Duffield, "Evolution of NATO's Strategy of Flexible Response"; and Gregory Pedlow, "The Evolution of NATO Strategy, 1949–1969," in *NATO Strategy Documents*, http://www.nato.int/archives/strategy.htm.

14. Of course, it is often forgotten that the Eisenhower period ended with his secretary of state Christian Herter asking NATO to embrace "flexibility of response." Airgram from NAC delegation to State, 17 December 1960, *FRUS:* 1958–1960, vol. 7, pt. 1, 674–82.

15. "Remarks by Secretary McNamara, NATO Ministerial Meeting, May 5, 1962, Restricted Session," 5 May 1962, OSD-FOIA (Office of Secretary of Defense-Freedom of Information Act), 79–481.

16. Wainstein, et al., "Evolution of U.S. Strategic Command and Control," 288. See also Lemnitzer to McNamara, 18 April 1961, *FRUS:* 1961–1963, vol. 8, 74.

17. See *FRUS:* 1961–1963, vol. 8, 1965, describing the contents of "A Study of Requirements for U.S. Strategic Systems: Final Report," 1 December 1961.

18. Rosenberg, "Reality and Responsibility."

19. Marc Trachtenberg was the first scholar to find this document and argue convincingly about its significance. Oral History, Bruce Holloway, 359, as cited in Trachtenberg, *Constructed Peace*, 318–19.

20. Wainstein, et al., "Evolution of U.S. Strategic Command and Control," 430.

21. Ibid., 432.

22. Testimony of Hon. James R. Schlesinger, Secretary of Defense, Subcommittee on Arms Control, Committee on Foreign Relations, "U.S.-U.S.S.R. Strategic Policies," 4 March 1974, 9.

23. Henry S. Rowen, "The Evolution of Strategic Nuclear Doctrine," in *Strategic Thought in the Nuclear Age*, ed. Lawrence Martin (Baltimore: Johns Hopkins University Press, 1979), 151.

24. Wainstein, et al., "Evolution of U.S. Strategic Command and Control," 415.

25. Ibid., 436.

26. Committee on Foreign Relations, "U.S.-U.S.S.R. Strategic Policies," 9.

27. Interview with Carl Kaysen by Joseph O'Conner, 11 July 1966, John F. Kennedy Library, Boston, Massachusetts (hereafter cited as JFK Library). See also May, Steinbruner, and Wolfe, "History of the Strategic Arms Competition," 1981, OSD Historical Office, OSD-FOIA, 520.

28. Memorandum, Nitze to McNamara, 5 June 1962, *FRUS:* 1961–1963, vol. 8, 303n3. See Memorandum for the Secretary of Defense, 20 April 1963, *FRUS:* 1961–1963, vol. 7, 481n4.

29. Minister of Defense's Visit to the US, September 1962, "Counter Force Strategy," 19 September 1962, Prime Minister File) 11/3779, Public Records Office (PRO); Minister of Defense's Visit to the US, note on Meeting with McNamara, 19 September 1962, DEFE 13/323, PRO; and "NATO Strategy—Statement by Mr. McNamara at the Ministerial Meeting on 5 May 1962," 15 August 1962, DEFE 6/83, PRO.

30. The incentive for preemption is obvious if both sides did, in fact, have soft targets. But if the United States had survivable forces and the Soviets knew this to be the case, why would the Soviets preempt if doing so guaranteed suicide? One would imagine that the Soviets would launch their forces regardless of whether their targets were hard or soft if they had warning of a US first strike (an uncertain proposition in 1962). This conversation seems to indicate that McNamara's real concern rested in preventing any US thoughts of a preemptive attack against the Soviets.

31. JFK Library, tape no. 102/A38, 30 July 1963. Marc Trachtenberg was the first scholar to transcribe this tape and argue convincingly about its significance.

32. Comments, McGeorge Bundy, Harvard University's Center for Science and International Affairs, 12 October 1983. I am grateful to Marc Trachtenberg for providing me with this quotation.

33. See Draft Memorandum from McNamara to Johnson, 6 December 1963, *FRUS: 1961–1963*, vol. 8, 550; and Keeny to Bundy, 22 November 1963, *FRUS: 1961–1963*, vol. 8, 534.

34. Trachtenberg, *Constructed Peace*, 292–97.

35. Memcon with Kennedy, 27 July 1961, *FRUS: 1961–1963*, vol. 8, 123.

36. Transcript of Meeting, Monday, 29 October, 1962, 10:10 a.m., in Ernest May and Philip Zelikow, eds., *The Kennedy Tapes: Inside the White House during the Cuban Missile Crisis* (Cambridge: Harvard University Press, 1997), 657.

37. 517th Meeting of the NSC, "Report of the Net Subcommittee, 12 September 1963, *FRUS*: 1961–1963, vol. 13, 499–507.

38. There is a somewhat misleading account of this limited preemptive strike plan in Kaplan, *Wizards of Armageddon*, 297 and 301.

39. *FRUS:* 1961–1963, vol. 8, 128–31.

40. Marc Trachtenberg and David Rosenberg's unpublished interview with Carl Kaysen at his office in Cambridge, Massachusetts, August 1988 (in author's possession).

41. This is one of the most important discoveries to emerge from Marc Trachtenberg's *Constructed Peace*. See also Trachtenberg, chapter 4, "The Nuclearization of NATO and U.S.-West European Relations" and chapter 5, "The Berlin Crisis," in *History and Strategy* (Princeton: Princeton University Press, 1991), esp. 163–68 and 180–91.

42. "Remarks by Secretary McNamara, NATO Ministerial Meeting, 5 May 1962, Restricted Session," 5 May 1962, OSD-FOIA, 79–481, 12.

43. Kohler to Rusk, "Secretary McNamara's Views on Nuclear Sharing," 12 April 1962, RG 59, 740.5611, p. 1, U.S. National Archives, College Park, Maryland (hereafter cited as USNA). See also Minutes of Meeting, the President, Rusk, McNamara, and Bundy, 16 April 1962, *FRUS*: 1961–1963, vol. 13, 2–4.

44. Bundy, Memo to the President, "Action on Nuclear Assistance to France," 7 May 1962, President's Office Files (POF) Box 116a, France-Security, JFK Library.

45. Ibid., 6.

46. See "Minutes of the 505th Meeting of the NSC," 20 October, 1962, *FRUS:* 1961–1963, vol. 11, 136; and "Minutes of the 506th Meeting of the NSC," 20 October 1962, *FRUS:* 1961–1963, vol. 11, 141–49.

47. For a full account of this story, see Richard Neustadt's "Skybolt and Nassau: American Policy-Making and Anglo-American Relations," 15 November 1963, Papers of Francis Bator, Lyndon B. Johnson Presidential Library, Austin, Texas (hereafter cited as LBJ Library).

My interpretation of this incident is based on Trachtenberg, *Constructed Peace*, 359–67.

48. "A USSR-US Enforced Non-Proliferation Agreement—the probable positions of the FRG, France, Italy, Norway, Belgium, and the Netherlands," 3, n.d. (but presumably June 1963), National Security Files, Carl Kaysen, Nuclear Energy Matters, 6/63, box 376, JFK Library. See also "On Nuclear Diffusion, vol. 2," NSF, Carl Kaysen, Briefing Book, vol. 2, box 376, JFK Library.

49. Interview, Joseph E. O'Conner with Carl Kaysen, 11 July 1966, 131, JFK Library.

50. Meeting between Kennedy, Macmillan, and other officials, at Nassau, 19 December 1962, Record of Nassau Conference, Prem 11/4229, PRO.

51. Taylor to McNamara, 25 April 1962, Maxwell D. Taylor Papers, box 35, National Defense University, Department of Special Collections, Ft. McNair, Washington, DC.

52. McNamara to Chairman, JCS, 23 May 1962, Maxwell D. Taylor Papers, National Defense University, Department of Special Collections, Ft. McNair, Washington, DC.

53. For arguments in favor of tactical nuclear weapons to support a conventional strategy, see "Further Study of Requirements for Tactical Nuclear Weapons," prepared by Special Studies Group (JCS), April 1963, *FRUS:* 1961–1963, vol. 8, microfiche supplement, document 291. For an argument that tactical nuclear weapons would not be useful in a conventional battle in Europe against the Soviets, see "Views of Dr. Enthoven on Tactical Nuclear Warfare," 7 February 1963, *FRUS:* 1961–1963, vol. 8, microfiche supplement, document 289.

54. Ibid., 4.

55. W. Y. Smith for General Goodpaster, "US Policy on Tactical Nuclear Weapons in Europe," 6 February 1963, *FRUS:* 1961–1963, vol. 8, microfiche supplement, document 288.

56. Daily White House Staff Meeting, 23 January 1962, *FRUS:* 1961–1963, vol. 8, microfiche supplement, document 287.

57. For the increase in tactical nuclear weapons in Europe during the 1960s, see J. Michael Legge, *Theater Nuclear Weapons and the NATO Strategy of Flexible Response*, Rand paper R-2964-FF, April 1983, 16.

58. Taylor for McNamara, "Preliminary Comments on the Department of Defense FY '63 Budget and 1963–1967 Program," NSF, Department and Agencies, box 275, JFK Library.

59. Rusk to Taylor, 29 October 1961, *FRUS:* 1961–1963, vol. 8, 191.

60. Kaysen to Bundy, "Secretary McNamara's Memorandum on the Defense Budget dated October 6, 1961," 13 November 1961, NSF, box 275, JFK Library.

61. For complaints about McNamara's funding for conventional forces, see Bundy to the President, "Washington News," 28 September 1961, *FRUS:* 1961–1963, vol. 8, microfiche supplement, document 245; Memo for the President, "FY 1963 Defense Budget Issues," 13 November 1961, *FRUS:* 1961–1963, vol. 8, microfiche supplement, document 247; Rusk to McNamara, 20 January, 1962, *FRUS:* 1961–1963, vol. 8, microfiche supplement, document 256; Kaysen to Bell, 23 January 1962, *FRUS:* 1961–1963,

vol. 8, microfiche supplement, document 257; Taylor to the President, "Scheduled Reduction in Strength of the U.S. Army in Fiscal Year 1963," 17 April 1962, *FRUS:* 1961–1963, vol. 8, microfiche supplement, document 264.

62. Kaysen to Taylor, 23 January 1962, *FRUS:* 1961–1963, vol. 8, microfiche supplement, document 258.

63. See Gavin, "Gold Battles." See also Arthur Schlesinger, Jr., *A Thousand Days: John F. Kennedy in the White House* (New York: Fawcett Premier, 1965), 601; W. W. Rostow, *The Diffusion of Power: An Essay in Recent History* (New York: Macmillan, 1972), 136; Memo of Conversation between Kennedy and Adenauer, 24 June 1963, *FRUS:* 1961–1963, vol. 9, 170; and George Ball Oral History, no. 2, AC 88–3, 29, LBJ Library.

64. Gesprach des Botschafters Freiherr von Welck mit Staatspasident Franco in Madrid, May 29, 1963 *Akten zur Auswartigen Politik der Bundesrepublik Deutschland*, 1963, vol. 1, #185, fn. 9.

65. Remarks of President Kennedy to the National Security Meeting, 22 January 1963, *FRUS:* 1961–1963, vol. 13, 486.

66. Gesprach des Botschafters Freiherr von Welck mit Staatspasident Franco in Madrid, 29 May 1963, *Akten zur Auswartigen Politik der Bundesrepublik Deutschland*, 1963/1, no. 185. For more details on Kennedy's threat to pull US troops out of Europe as a result of America's dollar and gold outflow, see Gavin, "Gold Battles," 61–64.

67. Visit to the United States, 9–17 September 1962, DEFE 13/323, PRO.

68. Memo of Conversation, "Trade and Fiscal Policy Matters," 24 June 1963, *FRUS:* 1961–1963, vol. 9, 170.

69. Memorandum of Conversation, "U.S. Troop Reductions in Europe," 24 September 1963, *FRUS:* 1961–1963, vol. 9, 187.

70. Schaetzel to Kitchen, "Balance of Payments and Force Withdrawal," 24 July 1963, *FRUS:* 1961–1963, vol. 8, microfiche supplement, document 336. The plate glass doctrine was similar to "tripwire" strategy—the idea that conventional forces were not in place to offer a legitimate, robust defense against a Warsaw Pact invasion; rather, they were there to "trigger" a nuclear response by the United States.

71. Kaysen to Bundy, 10 May 1963, *FRUS:* 1961–1963, vol. 8, microfiche supplement, document 326.

72. Klein to Bundy, 10 May 1963, *FRUS:* 1961–1963, vol. 8, microfiche supplement, document 323. Underlining in the original.

73. JCS Meeting with the President, 27 December 1962, *FRUS:* 1961–1963, vol. 8, 453.

74. JCS Meeting with the President, "Force Strength in Europe," 28 February 1963, *FRUS:* 1961–1963, vol. 13, 517.

75. For more details on the struggle over troop withdrawals during the Kennedy period, see Gavin, "Gold Battles," passim.

76. See, for example, Kennedy-Bundy-Rusk-McNamara meeting, 10 December 1962, *FRUS:* 1961–1963, vols. 13–14, microfiche supplement, document 27; and Kennedy-McNamara-JCS meeting, 27 December 1962, *FRUS:* 1961–1963, vol. 8, 449; and Memorandum for the Record, "Joint Chiefs of Staff Meeting with the President, 28 February 1963—Force Reductions in Europe," 28 February 1963, *FRUS:* 1961–1963, vol. 13.

77. Kennedy-Bundy-Rusk-McNamara meeting, 10 December 1962, *FRUS:* 1961–1963, vols. 13–15, microfiche supplement, document 27.

78. Memorandum from William Y. Smith to Taylor, 9 August 1962, *FRUS:* 1961–1963, vol. 15, 268–69.

79. Conversation between President John F. Kennedy and Dwight D. Eisenhower, 10 September 1962, Presidential Recordings (transcribed by Erin Mahan), JFK Library.

80. Meeting, JFK and Mayor Willy Brandt, 5 October 1962, *FRUS:* 1961–1963, vol. 15, document 128.

81. Conversation between JFK, Maxwell Taylor, Robert McNamara, George Ball, Averell Harriman, Gen. Lyman Lemnitzer, William Bundy, Michael Forrestal, and others, 25 September 1962 (transcribed by George Eliades; in author's possession).

82. Kennedy-Bundy-Rusk-McNamara meeting, 10 December 1962, *FRUS:* 1961–1963, vols. 13, microfiche supplement for volumes 13–15, document 27.

83. JCS Meeting with the President, "Force Strength in Europe," 28 February 1963, *FRUS:* 1961–1963, vol. 14, 517. See also, Memcon, the President and Couve de Murville, 9 October 1962, *FRUS:* 1961–1963, vol. 15, document 130.

84. Summary of President's Remarks to the NSC, 7 January 1962, NSF, box 313, NSC Meetings, 1962, JFK Library.

85. Memcon, President Kennedy and Mayor Willy Brandt of West Berlin, 5 October 1962, *FRUS:* 1961–1963, vol. 15, 347.

86. Chiefs of Staff Committee, Joint Planning Staff, "Reductions in NATO Deployed Forces," 2 May 1963, DEFE 6/84, PRO.

87. Transcript of Meeting, 18 October 1962, 11:00 a.m., in May and Zelikow, *Kennedy Tapes,* 144.

88. Transcript of Meeting, 19 October 1962, 9:45 a.m., in May and Zelikow, *Kennedy Tapes,* 176.

89. President's Office Files, Presidential Recordings, tapes 33.2 and 33A.1, 22 October 1962, 5:30–6:30 p.m., JFK Library.

90. See Gavin, "Gold Battles."

91. The political side of this story is told in Trachtenberg, *Constructed Peace.* The international and economic sides of this story—involving West Germany offset payments—is told in Francis J. Gavin, *Gold, Dollars and Power: The Politics of US Monetary Relations,* 1958–1971 (Chapel Hill: University of North Carolina Press, 2004), chap. 6.

92. On 31 August, 1966, Senate Majority Leader Mike Mansfield along with twelve other senators offered a nonbinding resolution recommending unspecified cuts in US forces in Europe. For LBJ's response, see telephone conversation between President Johnson and Senator Russell Long, 1 September 1966, *FRUS:* 1964–1968, vol. 15, 398–440.

93. Rostow, Bowie, Leddy, and Kitchen for Rusk, "OSD Proposal for Reducing U.S. Forces in Europe," n.d., Papers of Francis Bator, Trilateral/Military, box 17, LBJ Library.

94. Bator for LBJ, "The U.S. Position in the Trilateral Negotiations," 23 February 1967, NSF, Trilateral Negotiations and NATO, box 51, LBJ Library.

95. Telephone conversation between President Johnson and Secretary of Defense McNamara, 26 September, 1966, *FRUS:* 1964–1968, vol. 15, 434–35.

96. Knappstein, "Conversation with Secretary of State Rusk; Here, New Rumors about Troop Withdrawal," 23 July 1966, *Akten zur Auswaertigen Politik der Bundesrepublik Deutschland*, 1966/2, document 233.

97. Note of the Secretary of State Carsten, Conversation with General Heusinger, 31 May 1966, *Akten zur Auswaertigen Politik der Bundesrepublik Deutschland*, 1966/2, document 171.

98. Envoy of Lilienfeld, Washington, to the Office of Foreign Affairs, 19 September 1966, *Akten zur Auswaertigen Politik der Bundesrepublik Deutschland*, 1966/2, document 294.

99. Knappstein to Schroeder, 10 June 1966, *Akten zur Auswaertigen Politik der Bundesrepublik Deutschland*, 1966/2, document 189.

100. Ibid.

101. Conversation between Federal Chancellor Erhard and American Special Envoy McCloy, 20 October 1966, *Akten zur Auswaertigen Politik der Bundesrepublik Deutschland*, 1966/2, document 342.

102. Bator for LBJ, "The U.S. Position in the Trilateral Negotiations," 23 February 1967, NSF, Trilateral Negotiations and NATO, box 51, LBJ Library. Bator ended the memo by telling the president "my bad dream is another Skybolt," which is a clear indication that "European and German politics," rather than the Soviet threat, was the main issue when considering US troop withdrawals from Europe. Skybolt was an intra-alliance crisis.

103. Garthoff and Sonnefeldt, "Soviet Intentions: Possible Soviet Uses of Military Force in Europe," 24 October 1966, NSF, Trilateral Negotiations and NATO, box 51, LBJ Library.

104. "The Threat: Warsaw Pact Capabilities in the Central Region," date unknown but likely late 1966–early 1967, NSF, Trilateral Negotiations and NATO," box 51, LBJ Library.

105. Garthoff and Sonnefeldt, "Soviet Intentions," 10.

106. For shared US and Soviet concerns about a rearmed West Germany intervening in East Germany, see Averell Harriman, "Outlook for Future Discussions with USSR," 30 July 1963, NSF; Carl Kaysen, "Test Ban and Related Negotiations," box 376, JFK Library; and Memcon, Kissinger and Strauss, 10 May 1961, NSF, box 320, JFK Library.

107. Background Paper, Trilateral Talks, "Political Significance of NATO: U.S. Protection of and Political Predominance Exercised Through NATO," 18 November 1966, NSF, Trilateral Negotiations and NATO, LBJ Library.

108. "A USSR-US Enforced Non-Proliferation Agreement—the Probable Positions of the FRG, France, Italy, Norway, Belgium and the Netherlands," 12 June 1963, NSF; Carl Kaysen, "Test Ban and Related Negotiations," box 376, JFK Library.

109. "On Nuclear Diffusion," 20 June 1963, NSF; Carl Kaysen, "Test Ban and Related Negotiations," box 376, JFK Library.

110. Department of State Policy Planning Council, "Implications of a More Independent German Foreign Policy," 16 November 1967, Papers of Francis Bator, box 22, LBJ Library. See also Department of State Policy Planning Council, "The Future of NATO: A Pragmatic View," 1 November 1967, Papers of Francis Bator, box 22, LBJ Library; Memo, no author, "Key Issues in U.S.-European Relations," 8 November 1967, Papers of Francis Bator, box 22, LBJ Library. Ambassador McGhee revealed

that the West Germans were complaining that the Americans were making them the "Pruegelknabe" or whipping boy. See McGhee to State, 17 August 1966, *FRUS:* 1964–1968, vol. 15, 390.

111. For US assessments of the FRG's waning confidence in America's security commitment, see McGhee to State, 17 August 1962, *FRUS:* 1964–1968, vol. 15, 389–92; McGhee to Rusk, 25 August 1962, *FRUS:* 1964–1968, vol. 15, 394–96; McGhee to State, 20 September 1966, *FRUS:* 1964–1968, vol. 15, 417–20; and McGhee to State, 26 February 1967, *FRUS:* 1964–1968, vol. 15, 493–96.

112. Department of State Policy Planning Council, "Germany and the Future of Western Europe," 23 February 1968, Papers of Francis Bator, box 22, LBJ Library.

113. Ball, Memo for the President, "Handling the Offset Issue During Erhard's Visit," 21 September 1966, Papers of Francis Bator, box 21, LBJ Library.

114. Note of Ambassador Schnippenkoetter, 4 January 1967, *Akten zur Auswaertigen Politik der Bundesrepublik Deutschland*, 1967, document 6.

115. Background Paper, "Factors Arguing for and against UK Troop Cutbacks in Germany," n.d. but probably November 1966, Trilateral Negotiations and NATO, LBJ Library.

116. See J. B. Martin Interview with Robert F. Kennedy, 29 February and 1 March 1964, JFK Library.

117. Memo, Transfer, 19 January 1961 Meeting of the President and Senator Kennedy, 19 January, 1961, Whitman file, Presidential Transition Series, box 1, item no. 7, Dwight D. Eisenhower Presidential Library.

118. Letter, Thomas S. Gates to Robert S. McNamara, 15 September 1964, Thomas S. Gates Jr. Collection, Annenberg Rare Book and Manuscript Library, box 12: "McNamara—Secretary of Defense, Van Pelt-Dietrich Library Center, University of Pennsylvania, Philadelphia.

119. McGee to Rusk, 25 August 1966, *FRUS:* 1964–1968, vol. 15, 395.

120. McGhee to State, 25 February 1967, *FRUS:* 1964–1968, vol. 15, 493-94. For more on the widening gap between Soviet and East German interests, see the comments between Willy Brandt and Couve de Murville, Memcon, Quadripartite Dinner Discussion of East-West Relations; Berlin; The German Question, 14 December 1966, *FRUS:* 1964–1968, vol. 15, 467 and 469.

3. Nuclear Weapons, Statecraft, and the Berlin Crisis, 1958–1962

1. Memorandum of Conference with President Eisenhower, 11 December 1958, *Foreign Relations of the United States*, 1958–196, vol. 8 (Washington, DC: U.S. Government Printing Office, 1993), 173 (hereafter cited as *FRUS*, with appropriate year, volume, and page numbers).

2. Memorandum of Conference with President Eisenhower, 6 March 1959, *FRUS:* 1958–1960, vol. 8, 433.

3. President's Trip to Europe, 29 August 1959, *FRUS:* 1958–1960, vol. 9, 28.

4. Memorandum of Conversation, 13 March 1961, *FRUS:* 1961–1963, vol. 14, 25.

5. The President's Meeting with Prime Minister MacMillan, *FRUS:* 1961–1963, vol. 14, 42.

6. Memorandum from George A. Morgan of the Policy Planning Staff to the Assistant Secretary of State for Policy Planning (Smith), 8 December 1958, *FRUS: 1958–1960*, vol. 8, 158.

7. Memorandum of Conference with President Eisenhower, 11 December 1958, *FRUS: 1958–1960*, vol. 8, 173.

8. Memorandum of Conversation with President Eisenhower and Secretary of State Dulles, 30 November 1958, *FRUS: 1958–1960*, vol. 8, 143.

9. Frederick Kempe, *Berlin 1961* (New York: Putnam, 2011), 220.

10. There have been several impressive additions to this literature, including: John Gearson and Kori Schake, *The Berlin Wall Crisis: Perspectives on Cold War Alliances* (New York: Palgrave Macmillan, 2002); Kempe, *Berlin 1961*; W. R. Smyser, *Kennedy and the Berlin Wall* (New York: Rowman and Littlefield, 2009); and Frederick Taylor, *The Berlin Wall: A World Divided, 1961–1989* (New York: Harper Collins, 2007). There are two recent books that provide excellent insight into the previously murky decision making in the Communist bloc: Aleksandr Fursenko and Timothy Naftali, *Khrushchev's Cold War: The Inside Story of an American Adversary* (New York: W. W. Norton, 2006); and Hope M. Harrison, *Driving the Soviets up the Wall: Soviet-East German Relations, 1953–1961* (Princeton: Princeton University Press, 2005). By far the best integrated international history of the fundamental issues behind the origins and outcome of the crisis is Marc Trachtenberg's *A Constructed Peace: The Making of the European Settlement, 1945–1963* (Princeton: Princeton University Press, 1999).

11. In addition to the Betts and Jervis books on nuclear statecraft, the best (though differing) analyses of the role of nuclear weapons during the Berlin Crisis are Campbell Craig, *Destroying the Village: Eisenhower and Thermonuclear War* (New York: Columbia University Press, 1998), and Trachtenberg, chap. 5, "The Berlin Crisis," in *History and Strategy* (Princeton: Princeton University Press, 1991), 169–234.

12. I make this argument in chapter 7 of this book.

13. John Lewis Gaddis, "The Long Peace: Elements of Stability in the Postwar International System," chapter 8 in *The Long Peace: Inquiries into the History of the Cold War* (New York: Oxford University Press, 1987), 215–46; and John J. Mearsheimer, "Back to the Future: Instability in Europe after the Cold War," *International Security* 15, no. 1 (Summer 1990): 5–56.

14. In addition to the famous article by John Lewis Gaddis and the arguments of Kenneth Waltz, my analysis of the nuclear revolution is based largely on Robert Jervis's *The Meaning of the Nuclear Revolution: Statecraft and the Prospect of Armageddon* (Ithaca: Cornell University Press, 1989).

15. Jervis, *Nuclear Revolution*, 45. There is a controversy over *when* this period of mutual vulnerability began. Jervis does not indicate a date but seems sympathetic to McGeorge Bundy's idea of "nuclear danger" creating conditions of mutual vulnerability during this period. In opposing the idea that the strategic nuclear balance was decisive, Bundy argues that "large-scale nuclear war between the Soviet Union and the United States in the years of the Berlin crisis would have produced an exchange of death and destruction in which both nations would have been ghastly losers, not only as against their own condition before the war but also in their postwar relation to the rest of the world. This reality was deeply understood by the men at the top on both sides." *Danger and Survival: Choices about the Bomb in the First Fifty Years* (New York: Random House, 1988), 380–81. Daryl Press, on the other hand, believes the nuclear balance changed significantly between 1958 and 1962 "from a condition that

favored the United States to a condition of nuclear stalemate." *Calculating Credibility: How Leaders Assess Military Threats* (Ithaca: Cornell University Press, 2005), 91. Press believes that in 1958 if the United States had destroyed the Soviet Union's long-range nuclear systems, Russia would have retained "hundreds of nuclear weapons to retaliate in devastating fashion against America's European allies" (ibid., 86). Trachtenberg's assessment on this issue—which I find convincing—is that the United States possessed a meaningful nuclear primacy throughout this period that played a large role in driving US policy between 1958 and 1962 and in Soviet reactions. See chapters 5 and 6 of Trachtenberg, "History and Strategy."

16. Stephen Van Evera, "Offense, Defense, and the Causes of War," in *Offense, Defense, and War*, ed. Michael E. Brown, Owen R. Cote, Jr., Sean M. Lynn-Jones, and Steven E. Miller (Cambridge: MIT Press, 2004), 255.

17. For an excellent look at this side of the question, see Harrison, *Driving the Soviets up the Wall.*

18. This is one of the central arguments in *Constructed Peace.*

19. For the Cuban Missile Crisis as connected to and in fact an extension of the Berlin Crisis, see *The Presidential Recordings: John F. Kennedy*, vol. 3, ed. Ernest R. May, Timothy Naftali, Philip D. Zelikow (New York: W. W. Norton, 2001), xxiii–xxiv.

20. For the 1963 settlement, see the final chapter of Trachtenberg's *Constructed Peace.*

21. Memorandum of Conversation between President Eisenhower and Secretary of State Dulles, 18 November 1958, *FRUS:* 1958–1960, vol. 8, 85.

22. The President's Meetings with Prime Minister MacMillan, 6 April 1961, *FRUS:* 1961–1963, vol. 14, 42.

23. Smyser, *Kennedy and the Berlin Wall*, 75.

24. Telegram from the Embassy in the Soviet Union to the Department of State, 2 January 1960, *FRUS:* 1958–1960, vol. 9, 162.

25. Memorandum from George A. Morgan of the Policy Planning Staff to the Assistant Secretary of State for Policy Planning (Smith), 8 December 1958, *FRUS:* 1958–1960, vol. 8, 158.

26. Letter from the Ambassador of Yugoslavia (Kennan) to the Ambassador to the Soviet Union (Thompson), 9 February 1962, *FRUS:* 1961–1963, vol. 14, 803.

27. President's Report of His Private Session with Khrushchev, 27 September 1959, *FRUS:* 1958–1960, vol. 9, 46.

28. Khrushchev's Visit to the United States and Related Matters, 17 September 1959, *FRUS:* 1958–1960, vol. 9, 32.

29. Germany, 9 December 1964, *FRUS:* 1964–1968, vol. 15, 178.

30. Meeting between the President and Chairman Khrushchev in Vienna, 4 June 1961, *FRUS:* 1961–1963, vol. 14, 91.

31. Dale Copeland, *The Origins of Major War* (Ithaca: Cornell University Press, 2001), 182.

32. Fursenko and Naftali, *Khrushchev's Cold War*, 369.

33. Kempe, *Berlin* 1961, 217.

34. Taylor, *Berlin Wall*, 130.

35. Telegram from the Embassy in the Soviet Union to the Department of State, 19 February 1959, *FRUS:* 1958–1960, vol. 8, 381.

36. Kempe, *Berlin* 1961, 293.

37. Telegram from the Embassy in Germany to the Department of State, 2 March 1959, *FRUS:* 1958–1960, vol. 8, 407.

38. Memorandum of Conversation, 8 February 1959, *FRUS:* 1958–1960, vol. 8, 346.

39. Memorandum of the Discussion at a Special Meeting of the National Security Council, 23 April 1959, *FRUS:* 1958–1960, vol. 8, 631.

40. Memorandum of Conference with President Eisenhower, 11 December 1958, *FRUS:* 1958–1960, vol. 8, 173.

41. Memorandum of Telephone Conversation between Secretary of State Dulles and Acting Secretary of State Herter, 6 March 1959, *FRUS:* 1958–1960, vol. 8, 437.

42. President's Visit, 31 May 1961, *FRUS:* 1961–1963, vol. 14, 83.

43. Craig, *Destroying the Village*, 139.

44. Memorandum from the Joint Chiefs of Staff to Secretary of Defense McElroy, 11 March 1959, *FRUS:* 1958–1960, vol. 8, 455.

45. Memorandum of Meeting with President Eisenhower, 13 July 1959, *FRUS:* 1958–1960, vol. 8, 984.

46. Memorandum from Secretary of Defense McNamara to President Kennedy, June 1962, *FRUS:* 1961–1963, vol. 15, 194.

47. Meeting between President Kennedy and Chancellor Adenauer in the President's Office, 21 November 1961, *FRUS:* 1961–1963, vol. 14, 592.

48. Telegram from the Embassy in Germany to the Department of State, 2 March 1959. *FRUS:* 1958–1960, vol. 8, 404.

49. Press, *Calculating Credibility*, 93.

50. Memorandum of Conversation, 8 February 1959, *FRUS:* 1958–1960, vol. 8, 347.

51. Betts, *Nuclear Blackmail and Nuclear Balance*, 85.

52. Record of Meeting of the Interdepartmental Coordinating Group on Berlin Contingency Planning, 16 June 1961, *FRUS:* 1961–1963, vol. 14, 119–20.

53. Gearson and Schake, *Berlin Wall Crisis*, 62.

54. Report by Dean Acheson, 28 June 1961, *FRUS:* 1961–1963, vol. 14, 140.

55. Record of Meeting of the Interdepartmental Coordinating Group on Berlin Contingency Planning, 16 June 1961, *FRUS:* 1961–1963, vol. 14, 121.

56. Betts, *Nuclear Blackmail and Nuclear Balance*, 85.

57. McGeorge Bundy, cited in Craig, *Destroying the Village*, 132.

58. Wednesday Afternoon Talks, 31 May 1961, *FRUS:* 1961–1963, vol. 14, 85; and Record of Conversation, 5 June 1961, *FRUS:* 1961–1963, vol. 14, 102.

59. Ministerial Consultations on Berlin, August 1962, *FRUS:* 1961–1963, vol. 14, 283.

60. Letter from the Ambassador to Yugoslavia (Kennan) to the Ambassador to the Soviet Union (Thompson), 9 February 1962, *FRUS:* 1961–1963, vol. 14, 802.

61. Fursenko and Naftali, *Khrushchev's Cold War*, 6.

62. Ibid., 243.

63. Ibid., 243–44.

64. Taylor, *Berlin Wall*, 105.

65. Ibid., 116.

66. Press, *Calculating Credibility*, 105.

67. Telegram from the Embassy in the Soviet Union to the Department of State, 27 May 1961, *FRUS:* 1961–1963, vol. 14, 77.

68. Position Paper Prepared in the Department of State, "Berlin and Germany," 25 May 1961, *FRUS:* 1961–1963, vol. 14, 74.

69. Smyser, *Kennedy and the Berlin Wall*, 160.

70. Telegram from the Embassy in the Soviet Union to the Department of State, 24 May 1961, *FRUS:* 1961–1963, vol. 14, 67.

71. Kempe, *Berlin* 1961, 201.

72. Quadripartite Foreign Ministers Meeting, 11 December 1961, *FRUS:* 1961–1963, vol. 14, 656.

73. Copeland, *Origins of Major War*, 3.

74. For the argument that fear of West Germany's nuclear ambitions was the key motivator of Soviet policy during the Berlin Crisis, see Trachtenberg, *Constructed Peace*.

75. Memorandum Prepared by the Ambassador to Germany, 31 October 1968, *FRUS:* 1969–1976, vol. 40, 2–3.

76. Memorandum from the President's Assistant for National Security Affairs (Kissinger) to President Nixon, 24 January 1969, *FRUS:* 1969–1976, vol. 40, 9.

77. Draft Memorandum of Conversation, Bonn, 2 February 1969, *FRUS:* 1969–1976, vol. 40, 44.

78. Telegram from the Mission in Berlin to the Department of State, 8 January 1969, *FRUS:* 1969–1976, vol. 40, 5.

79. Editorial Note, 3 March 1969, *FRUS:* 1969–1976, vol. 40, 49.

80. Editorial Note, 22 October 1970, *FRUS:* 1969–1976, vol. 40, 377.

81. Memorandum from the President's Assistant for National Security Affairs (Kissinger) to President Nixon, 25 January 1971, *FRUS:* 1969–1976, vol. 40, 495.

82. Conversation among President Nixon, German Chancellor Brandt, the President's Assistant for National Security Affairs, and the German State Secretary for Foreign, Defense, and German Policy, 15 June 1971, *FRUS:* 1969–1976, vol. 40, 741–48.

83. "In the 1950s, the German question was still an open issue. In the 1960s, the division of Germany was accepted as a fact of life. In the late 1950s, it seemed West Germany was well on its way to acquiring nuclear weapons. By the early 1960s, it had become clear that the Federal Republic was not going to control nuclear forces on its own. . . . In general, it had seemed in the 1950s that events were in flux, but by the 1960s, the system of great power relations in Europe had acquired a certain permanence, and a certain stability." Trachtenberg, *History and Strategy*, 230. Furthermore, the East German regime was far more stable by the Nixon period, in part because the 1961 erection of the Berlin Wall had largely ended the debilitating exodus of East Germans.

84. Memorandum from the President's Assistant for National Security Affairs to President Nixon, 14 October 1970, *FRUS:* 1969–1976, vol. 40, 360.

4. Blasts from the Past

1. George W. Bush, The National Security Strategy of the United States, September 2002, http://www.whitehouse.gov/nsc/nss.html, 13–15.

2. Mao Zedong, "We Must Not Fear Nuclear War," cited in Richard Wyn Jones, *Security, Strategy, and Critical Theory* (Boulder, CO: Lynne Rienner, 1999), chap. 5. For the quotation, see http:// www.ciaonet.org/book/wynjones/wynjones05.html.

3. Accounts that underplay the influence of the Gilpatric committee on US nonproliferation strategy include Shane Maddock, "The Nth Country Conundrum: The American and Soviet Quest for Nuclear Nonproliferation, 1945–1970" (PhD diss., University of Connecticut, 1997); Raymond L. Garthoff, *A Journey through the Cold War: A Memoir of Containment and Coexistence* (Washington, DC: Brookings Institution Press, 2001), 194; and Glenn T. Seaborg, *Stemming the Tide: Arms Control in the Johnson Years* (Lexington, MA: D. C. Heath, 1987), 148. Two accounts that recognize the importance of the committee are George Perkovich, *India's Nuclear Bomb: The Impact on Global Proliferation* (Berkeley: University of California Press, 1999), 103; and Thomas Schwartz, *Lyndon Johnson and Europe: In the Shadow of Vietnam* (Cambridge: Harvard University Press, 2003).

4. Notes of Arthur H. Dean to Roswell Gilpatric, John J. McCloy, and Arthur Watson Jr., 13 December 1964, National Security Files (hereafter cited as NSF), Committee on Non-Proliferation, box 1, Lyndon Baines Johnson Library, Austin, Texas (hereafter cited as LBJ Library).

5. See William Burr and Jeffrey T. Richelson, "Whether to 'Strangle the Baby in the Cradle': The United States and the Chinese Nuclear Program, 1960–64," *International Security* 25, no. 3 (Winter 2000/01): 54–99.

6. Memo, Bundy to Kennedy, 8 November 1962, *Foreign Relations of the United States, 1961–1963*, vol. 7 (Washington, DC: U.S. Government Printing Office, 1995), 598 (hereafter cited as *FRUS*, with appropriate year, volume, and page numbers).

7. Glen Seaborg diary, entry 8 February 1963, quoted in Marc Trachtenberg, *A Constructed Peace: The Making of the European Settlement*, 1945–1963 (Princeton: Princeton University Press, 1999), 384.

8. "China as a Nuclear Power (Some Thoughts Prior to the Chinese Test)," author unknown, 7 October 1964, NSF, Committee on Non-Proliferation, box 5, LBJ Library.

9. John McCloy, untitled and undated memo, 7, Papers of John J. McCloy (hereafter cited as PJM), box DA1, folder 86A, Amherst College, Amherst, Massachusetts (hereafter cited as AC).

10. National Security Council, "The Value and Feasibility of a Nuclear Non-Proliferation Treaty," 12 December 1964, NSF, Committee on Non-Proliferation, box 2, LBJ Library.

11. Russell Murray, "Problems of Nuclear Proliferation outside Europe (Problem 2)," 7 December 1964, Declassified Documents Reference System (hereafter cited as DDRS), document no. CK3100281620, NSF, Committee on Non-Proliferation, box 5, LBJ Library.

12. Memcon, Couve de Murville, Charles Lucet, George Ball, and Charles Bohlen, 2 December 1964, record group (RG) 59, lot 67D2, box 7, U.S. National Archives, College Park, Maryland (hereafter cited as USNA).

13. Ibid.

14. For Indonesia's threat to detonate a nuclear device, see Ropa for Bundy, "The Asia Week," 20 September 1965, DDRS, document no. CK3100238073, 6. For a later threat by the Romanian leader Nicolae Ceausescu, see Cover Note, Sonnenfeldt to Kissinger, and Intelligence Note, "Romanians Will Ratify NPT but Will Want Something for It," 20 October 1969, National Security Council Files (hereafter cited as NSCF), box 366, Nixon Presidential Materials, USNA.

15. Murray, "Problems of Nuclear Proliferation outside Europe (Problem 2)."

16. NSC, "Value and Feasibility of a Nuclear Non-Proliferation Treaty," 14.

17. "Position Paper on a Non-Proliferation Agreement," author unknown, 16 July 1965, DDRS, document no. CK3100079658.

18. NSC, "Value and Feasibility of a Nuclear Non-Proliferation Treaty," 14.

19. "Disarmament Issues Discussed with Mikoyan," undated, RG 59, lot 67D2, box 5, USNA.

20. Record of Rusk-Khrushchev Meeting, 8 August 1963, *FRUS:* 1961–1963, vol. 15, 567.

21. Couve de Murville, Charles Lucet, George Ball, and Charles Bohlen, "Memorandum of Conversation," 2 December 1964, RG 59, lot 67D2, box 7, USNA.

22. The MLF was a proposal, championed by the U.S. State Department, to develop a seaborne nuclear force that would be manned by NATO countries that wanted to participate. Robert Bowie first proposed the concept in the last year of the Eisenhower administration, and different versions circulated with varying degrees of presidential support during the Kennedy and Johnson administrations. While the United States would retain a veto over the firing of the weapons, the idea was to give the NATO allies—in particular, West Germany—a role in nuclear policy and even some limited access to the weapons. With the exception of the FRG, there was little enthusiasm for the proposal; the Soviet Union and France were adamantly opposed. Many State Department officials, however, feared that without the MLF, the West Germans would be unable to resist pressures to acquire their own nuclear force. For an analysis of the MLF proposals, see Trachtenberg, *Constructed Peace*, 312–15.

23. Notes of President's Meeting with Consultants on Foreign Policy, 21 October 1964, DDRS, document no. CK3100066700.

24. In a telephone conversation between National Security Advisor Bundy and Under Secretary of State Ball on October 29, Bundy stated, "There was lots of feeling by the president that we should take a higher-level, harder look at the problem of nuclear spread—a better policy than we would be able to get by using our inter-house machinery. The thought has been expressed that a nuclear spread task force be established. He mentioned Ros Gilpatric in this regard." Transcript of Conversation, McGeorge Bundy and George Ball, 29 October 1964, Personal Papers of George Ball, Disarmament, box 3, LBJ Library.

25. Seaborg, *Stemming the Tide*, 137.

26. "Selected Issues," author and date unknown, NSF, Committee on Non-Proliferation, box 5, LBJ Library.

27. "Problems concerning Alternative Courses of Action," author and date unknown, Personal Papers of Roswell Gilpatric (hereafter cited as PPRG), box 11, John F. Kennedy Library, Boston, Massachusetts (hereafter cited as JFK Library).

28. "Probable Consequences: Permissive or Selective Proliferation," author and date unknown, PPRG, box 11, JFK Library; and "Permissive or Selective Proliferation author and date unknown, PPRG, box 11, JFK Library.

29. "All-Out Efforts to Stop Proliferation," author and date unknown, PPRG, box 11, JFK Library; and "Probable Consequences: All-Out Efforts to Stop Proliferation," author and date unknown, PPRG, box 11, JFK Library.

30. Ibid.

31. Roger Fisher, "Memo on Possible Action: Action Directed against Further French Atmospheric Tests," 19 December 1964, PPRG, box 10, JFK Library.

32. "Probable Consequences: All-Out Efforts to Stop Proliferation."

33. "Present 'Prudent' Course," author and date unknown, PPRG, box 11, JFK Library.

34. "Present 'Prudent' Course," author and date unknown (same title but different document from that cited in n. 219, PPRG, box 11, JFK Library.

35. "Course III," author and date unknown, PPRG, box 11, JFK Library.

36. "A Comparable Rationale for Course III (and Beyond)," author and date unknown, PPRG, box 10, JFK Library.

37. "Probable Consequences" author and date unknown, PPRG, box 11, JFK Library.

38. "Minutes of Briefing by Hon. Wm. C. Foster to Gilpatric Committee on January 7, 1965," 7 January 1965, PPRG, box 10, JFK Library.

39. "RLG's Notes on Luncheon Conf. with George Ball," 14 December 1964, PPRG, box 10, JFK Library.

40. "Secretary's Meeting with the Gilpatric Committee on Non-Proliferation," 7 January 1965, RG 59, lot 67D2, box 24, USNA.

41. "Notes on RLG's Talk with RS McN," 12 December 1964, PPRG, box 10, JFK Library.

42. Walt W. Rostow, "A Way of Thinking about Nuclear Proliferation," 19 November 1964, PPRG, box 11, JFK Library, 1.

43. "Tentative Thoughts on Certain Proliferation Problems," author and date unknown, PPRG, box 10, JFK Library.

44. Notes of AHD to RG, JJM, and AW Jr., 13 December 1964, NSF, Committee on Non-Proliferation, box 1, LBJ Library.

45. "Probable Consequences IV: All-Out Efforts to Stop Proliferation, author and date unknown, PPRG, box 11, JFK Library.

46. "Problems concerning Alternative Courses of Action," 4.

47. Memcon, "Non-Proliferation of Nuclear Weapons—Course of Action for UNGA—Discussed by the Committee of Principals," 23 November 1964, *FRUS: 1964–1968*, vol. 11; and Arms Control and Disarmament (Washington, DC: U.S. Department of State, n.d.), document no. 50, http://www.state.gov/www/about_state/history/vol_xi/f.html.

48. Memorandum, RWK to McGeorge Bundy, 26 October 1964, NSF, Subject File: Nuclear Weapons, box 34, LBJ Library.

49. Memorandum, Dean Rusk to President Johnson, January 1965, NSF, Country File: Japan, box 253, LBJ Library.

50. Memorandum of Conversation, PM Sato and President Johnson, January 1965, NSF, Country File: Japan, box 253, LBJ Library.

51. "Japan's Prospects in the Nuclear Weapons Field: Proposed U.S. Courses of Action," 24 June 1965, RG 59, lot 67D2, box 24, USNA.

52. Memorandum, George McGhee to Dean Rusk, 13 September 1961, Freedom of Information Act Files: India, USNA.

53. "A Report to the President by the Committee on Nuclear Proliferation," position paper, author unknown, 21 January 1965, PPRG, box 10, JFK Library.

54. "Professor Roger Fisher's Comments on Selected Portions of Course Three," n.d., NSF, Committee on Non-Proliferation, box 5, LBJ Library.

55. Thompson for Rusk, "Talking Points for Meeting with the Gilpatric Committee," 7 January 1965, RG 59, lot 67D2, box 24, USNA.

56. William Bundy to Ambassador Thompson, "Nuclear Assurances to India," 16 March 1965, RG 59, lot 67D2, box 24, USNA.

57. Ibid.

58. "Problems concerning Alternative Courses of Action," 3.

59. "Japan's Prospects in the Nuclear Weapons Field," 12.

60. "Europe, NATO, Germany, and the MLF," author and date unknown, NSF, Committee on Nuclear Proliferation, box 1, LBJ Library.

61. Fisher to Gilpatric, "A Proposed Decision on the General U.S. Policy toward Nuclear Weapons," 17 December 1964, PPRG, box 10, JFK Library.

62. "Background Paper on Factors Which Could Influence National Decisions concerning Acquisition of Nuclear Weapons," Department of State, 12 December 1964, RG 59, lot 68D452, box 199, USNA.

63. The Johnson administration made the decision to deploy a "light" system in December 1966. (A light system could be oriented against small nuclear powers or accidental missile launches from the Soviet Union. In contrast, a full-scale system could counter a full-scale Soviet attack.) Secretary of Defense McNamara announced the controversial decision in a speech in San Francisco in September 1967. McNamara justified the deployment by emphasizing the Chinese, not Soviet, threat.

64. "Probable Consequences: Permissive or Selective Proliferation."

65. "Present 'Prudent' Course," PPRG, box 11, JFK Library.

66. "Course III."

67. "Handwritten Notes on RLG's Talk with RS McN," 12 December 1964, PPRG, box 11, JFK Library.

68. Gerald W. Johnson, associate director of Plowshare, to Gilpatric, 7 December 1964, PPRG, box 10, JFK Library.

69. "Contingency Paper on the Arms Control Considerations of a U.S. ABM Deployment Decision," 25 August 1967, NSF, Country File: USSR, box 231, folder: USSR-ABM Negotiations (II) 1/ 67–9/68, LBJ Library.

70. Committee on Nuclear Proliferation, Minutes of Discussion, 13–14 December 1965, NSF, Committee on Nuclear Proliferation, box 7, LBJ Library.

71. Notes of Ministerial Director Diehl, 1 February 1967, document no. 40, 213, in *Akten zur Auswaertigen Politik der Bundesrepublik Deutschland,* 1966, vol. 2, ed. Matthias Peter and Harald Rosenbach (Munich, Germany: Oldenbourg Verlag, 1997).

72. Soviet Ambassador to the United States Anatoly F. Dobrynin and President's Special Assistant Walt W. Rostow, Memo of Conversation, 27 January 1967, *FRUS: 1964–1968*, vol. 14, 455.

73. Strategic Military Panel, President's Science Advisory Committee, "Proposed Army-BTL Ballistic Missile Defense System," 29 October 1965, http://www.gwu.edu/?nsarchiv/NSAEBB/ NSAEBB36/01-01.htm.

74. Spurgeon Keeny to Dr. Donald F. Hornig, "ABM Deployment," 4 January 1967, DDRS, document no. CK3100183292.

75. Murray, "Problems of Nuclear Proliferation outside Europe," 7.

76. Burr and Richelson, "Whether to 'Strangle the Baby in the Cradle,'" 67.

77. Trachtenberg, *Constructed Peace*, 320.

78. Henry Rowen, "Effects of Chinese Bomb on Nuclear Spread," 2 November 1964, RG 59, lot 70D, box 199, USNA.

79. Memo, Rostow to Rusk, "Nuclear Proliferation and the Crises in South-east Asia and the Atlantic," 4 November 1964, RG 59, lot 70D, box 199, USNA.

80. Rostow, "A Way of Thinking," 15.

81. "Statement by the President on Chinese Communist Detonation of Nuclear Devices," 16 October 1964, RG 59, lot 70D, book 199, USNA.

82. "Position Paper on a Non-Proliferation Agreement," 16 July 1965, DDRS, document no. CK3100079658, 11.

83. Ibid., 13

84. Thomas Hughes to Acting Secretary, "Communist China: Lo Jui-ch'ing on War—Nuclear and Conventional," 13 May 1965, DDRS, document no. CK 3100363074.

85. Committee on Nuclear Proliferation, Minutes of Discussion, Third Meeting, 7–8 January 1965, PPRG, box 10, JFK Library. In the LBJ Library's copy of this document, the last line (and much else) has been redacted.

86. McCloy to Gilpatric, cover letter and "Memorandum for the Chairman," 11 January 1965, PJM, box DA1, folder 87, AC.

87. "London Meeting of McNamara and Ball with Secretary of State for Defence Denis Healy and Foreign Secretary Michael Stewart," 26 November 1965, RG 59, box 1592, Defe 18–3, USNA.

88. Ibid.

89. Letter, McCloy to Pastore, 28 February 1966, PJM, box DA1, folder 108, 1, AC. China had been an ally of the Soviet Union but was now an adversary. The change from friend to foe caused the Soviet leadership to regret any assistance the Soviets had provided to China's nuclear program.

90. McCloy to Kennedy, 2 March 1966, PJM, box DA1, folder 107, 1, AC.

91. Letter, Robert Kennedy to John McCloy, 15 April 1966, PJM, box DA1, folder 107, 1–2, AC.

92. Owen to McCloy, 16 October 1965, PJM, box DA1, folder 110, 1–2, AC.

93. Bowie to McCloy, "Article on Non-Proliferation," cover letter and memo, 3 November 1965, PJM, box DA1, folder 105, AC.

94. Robert Bowie, "European Policy," attached to 15 February 1966 letter to John McCloy, PJM, box DA1, folder 105, 1, AC.

95. Memcon, Dr. Horst Blomeyer-Bartenstein and Mr. Richard B. Freund, "Observation Posts and Non-Acquisition of Nuclear Weapons," 19 February 1964, RG 59, box 1592, Defe 18–6, 3, USNA.

96. Telegram from State, 26 October 1966, box 56, History of the NPT, NSF, National Security File, LBJ Library.

97. Henry Kissinger, Memcon with Chancellor Erhard, 28 January 1966, DDRS, document no. CK3100383582.

98. Notes of Ambassador Schnippenkoetter, "Nonproliferation of Nuclear Weapons (NP)," 7 September 1966, document no. 277, in *Akten zur Auswaertigen Politik der Bundesrepublik Deutschland*, 1966, vol. 2, ed. Matthias Peter and Harald Rosenbach (Munich, Germany: Oldenbourg Verlag, 1997).

99. Memorandum, Robert Neumann of UCLA to Lawrence S. Finkelstein, Deputy Assistant Secretary of Defense, 1 November 1965, box 26, Papers of Francis M. Bator, LBJ Library.

100. Conversation between Federal Chancellor Kiesinger and President de Gaulle, Köln, Germany, 25 April 1967, document no. 142, in *Akten zur Auswaertigen Politik der Bundesrepublik Deutschland*, 1967, ed. Ilse Dorothee Pautsch, Jurgen Klockler, Matthias Peter, and Harald Rosenbach (Munich: Oldenbourg Verlag, 1998), 645–46.

101. Conversation between Federal Chancellor Kiesinger and the American Vice President Humphrey," 5 April 1967, document no. 120, in ibid., 550.

102. Ambassador Schnippenkoetter to Secretary of State Carstens, 15 September 1966, document no. 291, in *Akten zur Auswaertigen Politik der Bundesrepublik Deutschland*, 1966, vol. 2, 1216–17. According to this document, President Johnson "gave the order in June to formulate the position of the State Department, Pentagon, and Disarmament Commission. In so doing, he encountered significant differences of opinion. He then entered a long chain of advisory discussions and wrote memoranda with his own hand—an action that is unique in substantive questions about foreign affairs. The president needs progress in the NP [because] of the objective dangers of proliferation" and to demonstrate US-Soviet good relations "despite the Vietnam War."

103. Telegram, State to Bonn, 22 July 1965, DDRS, document no. CK3100054575.

104. "A Report to the President by the Committee on Nuclear Proliferation," 21 January 1965, *FRUS:* 1964–1968, vol. 11, 173–82.

105. Ibid., 179.

106. Seaborg, *Stemming the Tide*, 145.

107. E. W. Kenworthy, "Kennedy Proposes Treaty to Check Nuclear Spread," *New York Times*, 24 June 1965.

108. "President Johnson's Conversation with McGeorge Bundy," 24 June 1965, 10:00 a.m., White House tape WH6506.07, program no. 2, LBJ Library.

109. Seaborg, *Stemming the Tide*, 149. Seaborg wrote, "I was surprised and disappointed that the AEC-written passages on scientists providing a common ground between nations and extolling the IAEA, which were present in earlier drafts, had been omitted. White House assistant Horace Busby told me in confidence that the material had been deleted at the last moment, along with words about halting nuclear spread, because the president had been annoyed by Kennedy's speech, which contained some of the same language as had been in the president's draft speech." Ibid., 146–47.

110. Schwartz, *Lyndon Johnson and Europe*, 52–63.

111. National Security Action Memorandum no. 355, 28 June 1965, *FRUS:* 1964–1968, vol. 11, 216–17.

112. See chapter 2 of this book.

113. See the internet supplement to Trachtenberg's *Constructed Peace* at http://www polisci.ucla.edu/faculty/trachtenberg/appendices/appendixVIII.html.

114. Perkovich, *India's Nuclear Bomb*, 52–53.

115. "Summary of NPT Issues Paper," 28 January 1969, NSCF, box H-019, Nixon Presidential Materials, USNA.

116. Sonnenfeldt to Kissinger, 27 January 1969, NSCF, box 366, Nixon Presidential Materials, USNA.

117. Cover Note from Haig to Kissinger, with cable, Tokyo to Washington, DC, September 1969, NSCF, box 366, Nixon Presidential Materials, USNA.

118. Minutes of the NSC, 29 January 1969, NSCF, box H-12, Nixon Presidential Materials, USNA.

119. "List of Actions Resulting from Meeting of the NSC on January 29, 1969," NSCF, box H-019, Nixon Presidential Materials, USNA.

120. See Thompson to Fisher, "Nuclear Non-Proliferation Agreement," 20 May 1964, RG 59, lot 67D2, box 5, USNA; and Thompson to the Secretary, "Talking Points for Meeting with the Gilpatric Committee," n.d., RG 59, lot 67D2, box 24, USNA.

121. Thompson to Weiss, "Implications of a Major Soviet Conventional Attack in Central Europe," 29 December 1964, RG 59, lot 67D2, box 21, USNA.

122. Stevenson to the President, "A Reassessment of United States Foreign Policy, 1965–70," 18 November 1964, DDRS, document no. CK3100352013.

123. Ernest May, *"Lessons" of the Past: The Use and Misuse of History in American Foreign Policy* (Oxford: Oxford University Press, 1973), xi.

124. Roger Cohen, "A New German Assertiveness on Its Foreign Policy Stance," *New York Times*, 12 September 1999, accessed 12 December 2011, http://www.nytimes.com/1999/09/12/world/a-new-german-assertiveness-on-its-foreign-policy-stance.html.

125. Howard W. French, "Japan Faces Burden: Its Own Defense," *New York Times*, 22 July 2003, accessed 12 December 2011, http://www.nytimes.com/2003/07/22/world/japan-faces-burden-its-own-defense.html?pagewanted=all&src=pm.

5. Nuclear Nixon

1. Conversation between President Nixon and his Assistant for National Security (hereafter cited as Kissinger), 4 April 1972, *Foreign Relations of the United States*, 1969–1972, vol. 14 (Washington, DC: U.S. Government Printing Office, 2006), 258 (hereafter cited as *FRUS*, with appropriate year, volume, and page numbers).

2. For a fascinating history of the development of these ideas, see Fred Kaplan, *The Wizards of Armageddon* (New York: Simon and Schuster, 1983); for the best intellectual treatment of the nuclear revolution and its significance for world politics, see Robert Jervis, *The Meaning of the Nuclear Revolution: Statecraft and the Prospect of Armageddon*, (Ithaca: Cornell University Press, 1989).

3. Spurgeon M. Keeny, Jr., "Fingers on the Nuclear Trigger," review of *At the Borderline of Armageddon: How American Presidents Managed the Atom Bomb* by James E. Goodby, *Arms Control Today*, October 2006, accessed 16 June 2007, http://www.armscontrol.org/act/2006_10/BookReview.asp?print.

4. David Hoffman, "1983: Turning Point of the Cold War," *Security Index: Russian Journal on International Security* 13, no. 1 (81) (Spring 2007): 135–46.

5. McGeorge Bundy, *Danger and Survival: Choices about the Bomb in the First Fifty Years* (New York: Random House, 1988), 552.

6. Sidney D. Drell, "The Impact of a U.S. Public Constituency on Arms Control," in *Breakthrough*, ed. Anatoly Gromyko and Martin Hellman (New York: Walker and Co., 1988).

7. Joan Hoff, *Nixon Reconsidered* (New York: Basic Books, 1994), 201.

8. Richard Nixon, *RN: Memoirs*, 617–18, cited in *FRUS:* 1969–1972, vol. 14, 1144.

9. Henry Kissinger, *White House Years*, 1253–54, cited in *FRUS:* 1969–1972, vol. 14, 1144.

10. Conversation between President Nixon and Kissinger, 19 April 1972, *FRUS:* 1969–1972, vol. 14, 439.

11. Memorandum from Kissinger to President Nixon, 15 February 1969, *FRUS:* 1969–1976, vol. 12, 33.

12. Ambassador Dobrynin's Initial Call on the President, 17 February 1969, 11:45–12:45 a.m. *FRUS:* 1969–1976, vol. 12, 40.

13. Richard Nixon's Meeting with NATO Ambassadors, 30 June 1973, Digital National Security Archive (hereafter cited as DNSA), no. KT00767, 12.

14. Kissinger to Nixon, Analysis of Dobrynin Message, 18 February 1969, *FRUS:* 1969–1976, vol. 12, 51.

15. Letter from President Nixon to Secretary of State Rogers, 4 February 1969, *FRUS:* 1969–1976, vol. 12, 27.

16. Memorandum of Telephone Conversation between President Nixon and Kissinger, 14 May 1972, *FRUS:* 1969–1972, vol. 14, 841.

17. Journal/Diary of H. R. Haldeman, entry April 27,1970, as found in Jeffrey Kimball, *The Vietnam War Files: Uncovering the Secret History of Nixon-Era Strategy* (Lawrence: University of Kansas Press, 2003), 132.

18. Transcript of Telephone Conversation between President Nixon and Kissinger, 6 May 1972, *FRUS:* 1969–1972, vol. 14, 752.

19. Meeting between President Nixon and Committee on Arms Control and Disarmament, 21 March 1972, editorial note, *FRUS:* 1969–1972, vol. 14, 218.

20. Memorandum of Telephone Conversation between President Nixon and Kissinger, 14 May 1972, *FRUS:* 1969–1972, vol. 14, 835.

21. Conversation between President Nixon and Kissinger, 19 April 1972, *FRUS:* 1969–1972, vol. 14, 243.

22. Ibid., 444.

23. Conversation, Nixon and Kissinger, 10 April 1972, 8:57 a.m., editorial note, *FRUS:* 1969–1972, vol. 14, 281.

24. Meeting between President Nixon and Committee on Arms Control and Disarmament, 21 March 1972, editorial note, *FRUS:* 1969–1972, vol. 14, 219.

25. Richard Nixon's Meeting with NATO Ambassadors, 30 June 1973, DNSA, item no. KT00767, 7.

26. Ibid., 12.

27. Meeting between President Nixon and Committee on Arms Control and Disarmament, 21 March 1972, editorial note, *FRUS:* 1969–1972, vol. 14, 218.

28. Memorandum from President Nixon to Haig, 20 May 1972, *FRUS:* 1969–1972, vol. 14, 965.

29. Richard Nixon's Meeting with NATO Ambassadors, 30 June 1973, DNSA, item no. KT00767, 2.

30. Memorandum for the President's Files, 8 May 1972, *FRUS:* 1969–1972, vol. 14, 769.

31. Notes on NSC Meeting, 14 February 1969, DNSA, item no. KT00006, 3.

32. Meeting between President Nixon and Committee on Arms Control and Disarmament, 21 March 1972, editorial note, *FRUS:* 1969–1972, vol. 14, 218.

33. Richard Nixon's Meeting with NATO Ambassadors, 30 June 1973, DNSA, item no. KT00767, 2.

34. NSC Meeting, 19 February 1969, DNSA, item no. KT00006, 1.

35. Ibid., 3–5.

36. Notes on NSC Meeting, 14 February 1969, DNSA, item no. KT00003, 5.

37. For an early scholarly description of Nixon's use of the "madman" theory, see Raymond Garthoff, *Détente and Confrontation: American-Soviet Relations from Nixon to Reagan* (Washington, DC: Brookings Institution Press, 1985), 251. For manipulation of risk, see Thomas Schelling, *Arms and Influences* (New Haven: Yale University Press, 1966), 92–125. For "the threat that leaves something to chance," see Thomas Schelling, *The Strategy of Conflict* (Cambridge: Harvard University Press, 1960), 187–204. For an interesting analysis, see Jeffrey Kimball, "Did Thomas C. Schelling Invent the Madman Theory?" published on the History News Network, 24 October 2005, accessed 10 July 2007, http://hnn.us/articles/17183.html.

38. William Burr, "The Nixon Administration, the 'Horror Strategy,' and the Search for Limited Nuclear Options, 1969–1972," *Journal of Cold War Studies* 7, no. 3 (Summer 2005): 34–78; Terry Terriff, *The Nixon Administration and the Making of U.S. Nuclear Strategy* (Ithaca: Cornell University Press, 1995).

39. See chapter 2 of this book.

40. Henry Kissinger, *The White House Years* (Boston: Little, Brown, 1979), 198.

41. See Burr, "Nixon Administration" and Terriff, *Nixon Administration.*

42. Burr, "Nixon Administration," 71.

43. National Security Decision Memorandum 242, accessed 12 September 2007, http://www.gwu.edu/~nsarchiv/NSAEBB/NSAEBB173/SIOP-24b.pdf.

44. Jeffrey Kimball, *Nixon's Vietnam War* (Lawrence: University of Kansas Press, 1998), esp. 23, 27, 68–69. For Haldeman's views, see Kimball, *Nixon's Vietnam War,* 76–77, and Kimball, *Vietnam War Files,* 132.

45. NSC Meeting, 19 February 1969, DNSA, item no. KT00006, 1.

46. See William Burr and Jeffrey Kimball, "Nixon's Nuclear Ploy: To Help End the War in Vietnam, the United States Thought a Secret, Yet Massive, Nuclear Alert Would Get the Soviets' Attention and Assistance," *Bulletin of the Atomic Scientists* 59, no. 1 (2003): 28–39; Scott Sagan and Jeremi Suri, "The Madman Alert: Secrecy, Signaling, and Safety in October 1969," *International Security* 27, no. 4 (2003): 150–83.

47. This is a consistent theme throughout *FRUS:* 1969–1972, vol. 14, documents 73–124.

48. Kissinger, as quoted in Jervis, *Meaning of the Nuclear Revolution*, 43.

49. For an excellent early treatment of this episode, see Barry Blechman and Douglas Hart, "The Political Utility of Nuclear Weapons: The 1973 Middle East Crisis," in *Strategy and Nuclear Deterrence*, ed. Steven E. Miller (Princeton: Princeton University Press, 1984), 273–97. For an excellent treatment of the efficacy of nuclear threats during the Cold War, see Richard K. Betts, *Nuclear Blackmail and Nuclear Balance* (Washington, DC: Brookings Institution Press, 1987).

50. Conversation between Nixon and Kissinger, 4 April 1972, *FRUS:* 1969–1972, vol. 14, 258.

51. President Nixon's Meeting with Bipartisan Congressional Leadership, 20 June 1974, DNSA, item no. KT01227, 2.

52. Conversation between President Nixon and Kissinger, 23 April 1971, *FRUS:* 1969–1976, 1972, vol. 7, 581.

53. Oval Office Conversation no. 637–3, 8:45–9:42 a.m., 12 December 1971, editorial note, *FRUS:* 1969–1972, vol. 14, 74.

54. Conversation between President Nixon and Kissinger, 19 April 1972, *FRUS:* 1969–1972, vol. 14, 433.

55. "Executive Office Building Conversation no. 332–35, Nixon and Kissinger, 12–12:28 a.m.," 15 April 1972, in Kimball, *Nixon's Vietnam War*, 217.

56. See chapter 4 of this book.

57. Kissinger, *Nuclear Weapons and Foreign Policy* (New York: Harper and Brothers, 1957), 213.

58. Minutes of the NSC, 29 January 1969, National Security Council Draft Minutes, box H-12, Nixon Presidential Materials, U.S. National Archives, College Park, Maryland (hereafter cited as USNA).

59. Summary of NPT Issues Paper, 28 January, 1969, National Security Council Meetings File, NSCF, box H-019, Nixon Presidential Materials, USNA.

60. Roger Kelly Smith, "The Origins of the Regime, Nonproliferation, National Interest, and American Decision-Making, 1943–1976." (PhD diss., Georgetown University, 1990), 370.

61. Minutes of NSC Meeting on Post-de Gaulle France, 23 February 1970, DNSA, item no. KT00101, 2.

62. Discussion with Ambassador Kosciusko-Morizet of U.S. Relations with France and Western Europe, 13 April 1973, DNSA, item no. KT00702, 9.

63. The leading scholar on Israel's nuclear program, Avner Cohen, has put together an excellent briefing book on this question, which can be found on the National Security Archive's website, http://www.gwu.edu/~nsarchiv/NSAEBB/NSAEBB189/index.htm.

64. National Security Council Meeting, 19 February 1969, DNSA, item no. KT00006, 7.

65. Winston Lord, "The Nixon Doctrine for Asia: Some Hard Choices," 23 January 1970, DNSA, item no. KT00182, 4.

66. Garthoff, *Détente and Confrontation*, 286.

67. Robert Dallek, *Nixon and Kissinger: Partners in Power* (New York: HarperCollins, 2007), 139.

68. Kimball, *Nixon's Vietnam War*, xii.

69. For the best discussion of this fascinating question, see Marc Trachtenberg, "The Influence of Nuclear Weapons on the Cuban Missile Crisis," in *History and Strategy* (Princeton: Princeton University Press, 1991), 235–60.

70. For this critique, see Marc Trachtenberg, "The Past and Future of Arms Control," *Daedalus* (Winter 1991): 203–16; and Marc Trachtenberg, Comment on Robert Jervis in his, "Security Studies: Ideas, Policy, and Politics," in *The Evolution of Political Knowledge: Democracy, Autonomy, and Conflict in Comparative and International Politics*, ed. Edward D. Mansfield and Richard Sisson (Columbus: Ohio State University Press, 2004), 140–45. Both articles can be accessed at http://www.polisci.ucla.edu/faculty/trachtenberg/cv/cv.html.

71. Ernest R. May, John D. Steinbruner, and Thomas Wolfe, *History of the Strategic Arms Competition, 1945–1972*, part 2 (Washington, DC: Office of the Secretary of Defense, Historical Office, March 1981), 810, available on DNSA, http://nsarchive.chadwyck.com.

72. John Lewis Gaddis, chapter 6 "The Essential Relevance of Nuclear Weapons," in *The United States and the End of the Cold War: Implications, Reconsiderations, Provocations* (Oxford: Oxford University Press, 1992), 110.

73. The best articulation of this idea can be found in Kenneth N. Waltz, "More May Be Better," in *The Spread of Nuclear Weapons: A Debate*, ed. Scott D. Sagan and Kenneth N. Waltz (New York: W. W. Norton, 1995).

6. That Seventies Show

1. For popular accounts, in addition to Greg Herken, *Counsels of War* (New York: Oxford University Press, 1987), see Fred Kaplan, *The Wizards of Armageddon* (Stanford: Stanford University Press, 1991); and John Newhouse, *War and Peace in the Nuclear Age* (New York: Vintage Books, 1990).

2. For a trenchant analysis of these debates, see Bruce Kuklick, *Blind Oracles: Intellectuals and War from Kennan to Kissinger* (Princeton: Princeton University Press, 2006).

3. McGeorge Bundy, "To Cap the Volcano," *Foreign Affairs* 48, no. 1 (October 1969): 11.

4. Paul C. Warnke and Leslie H. Gelb, "Security or Confrontation: The Case for a Defense Policy," *Foreign Policy* 1 (Winter 1970–71): 23.

5. Robert Jervis, *The Meaning of the Nuclear Revolution: Statecraft and the Prospects of Armageddon* (Ithaca: Cornell University Press, 1989), 74–106.

6. William C. Foster, "Prospects for Arms Control," *Foreign Affairs* 47, no. 3 (April 1969): 416.

7. Alton Frye, "The Vindication of Robert McNamara," *Washington Post*, 6 July 1972, editorial section.

8. Robert Jervis, "Cooperation under the Security Dilemma" *World Politics* 30, no. 2 (1978): 167–214.

9. Quote from Lawrence Freedman, *The Evolution of Nuclear Strategy*, 2nd ed. (New York: St. Martin's Press, 1997), 349.

10. Paul H. Nitze, "Assuring Strategic Stability in an Era of Détente," *Foreign Affairs* 54, no. 2 (January 1976): 207

11. Richard Pipes, "Why the Soviet Union Thinks It Could Fight and Win a Nuclear War," *Commentary* 64, no. 1 (July 1977): 34.

12. Colin S. Gray, "Nuclear Strategy: The Case for a Theory of Victory," *International Security* 4, no. 1 (Summer 1979): 87.

13. For contrasting views, see Richard Betts, *Nuclear Blackmail and Nuclear Balance* (Washington, DC: Brookings Institution Press, 1987); and Gareth Porter, *Perils of Dominance: Imbalance of Power and the Road to War in Vietnam* (Berkeley: University of California Press, 2005).

14. See Marc Trachtenberg, chapter 6 "The Cuban Missile Crisis," in *History and Strategy* (Princeton: Princeton University Press, 1991), 235–60.

15. See Marc Trachtenberg, chapter 5 "The Berlin Crisis," in *History and Strategy*, 192–93; 218–21.

16. See chapter 5 of this book.

17. For an excellent assessment of this question, see Marc Trachtenberg, "The Past and Future of Arms Control," *Daedalus* 120, no. 1 (Winter 1991): 203–16.

18. Ernest May, John Steinbruner, and Thomas Wolfe, *History of the Strategic Arms Competition, 1945–1972*, part 2 (Washington, DC: Office of the Secretary of Defense, Historical Office, March 1981), 810.

19. Ibid., 828.

20. Lawrence Wittner, *Toward Nuclear Abolition: A History of the World Disarmament Movement, 1971 to the Present* (Stanford: Stanford University Press, 2003), 41–42.

21. Paul Lettow, *Ronald Reagan and His Quest to Abolish Nuclear Weapons* (New York: Random House, 2005), iv.

22. Nina Tannenwald, *The Nuclear Taboo: The United States and the Non-Use of Nuclear Weapons Since 1945* (Cambridge: Cambridge University Press, 2007).

23. John Mueller, *Retreat from Doomsday: The Obsolescence of Major War* (New York: Basic Books, 1989).

24. George P. Shultz, William J. Perry, Henry A. Kissinger, and Sam Nunn, "Toward a Nuclear-Free World," *Wall Street Journal* online, 15 January 2008, accessed 22 November 2011, http://www.cfr.org/proliferation/wsj-toward-nuclear-free-world/p15264.

7. Same as It Ever Was

1. Craig Gilbert, "Nuclear Threat Seen as Top Issue for Nation," *Milwaukee Journal Sentinel*, 10 October 2004.

2. John McCain, "Remarks by John McCain on Nuclear Security," University of Denver, Colorado, 27 May 2008, accessed 15 April 2012, http://carnegieendowment.org/2008/05/27/remarks-by-john-mccain-on-nuclear-security/mqy.

3. "Transcript: The Democratic Debate in New Hampshire," *New York Times* online, 5 January 2008, accessed 22 November 2011, http://www.nytimes.com/2008/01/05/us/politics/05text-ddebate.html?pagewanted=all.

4. Ibid.

5. Richard G. Lugar, "The Lugar Survey on Proliferation Threats and Responses," Office of Richard Lugar, Washington, DC, June 2005, accessed 22 November 2011, lugar.senate.gov/nunnlugar/pdf/NPSurvey.pdf.

6. William C. Potter and Gaukhar Mukhatzhanova, "Divining Nuclear Intentions: A Review Essay," *International Security* 33, no. 1 (Summer 2008): 159.

7. David Von Drehle, "The Yikes Years: Life as the World's Lone Superpower Is Beginning to Make the Cold War Look Easy," *Washington Post Magazine*, 21 November 2004, W16.

8. Derek D. Smith, *Deterring America: Rogue States and the Proliferation of Weapons of Mass Destruction* (Cambridge: Cambridge University Press, 2006), 10.

9. Abraham Denmark, quoted in Matthew B. Stannard, "Tauscher in Hot Seat for Key State Dept. Post," *San Francisco Chronicle*, 9 June 2009.

10. Schultz et al., "A World Free of Nuclear Weapons."

11. David Ignatius, "New World Disorder," *Washington Post*, 4 May 2007.

12. For an optimistic view of the effects of nuclear proliferation on peace and stability, see Kenneth N. Waltz, "The Spread of Nuclear Weapons: More May Be Better," Adelphi Papers, no. 171 (London: International Institute for Strategic Studies, 1981).

13. Most analysts agree that "the second nuclear age began in 1991": Michael Krepon, *Better Safe Than Sorry: The Ironies of Living with the Bomb* (Stanford: Stanford University Press, 2009), 94. Paul Bracken, however, suggests that it began with India's 1974 "peaceful" nuclear explosion. See Paul Bracken, *Fire in the East: The Rise of Asian Military Power and the Second Nuclear Age* (New York: HarperCollins, 1999), 109.

14. Ignatius, "New World Disorder."

15. Benjamin Frankel, "The Brooding Shadow: Systemic Incentives and Nuclear Weapons Proliferation," in *The Proliferation Puzzle: Why Nuclear Weapons Spread*, ed. Zachary S. Davis and Benjamin Frankel (London: Frank Cass, 1993), 36.

16. Joe Palca interview with Stephen D. Rosen, "Transcript: North Korea and Nuclear Proliferation," *Talk of the Nation*, National Public Radio, 9 October 2006, 6.

17. Greg Sheridan, "Nuclear-Armed Iran Changes World," *The Australian*, 3 July 2008, accessed 22 November 2011, http://www.theaustralian.com.au/news/nuclear-armed-iran-changes-world/story-e6frg6v6-1111116803241.

18. Ariel E. Levite, "Never Say Never Again: Nuclear Reversal Revisited," *International Security* 27, no. 3 (Winter 2002–3): 69–73.

19. Mitchell B. Reiss, "The Nuclear Tipping Point: Prospects for a World of Many Nuclear Weapons States," in *The Nuclear Tipping Point: Why States Reconsider Their Nuclear Choices*, ed. Kurt M. Campbell, Robert J. Einhorn, and Mitchell B. Reiss (Washington, DC: Brookings Institution Press, 2004), 4.

20. George Perkovich, Jessica T. Mathews, Joseph Cirincione, Rose Gottemoeller, and Jon B. Wolfsthal, "Universal Compliance: A Strategy for Nuclear Security," Carnegie Endowment for International Peace, Washington, DC, March 2005, 19, accessed 22 November 2011, carnegieendowment.org/files/univ_comp_rpt07_final1.pdf.

21. Michael Crowley, "The Stuff Sam Nunn's Nightmares Are Made Of," *New York Times*, 25 February 2007.

22. Bill Keller, "The Thinkable," *New York Times Magazine*, 4 May 2003.

23. John Lewis Gaddis, "The Long Peace: Elements of Stability in the Postwar International System," chapter 8 in *The Long Peace: Inquiries into the History of the Cold War* (New York: Oxford University Press, 1987), 215–46; and John J. Mearsheimer, "Back

to the Future: Instability in Europe after the Cold War," *International Security* 15, no. 1 (Summer 1990): 5–56.

24. Michael Dobbs, "The World's Most Terrifying Danger, Then and Now," *Washington Post*, 17 October 2004.

25. Thomas L. Friedman, "The Post-Post-Cold War," *New York Times*, 10 May 2006, accessed 22 November 2011, http://www.nytimes.com/2006/05/10/opinion/10friedman.html?scp=1&sq=Thomas%20L.%20Friedman,%20%E2%80%9CThe%20Post-Post-Cold%20War,&st=cse.

26. Dobbs, "World's Most Terrifying Danger."

27. Sheridan, "Nuclear-Armed Iran."

28. Keith B. Payne, "Nuclear Deterrence for a New Century," *Journal of International Security Affairs* 10 (Spring 2006): 53.

29. Ashton B. Carter and William J. Perry, "If Necessary, Strike and Destroy: North Korea Cannot Be Allowed to Test This Missile," *Washington Post*, 22 June 2006.

30. Fred C. Iklé, "Possible Consequences of a Further Spread of Nuclear Weapons," 2 January 1965, National Security Files, Committee on Nuclear Proliferation, box 7, Lyndon Baines Johnson Presidential Library, Austin, Texas.

31. Moeed Yusuf, "Predicting Proliferation: The History of the Future of Nuclear Weapons," Brookings Institution Foreign Policy Paper Series, no. 11 (Washington DC: Brookings Institution Press, January 2009), 25.

32. Ibid., 47

33. See Marc Trachtenberg, chapter 3, "A 'Wasting Asset': American Strategy and the Shifting Nuclear Balance, 1949–1954," in *History and Strategy* (Princeton: Princeton University Press, 1991), 100–152.

34. See chapter 4 of this book.

35. See Jeffrey Lewis, *The Minimum Means of Reprisal: China's Search for Security in the Nuclear Age* (Cambridge: MIT Press, 2007), 1–25.

36. Shahram Chubin, *Iran's Nuclear Ambitions* (Washington, DC: Carnegie Endowment for International Peace, 2006), 44.

37. Frank Procida, "Overblown: Why an Iranian Nuclear Bomb Is Not the End of the World," *Foreign Affairs*, 9 June 2009, accessed 22 November 2011, http://www.foreignaffairs.com/articles/65127/frank-procida/overblown.

38. Iran's desire for a nuclear deterrent likely increased after the surprise and devastation of the 1980–88 Iran-Iraq War, which included an Iraqi chemical weapons attack. The overwhelming victory of US forces against Iraq in the 1991 Persian Gulf War no doubt added fuel to this desire. Iran, a Persian and Shiite state, is viewed with suspicion and even hostility by many of its Arab Sunni neighbors. And, like France and India, for example, Iran takes great pride in its independence and in demonstrating its scientific prowess. Iran's interest in a nuclear deterrent was obviously heightened after 2002 by the increased presence of the United States in the region as a result of the wars in Afghanistan and Iraq. There is a broad consensus among Iranian political elites that the United States is a revolutionary state implacably hostile to its regime. Even though Iran and the United States are foes, they share important overlapping interests, including a desire to see a stable Afghanistan rid of the Taliban and a stable, unified, democratic Iraq (ruled by the Shiite majority). There is some evidence that Iran's abhorrent rhetoric about Israel and its support for Palestinian extremists is partly driven by domestic politics and a desire to gain

influence in the region by outflanking its Arab Sunni rivals. Few in Iran see the Palestinian question as core to Iranian national interests. Finally, Iran has likely learned a valuable lesson for itself in observing two decades of failed US and international efforts to keep North Korea nonnuclear. See Chubin, *Iran's Nuclear Ambitions*; and Procida, "Overblown." None of these facts should prevent the creation of a realistic strategy of how to deal with Iran, but few have been incorporated into the failed alarmist perspective.

39. Ronald Koven, "Many Nations Ready to Break into Nuclear Club," *Washington Post*, 15 June 1981.

40. Henry Rowen, "India's Nuclear Problem," memorandum, 24 December 1964, Declassified Documents Reference System (hereafter cited as DDRS), document no. CK3100154493, 6.

41. Russell Murray, "Problems of Nuclear Proliferation outside Europe," 7 December 1964, DDRS, document no. CK3100281620, 1.

42. "Prevention of the Proliferation of Nuclear Weapons," National Security Action Memorandum, 21 January 1965, Collection: Nuclear Non-Proliferation, Digital National Security Archives, item no. NP01103, 1.

43. See National Intelligence Council, "The Dynamics of Nuclear Proliferation: Balance of Incentives and Constraints," September 1985, accessed 22 November 2011, www.foia.cia.gov/docs/DOC_0000453458/DOC_0000453458.pdf.

44. Yusuf, "Predicting Proliferation," 61.

45. Potter and Mukhatzhanova, "Divining Nuclear Intentions," 166. See also 159n42, where works that discuss tipping points and chain reactions are listed.

46. Figures taken from Perkovich et al., "Universal Compliance," 19–20.

47. There is uncertainty about the nature and timeline of nuclear research in Syria. See "Nuclear Weapons Programs," GlobalSecurity.org., accessed 22 November 2011, http://www.globalsecurity.org/wmd/world/syria/nuke.htm.

48. Yusuf, "Predicting Proliferation," 49. Much of the nuclear terrorism literature is alarmist. A good if unduly pessimistic assessment, which evaluates past actions and recommends further measures, is Matthew Bunn, *Securing the Bomb* (Cambridge and Washington, DC: Project on Managing the Atom, Harvard University and Nuclear Threat Initiative, September 2008), accessed 22 November 2011, www.nti.org/e_research/securing_the_bomb08.pdf.

49. Although the Abdul Qadeer Khan case is disturbing, the network did not aid nonstate actors and was ultimately discovered and shut down. Michael Levi notes that Khan's trade did not involve nuclear weapons or explosive materials, the most sensitive part of the Pakistani nuclear program. See Michael Levi, *On Nuclear Terrorism* (Cambridge: Harvard University Press, 2007), 24.

50. Adam Garfinkle, "Does Nuclear Deterrence Apply in the Age of Terrorism?" Foreign Policy Research Institute Newsletter, *Footnotes* 14, no. 10 (May 2009), accessed 22 November 2011, http://www.fpri.org/footnotes/1410.200905.garankle.nucleardeterrenceterrorism.html.

51. Robin M. Frost, "Nuclear Terrorism after 9/11," Adelphi Papers, no. 378 (London: International Institute for Strategic Studies, 2005); and Garfinkle, "Does Nuclear Deterrence Apply in the Age of Terrorism?" See also, William Langewiesche, "How to Get a Nuclear Bomb," *Atlantic Monthly*, December 2006, 80–98, accessed

22 November 2011, http://www.theatlantic.com/magazine/archive/2006/12/how-to-get-a-nuclear-bomb/5402/. Langewiesche writes: "In the end, if you wanted a bomb and calculated the odds, you would have to admit that they were stacked against you, simply because of how the world works. . . . [For example,] the existence of suitcase bombs has never been proved, and there has never been a single verified case, anywhere, of the theft of any sort of nuclear weapon." Like Levi, Langewiesche shows the difficulty that terrorists would have at each stage in acquiring the needed nuclear materials and then assembling, transporting, delivering, and detonating a bomb in the United States.

52. Joseph Cirincione, *Bomb Scare: The History and Future of Nuclear Weapons* (New York: Columbia University Press, 2007), 91.

53. Chubin, *Iran's Nuclear Ambitions*, 52.

54. Levi, *On Nuclear Terrorism*, 141. The earlier quotes were taken from pages 144 and 151–52.

55. Anne Stenersen, *Al-Qaida's Quest for Weapons of Mass Destruction: The History behind the Hype* (Saarbrücken, Germany: VDM Verlag Dr. Müller Aktiengesellschaft, 2008), 89.

56. Ibid., 84.

57. Ibid., 69. Al-Qaida may also have had less money than is commonly thought, both before and after the September 11 terrorist attacks. See John Roth, Douglas Greenburg, and Serena Wille, National Commission on Terrorist Attacks upon the United States, "Monograph on Terrorist Financing: Staff Report to the Commission," accessed 22 November 2011, http://govinfo.library.unt.edu/911/staff_statements/911_TerrFin_Monograph.pdf; and Lawrence Wright, *The Looming Tower: Al-Qaeda and the Road to 9/11* (New York: Alfred A. Knopf, 2006), 194–97.

58. Levi, *On Nuclear Terrorism*, 11.

59. Frost, "Nuclear Terrorism after 9/11," 7.

60. Edward U. Condon, "The New Technique of Private War," in *One World or None: A Report to the Public on the Full Meaning of the Atomic Bomb*, ed. Dexter Masters and Katharine Way (New York: McGraw-Hill, 1946), quoted in Dan Stober, "No Experience Necessary," *Bulletin of the Atomic Scientists* 2, no. 59 (March/April 2003): 63.

61. Central Intelligence Agency, "Capabilities of the USSR to Employ Unconventional Attack Involving the Smuggling of Atomic Weapons into the United States," 19 January 1950, DDRS, document no. CK3100165674, 1.

62. "A Report on Strategic Developments over the Next Decade for the Interagency Panel," October 1962, National Security Files, box 376, 51–53, John F. Kennedy Presidential Library, Boston, Massachusetts.

63. Richard T. Kennedy, "Status of USG Actions against Terrorism," memo for Henry Kissinger, 25 November 1972, DDRS, document no. CK3100525361, 1.

64. Will Kriegsman to Peter Flanigan, "Saboteur or Terrorist Actions against Nuclear Installations," 23 October 1970, National Security Council Institutional Files, National Security Decision Memorandum, box H-180, Nixon Presidential Materials, U.S. National Archives, College Park, Maryland.

65. For the angry US response to this scenario—including an extraordinary threat by Secretary of State Rusk against France—see Marc Trachtenberg, *A Constructed Peace: The Making of the European Settlement, 1945–1963* (Princeton: Princeton University Press, 1999), 338n193.

66. See Trachtenberg, *History and Strategy*, 274.

67. Dale C. Copeland argues: "To make a theory of major war relevant to the nuclear era, as well as to the pre-nuclear era, we must explain why states would move from peaceful engagement to a destabilizing cold war rivalry, or from such a rivalry into crises with the types of risks witnessed in the Cuban missile crisis." Dale C. Copeland, *The Origins of Major War* (Ithaca: Cornell University Press, 2000), 3.

68. Keir A. Lieber explains: "The logic of extended deterrence required a first-strike capability." Keir A. Lieber, *War and the Engineers: The Primacy of Politics over Technology* (Ithaca: Cornell University Press, 2005), 145.

69. Joseph S. Nye Jr., "Soft Power," *Foreign Policy* 80 (Fall 1990): 153–71.

70. See William Burr and Jeffrey T. Richelson's excellent account in "Whether to 'Strangle the Baby in the Cradle': The United States and the Chinese Nuclear Program, 1960–64," *International Security* 25, no. 3 (Winter 2000/2001): 54–99.

71. Marc Trachtenberg, chapter 4 "The Nuclearization of NATO," in Trachtenberg, *History and Strategy*, 162.

72. Lieber, *War and the Engineers*, 140–48.

73. Marc Trachtenberg, "Waltzing to Armageddon?" *National Interest* 69 (Fall 2002): 144–52, quote at 149. Robert Jervis and other defensive realists acknowledge that balance-of-resolve considerations were paramount during these nuclear crises, but they do not see this fact as destabilizing. See Robert Jervis, *The Meaning of the Nuclear Revolution: Statecraft and the Prospect of Armageddon* (Ithaca: Cornell University Press, 1989), 38; and Stephen Van Evera, *The Causes of War: Power and the Roots of Conflict* (Ithaca: Cornell University Press, 1999), 245. But as Trachtenberg points out, "why would anyone think that a world of that sort, where political outcomes are up for grabs and victory goes to the side with the strongest nerves, would be particularly stable?" "Waltzing to Armageddon?," 149.

74. See the chapter titled "The Manipulation of Risk," in Thomas C. Schelling, *Arms and Influence* (New Haven: Yale University Press, 1966), 92–125.

75. Nor did the Soviet Union mobilize its strategic nuclear forces, despite the United States having done so. Daryl G. Press, *Calculating Credibility: How Leaders Assess Military Threats* (Ithaca: Cornell University Press, 2005), 193n37.

76. Aleksandr Fursenko and Timothy Naftali, *Khrushchev's Cold War: The Inside Story of an American Adversary* (New York: W. W. Norton, 2006), 6.

77. For details of how US policymakers came to this belief, see Fred Kaplan, "JFK's First-Strike Plan," *Atlantic Monthly*, October 2001, 81–86.

78. Fursenko and Naftali reveal that the Soviet premier believed, incorrectly, that the United States and its Western allies had backed down during the Suez Crisis in 1956 and in Iraq in 1958 because of Khrushchev's successful nuclear brinksmanship. Fursenko and Naftali, *Khrushchev's Cold War*, 137.

79. Western Foreign Ministers' Meeting, 11 December 1961, *Foreign Relations of the United States*, 1961–1963, vol. 14 (Washington, DC: U.S. Government Printing Office, 1975), 656.

80. For example, Kennedy would have publicly agreed to remove US missiles from Turkey and may not even have responded if the Soviets attacked them. Philip Nash, *The Other Missiles of October: Eisenhower, Kennedy, and the Jupiters, 1957–1963* (Chapel Hill: University of North Carolina Press, 1997), 126–27.

81. Fursenko and Naftali, *Khrushchev's Cold War*, 6.

82. See Scott D. Sagan and Jeremi Suri, "The Madman Nuclear Alert: Secrecy, Signaling, and Safety in October 1969," *International Security* 27, no. 4 (Spring 2003): 150–83; and chapter 5 of this book.

83. Eisenhower thought that it "had been a terrible mistake at the end of the war to create Berlin as a western island in the Soviet zone," and he was eager to work out a political compromise with the Soviets. Trachtenberg, *History and Strategy*, 204. For further evidence of Eisenhower's and Kennedy's lack of enthusiasm for the US commitment to Berlin, see Campbell Craig's fascinating account in *Destroying the Village: Eisenhower and Thermonuclear War* (New York: Columbia University Press, 1998).

84. For example, the major realist intellectuals of the postwar period—George Kennan, Hans Morgenthau, Reinhold Niebuhr, and Kenneth Waltz—were against the US military intervention in South Vietnam; none believed its loss would affect the balance of power vis-à-vis the Soviet Union. See Campbell Craig, *Glimmer of a New Leviathan: Total War in the Realism of Niebuhr, Morgenthau, and Waltz* (New York: Columbia University Press, 2003).

85. According to Jervis, the nuclear revolution meant that "small issues will often loom large, not because of their intrinsic importance, but because they are taken as tests of resolve." What happens "in peripheral areas . . . is not important; whether the United States and the Soviet Union are seen as having lived up to their commitments in these disputes may be crucial." See Jervis, *Meaning of the Nuclear Revolution*, 39. Jervis is correct, although it is hard to understand how this focus on resolve and credibility over material and geopolitical interests makes for a more stable, less crisis-prone and peaceful world order.

86. In a nonnuclear world, how could the United States protect a city deep in enemy territory, facing an adversary with substantial conventional superiority? And in the absence of nuclear weapons, the United States could have quickly and easily eliminated a Soviet military presence in Cuba.

87. For the importance of security guarantees in dampening proliferation, see Makreeta Lahti, "Security Cooperation as a Way to Stop the Spread of Nuclear Weapons?: Nuclear Nonproliferation Policies of the United States towards the Federal Republic of Germany and Israel, 1945–1968" (PhD diss., University of Potsdam, 2008).

88. Robert Jervis, "Cooperation under the Security Dilemma," *World Politics* 30, no. 2 (January 1978): 167–214. Interestingly, Jervis no longer appears to believe that the Cold War was an example of a security dilemma. See Robert Jervis, "Was the Cold War a Security Dilemma?" *Journal of Cold War Studies* 3, no. 1 (Winter 2001): 36–60.

89. For a summary of this view, see Copeland, *Origins of Major War*, 147. See also Melvyn Leffler, *A Preponderance of Power: National Security, the Truman Administration, and the Cold War* (Stanford: Stanford University Press, 1992).

90. See chapter 6 of this book.

91. See Lieber, *War and the Engineers*, 143–48.

92. Marc Trachtenberg, chapter 3 "A 'Wasting Asset': American Strategy and the Shifting Nuclear Balance, 1949–1954," in *History and Strategy*. See also Francis J. Gavin, "Politics, Power, and U.S. Policy in Iran, 1950–1953," *Journal of Cold War Studies* 1, no. 1 (Winter 1999): 56–89.

93. See Trachtenberg, *Constructed Peace*; and chapter 4 of this book.

94. See Fursenko and Naftali, *Khrushchev's Cold War*.

95. Jervis argues that the side defending the status quo enjoys the advantage in a nuclear crisis in *Meaning of the Nuclear Revolution*, 29–35. But in Berlin, it was not always clear who was defending and who was challenging the status quo: the Soviet Union, which wanted to end the West's legal rights in the city, or the United States, which appeared to be looking the other way as West Germany sought an independent nuclear capability. Furthermore, maintaining a defenseless city within enemy territory hardly seems an obvious definition of the status quo, nor is it clear what would be defined as moving first in a Berlin crisis.

96. Trachtenberg, *Constructed Peace*. See also Georges-Henri Soutou, *L'alliance incertaine: Les rapports politico-stratégiques franco-allemands*, 1954–1996 (Paris: Fayard, 1996), 203–65; and Hans-Peter Schwarz, *Konrad Adenauer: A German Politician and Statesman in a Period of War, Revolution, and Reconstruction*, trans. Louise Willmot (Providence: Berghahn, 1997), 513–712.

97. For an excellent account of President Johnson's efforts to achieve détente with the Soviets, see Thomas A. Schwartz, *Lyndon Johnson and Europe: In the Shadow of Vietnam* (Cambridge: Harvard University Press, 2003).

98. Yusuf, "Predicting Proliferation," 35.

99. Lewis, *Minimum Means of Reprisal*, 206.

100. "For instance, K. Subrahmanyam, India's most prominent strategic thinker, argued that the 'main purpose of a third world arsenal is deterrence against blackmail,' and that new nuclear powers had the benefit of learning from the 'highly risky and totally non-viable policies' of the superpowers and would not repeat their mistakes." Yusuf, "Predicting Proliferation," 45.

101. "A Report on Strategic Developments over the Next Decade for the Interagency Panel," October 1962 Camp David, 51.

102. For one of the first and best arguments calling for diplomatic historians to go beyond the "Cold War lens," see Matthew Connelly, *A Diplomatic Revolution: Algeria's Fight for Independence and the Origins of the Post–Cold War Era* (New York: Oxford University Press, 2002). See also, Akira Iriye, *Cultural Internationalism and World Order* (Baltimore: Johns Hopkins University Press, 1997); and the relevant chapters in Anthony G. Hopkins, ed., *Global History: Interactions between the Universal and the Local*(New York: Palgrave Macmillan, 2006). For a slightly different argument—that Cold War scholarship should be "de-centered" and focus on nonsuperpower actors—see Odd Arne Westad, *The Global Cold War: Third World Interventions and the Making of Our Times* (Cambridge: Cambridge University Press, 2005).

103. Jervis, *Meaning of the Nuclear Revolution*, 34.

104. Palca and Rosen, "North Korea and Nuclear Proliferation," 7.

105. Maurice Vaisse, *La France et l'atomique française*, 1945–1958 (Brussels: Bruylant, 1994); Jacques E.C. Hymans, *The Psychology of Nuclear Proliferation: Identity, Emotions, and Foreign Policy* (Cambridge: Cambridge University Press, 2006), esp. 85–113; Susanna Schrafstetter and Stephen Twigge, *Avoiding Armageddon: Europe, the United States, and the Struggle for Nuclear Nonproliferation*, 1945–1970 (Westport, CT: Praeger, 2004); and Lorna Arnold and Mark Smith, *Britain, Australia, and the Bomb: The Nuclear Tests and Their Aftermath* (New York: Palgrave Macmillan, 2006).

106. Palca and Rosen, "North Korea and Nuclear Proliferation," 7.

107. For a comparison of Iran to France in the 1950s and 1960s, see Serre Lodgaard, "Challenge from Within: The Case of Iran," 7n8, presented at the "Nobel Sympo-

sium: Peace, Stability, and Nuclear Order: Theoretical Assumptions, Historical Experiences, and Future Challenges," Drøbak, Norway, June 25–27, 2009.

108. Richard K. Betts, *Nuclear Blackmail and Nuclear Balance* (Washington, DC: Brookings Institution Press, 1987), 11.

109. This is one of the key points in John Mueller's trenchant analysis in *Overblown: How Politicians and the Terrorism Industry Inflate National Security Threats and Why We Believe Them* (New York: Free Press, 2006).

110. Richard Betts, summarized in Smith, *Deterring America*, 157.

111. Yusuf, "Predicting Proliferation," 68.

112. Alan Cullison, "Inside Al-Qaeda's Hard Drive," *Atlantic Monthly*, September 2004, 55–70, accessed 23 November 2011, http://www.theatlantic.com/doc/200409/cullison. See also the discussion of Secretary of Defense William Cohen's "bag of sugar" (anthrax) speech in Martin C. Libicki, Peter Chalk, and Melanie Sisson, *Exploring Terrorist Targeting Preferences* (Santa Monica, CA: RAND, 2006), 54.

8. Global Zero, History, and the "Nuclear Revolution"

1. Remarks by President Barack Obama, 5 April 2009, accessed 13 April 2012, http://www.whitehouse.gov/the_press_office/Remarks-By-President-Barack-Obama-In-Prague-As-Delivered/.

2. See http://www.hoover.org/publications/hover-digest/article/6109, accessed 13 April, 2012.

3. See http://www.stanleyfoundation.org/publications/report/Issues09.pdf, p. 10, accessed 13 April 2012.

4. See http://www.worldpublicopinion.org/pipa/articles/international_security_bt/577.php?lb=btis&pnt=577&nid=&id=, accessed 13 April 2012.

5. Harold Brown and John Deutch, "The Nuclear Disarmament Fantasy," *Wall Street Journal*, 19 November 2007, accessed 13 April 2012, http://www.wagingpeace.org/articles/2007/11/26_brown_article_responses.php.

6. Melanie Kirkpatrick, "Why We Don't Want a Nuclear-Free World: The Former Defense Secretary on the US Deterrent and the Terrorist Threat," *Wall Street Journal*, 13 July 2009, accessed 13 April 2012, http://online.wsj.com/article/SB124726489588925407.html.

7. Thomas Schelling, "A World without Nuclear Weapons," *Daedalus*, 138, no. 4 (Fall 2009: 124–29.

8. Charles L. Glaser, "The Instability of Small Numbers Revisited: Prospects for Disarmament and Nonproliferation," paper presented at the conference "Rebuilding the NPT Consensus," Center for International Security and Cooperation (CISAC), Stanford University, 16–17 October 2007, accessed 13 April 2012, http://iis-db.stanford.edu/docs/103/Glaser-summary.pdf.

9. See Robert Jervis, *The Meaning of the Nuclear Revolution: Statecraft and the Prospect of Armageddon* (Ithaca: Cornell University Press, 1989), 1–45.

10. Gregg Herken, *Counsels of War* (New York: Alfred Knopf, 1985), 9.

11. Kenneth N. Waltz and Scott Sagan, "The Great Debate: Is Nuclear Zero the Best Option?" *National Interest* 109 (September/October 2010): 93.

12. Ibid.

13. George P. Shultz, William J. Perry, Henry A. Kissinger, and Sam Nunn, "Deterrence in the Age of Nuclear Proliferation," *Wall Street Journal*, 7 March 2011, accessed 30 October 2011, http://online.wsj.com/article/SB10001424052748703300904576178760530169414.html.

14. These fears are expressed in the "Nuclear Posture Review," April 2010, accessed 24 October 2011, http://www.defense.gov/npr/.

15. Waltz and Sagan, "Great Debate," 94.

16. Dan Reiter argues that the preventive attacks that have occurred against nuclear, biological, and chemical weapons facilities have had limited success and rarely delay programs. "Preventive Attacks against Nuclear, Biological, and Chemical Weapons Programs: The Track Record," in *Hitting First: Preventive Force in U.S. Security Strategy*, ed. William Walton Keller and Gordon R. Mitchell (Pittsburgh: University of Pittsburgh Press, 2006), 28.

17. Fred Charles Iklé, "The Second Coming of the Nuclear Age," *Foreign Affairs* 75, no. 1 (January/February 1996): 119–28.

18. This is the theme of the documentary film by Errol Morris about Robert McNamara, *The Fog of War: Eleven Lessons from the Life of Robert S. McNamara*, December 2003.

19. For instance, see "Special Estimate: Soviet Capabilities for a Surprise Attack on the Continental United States before July 1952," (published 15 September 1951, declassified 12 February 1981). See also, Brian Michael Jenkins, "Nuclear Terror: How Real?" *Washington Times*, 13 May 2007, accessed 17 October 2011, http://www.rand.org/commentary/2007/05/13/WT.html.

20. For example, see John F. Kennedy, "1960 US Presidential Debate (no. 3) on Any Topics," 13 October 1960, John F. Kennedy Library, accessed 17 October 2011, http://www.archive.org/details/Kennedy-Nixon_third_debate_10_13_1960 .

21. See chapter 7 of this book.

22. Treaty Banning Nuclear Weapons Tests in the Atmosphere, in Outer Space, and Under Water (Limited Test Ban Treaty), 10 October 1963, 480 U.N.T.S. 43.

23. "Nuclear Posture Review," 6.

24. Dale C. Copeland, *The Origins of Major War* (Ithaca: Cornell University Press, 2001), 149.

25. David Sanger, "Officials Say Obama Has Offer for Iran," *New York Times*, 27 October 2010, accessed 13 April 2012, http://www.nytimes.com/2010/10/28/world/middleeast/28iran.html?hp.

26. See Jacques Hymans, *Implementing Nuclear Ambitions: The Political Foundations of Technical Achievement*(Cambridge, UK: Cambridge University Press, forthcoming). Even among those who argue about the potential of nuclear terrorism, there is still agreement that "it is extremely unlikely that a subnational terrorist group would be able to make its own nuclear bomb material." Matthew Bunn and Anthony Wier, "Terrorist Nuclear Weapon Construction: How Difficult?," *Annals of the American Academy of Political and Social Science* 267 (September 2006): 136. For a critical argument against the overstatement of nuclear threats, see John Mueller, "Why Nuclear Weapons Aren't as Frightening as You Think," *Foreign Policy* (January/February 2010), accessed 30 October 2011, http://www.foreignpolicy.com/

articles/2010/01/04/think_again_nuclear_weapons?print=yes&hidecomments=yes&page=full.

27. For a debate on the projections of the detonation on a nuclear weapon by terrorists, see Michael A. Levi and Graham T. Allison, "How Likely Is a Nuclear Terrorist Attack on the United States?," *Council on Foreign Relations*, 20 April 2007, accessed 24 October 2011, http://www.cfr.org/weapons-of-mass-destruction/likely-nuclear-terrorist-attack-united-states/p13097.

Index